After Snowden :privacy, secrecy, and
security in the information age

AFTER SNOWDEN

AFTER SNOWDEN

PRIVACY, SECRECY, AND SECURITY

IN THE INFORMATION AGE

RONALD GOLDFARB, EDITOR

THOMAS DUNNE BOOKS

ST. MARTIN'S PRESS

NEW YORK

THOMAS DUNNE BOOKS.
An imprint of St. Martin's Press.

www.thomasdunnebooks.com
www.stmartins.com

Designed by Steven Seighman

Library of Congress Cataloging-in-Publication Data

After Snowden : privacy, secrecy, and security in the information age /
edited by Ronald Goldfarb.—First edition.
    p. cm.
  ISBN 978-1-250-06760-9 (hardcover)
  ISBN 978-1-4668-7605-7 (e-book)
  1. Official secrets—United States.   2. Government information—
United States.   3. Electronic surveillance—United States.   4. Snowden,
Edward J., 1983–   I. Goldfarb, Ronald L., editor of complilation.
  JK468.S4A67 2015
  363.25'2—dc23

                                                    2015006047

First Edition: May 2015

10   9   8   7   6   5   4   3   2   1

CONTENTS

INTRODUCTION

RONALD GOLDFARB is a veteran Washington, D.C., attorney, author of thirteen books, and a literary agent. He worked in the Department of Justice prosecuting organized crime cases during the Kennedy administration, and served as trial counsel in the U.S. Air Force, JAG, for three years before that. He was special counsel to a congressional (House of Representatives) investigation, and was appointed to chair a special review committee established by a D.C. federal court dealing with the practices of the Department of Labor. His Web site, www.ronaldgoldarb.com, lists his biography in full detail.

THE NOTORIOUS REVELATIONS of Edward Snowden, former U.S. government employee and contractor, who stole and made public a deluge of classified government documents concerning U.S. surveillance practices, have generated passionate reactions worldwide. Most people have strong opinions about whether Snowden is a megalomaniacal traitor or a self-sacrificing patriot, and whether our nation's policies should err on the side of protecting national security or civil liberties. Use of the word "leak" to describe Snowden's disclosures, rather than geyser or waterfall, is as minimalizing of his action as the charge of espionage by the government seems a grandiose exaggeration of his offense.

Mediating the debate over the right judgment of Mr. Snowden's behavior is not the aim of this collection of essays by eminent scholars with expertise in relevant fields affected by the Snowden affair. Whatever the final verdict on Snowden may be—whether he is a public-spirited whistleblower, classic leaker, actor in a proud tradition of civil disobedience, or a vain and reckless vigilante, a treacherous criminal who has hurt his country—his behavior has raised important questions about our nation's dragnet surveillance practices and the proper agencies and manner of its review. These questions are the subject of this book.

What are the proper bounds of secrecy? Are current government surveillance practices justified as necessary measures of national security at a time of extraordinary provocation, or do they go too far, setting a dangerous precedent for our national policies of self-protection that could lead to a security state? And if so, who decides that, and what should be done about it?

A high school dropout and technical wizard, Snowden worked for the CIA, NSA, Defense Intelligence Agency, and recently for a private contractor (first Dell, then Booz Allen Hamilton) commissioned by the NSA, doing what has been described as cyber-counterintelligence. Once an idealistic participant in U.S. national security programs, Snowden became disillusioned by what he perceived as government excesses and abuses in its data gathering. Believing that he had no proper alternatives, Snowden fled from his carefree life in Hawaii, his well-paying job, his girlfriend, and his country, taking along four laptops with encrypted, top secret files. He claims he did so in order to protest what he viewed as major incursions on people's privacy and constitutional rights. "I took an oath to support and defend the Constitution and saw that the Constitution was being violated on a massive scale," he told a Texas teleconference.[1]

The Snowden Files, by *The Guardian* editor Luke Harding[2]—to be a movie by Oliver Stone—described the exciting, intense behind-the-scenes story of Snowden's dramatic flight to Hong Kong and his secret meetings with lawyer-journalist Glenn Greenwald, author of *No Place to Hide.*[3] Greenwald's book complements and expands on Harding's story, as does the work of documentary filmmaker Laura Poitras—Snowden's other chosen vehicle for telling his story to the world. Poitras's Academy Award–winning documentary covering that clandestine drama, *Citizenfour* (Snowden's code name for Poitras), was shown in New York City on October 2014.[4]

New Yorker columnist George Packer called it "a political thriller." Poitras considers it a "human drama."[6] The prize-winning reporter Barton Gellman would later join them in telling Snowden's story at *The Washington Post*.

For ten intense, perilous, around-the-clock days in Hong Kong, the three met secretly in Snowden's room at the Mira Hotel, joined by *The Guardian*'s expert on national security, Ewen MacAskill, to evaluate Snowden's story before they would eventually tell it to the world. Once satisfied with Snowden as a credible source (after forty-eight hours of "speed dating," as MacAskill called it),[5] *The Guardian* called the White House seeking a quick response before going public with Snowden's material. Getting none, *The Guardian* broke the story. Snowden hurriedly departed Hong Kong for refuge in South America, but finding his passport canceled by the United States ended up grounded en route at the airport in Russia.

At this time, Snowden, a thirty-one-year-old man without a country, remains in Russia under temporary asylum, recently joined by his girlfriend, regularly interviewed by visiting reporters, and broadcasting his story and viewpoints to audiences worldwide over the Internet. His residence permit recently was extended for three more years, as he negotiates safe harbor in other countries, evading extradition and facing an indictment in the United States for espionage and theft of government property for which he faces thirty years in prison. Reviled for recklessness and praised for self-sacrifice, his actions already have generated the beginnings of reforms.

Through his trusted journalistic confederates, he continues to expose the government's questionable surveillance practices. He certainly has generated a national debate about this subject in the United States, and engaged other countries in an international conversation by raising the public's consciousness about the practices of surveillance in the borderless world of cyberspace. In October 2014, the UN's top counterterrorism and human rights official formally reported to the General Assembly that questionable electronic surveillance by member states unjustifiably violated core privacy rights in violation of multiple treaties and conventions. Reformative bills are pending before the U.S. Congress. Reevaluation of House and Senate oversight practices are underway. Lawsuits have been filed. A high-level White House review panel already has proposed forty-six reform measures.

The Snowden affair raises a classic, fundamental question about how our three branches of government should synchronize their work, yet check and balance each other's powers. Is the executive branch's work on national security—arguably no more important role exists as part of its constitutional powers—properly overseen by the Congress and the courts? And how does the press monitor all three branches when national security is the question? Have surveillance technologies "outpaced democratic controls," as one of Snowden's attorneys claimed? A recent *Foreign Affairs* article concluded that "Snowden's revelations demonstrated how the implicit bargain that has governed the U.S. intelligence community since the 1970's has broken down." Has it? How so? What to do about it?[7]

This book aspires to inform the debates generated by the Snowden disclosures about critical policies: the role of the press in reporting about national security; the value of leaks and the need for whistleblowers; the proper bounds and treatment of civil disobedience; the roles of courts and Congress in overseeing executive practices taken in the defense of our nation; and the appropriate balance between privacy and government investigation and secrecy in this evolving era of invasive technology and metadata gathering.

How do we protect our nation's security without creating, in the words of Cato Institute official Julian Sanchez, "a nigh-omniscient, planet-spanning, electronic panopticon"?[8] And how do we deal with the conundrum described by James Clapper,

Director of National Intelligence?: "We are supposed to keep the country safe, predict anticipatory intelligence, with no risk and no embarrassment if revealed, and without a scintilla of jeopardy to privacy of any domestic person or foreign person. We call that 'immaculate collection.'"[9]

In the history of the United States—it could be said so about most, if not all, places—when national security, domestic terror, and personal provocation clash with people's civil liberties, the former prevail. That is human nature. The Constitution is not a suicide pact, the late Supreme Court Justice Robert Jackson said, capturing the human dilemma of this conundrum.[10,11] As Professor Jon L. Mills points out in his chapter, "The Future of Privacy in the Surveillance Age," the first words of the Constitution pronounce the need for national security. Over a century later judges declared that privacy, not a word that appears in the Constitution, is constitutionally protected by implication from other protections in the Constitution.

There is both wisdom and cynicism in the manner in which national security is enforced. A book, *America's War Machine,* by the late James McCartney and his wife, Molly, both experienced reporters, quoted a remarkable conversation that took place in 1946 after World War II that echoes today in the wake of 9/11 and this country's attempts to prevent its recurrence.

> *". . . it is always a simple matter to drag the people along, whether it is a democracy or a fascist dictatorship . . . ," the speaker said.*
>
> *But in a democracy, his questioner argued, ". . . the people have some say . . . through their elected representatives, and in the U.S. only Congress can declare wars."*
>
> *The challenged interviewer responded: "Oh, that is all well and good, but voice or no voice, the people can always be brought to the*

bidding of the leaders. That is easy. All you have to do is tell them they are being attacked and denounce the pacifists for lack of patriotism and exposing the country to danger. It works the same way in any country."

Ironically, the commentator quoted by the McCartneys was Hermann Goering, then a Nuremberg prisoner in an interview just before his execution. Some moral tutor to instruct on realpolitik![12]

History provides comparisons to current dilemmas—the internment of Japanese American citizens after the treacherous attack on Pearl Harbor, Hawaii, on December 7, 1941, was not one of this country's finest hours, and the infamous attack on America on 9/11 gave rise to draconian measures of extreme rendition, rationalized by some as necessary for national security, but condemned by others as excessive torture. In both instances, the provocation was clear, but the methods of response were questionable.

Materials provided by Snowden to Glenn Greenwald (reported in *The Daily Beast* and *The Intercept*) reported that the NSA and the FBI were monitoring e-mails of prominent Muslim Americans under secret procedures for targeting terrorists and foreign spies.[13] Should ethnic profiling of American Muslim citizens today be condoned as a rational necessity, or compared with the excessive intelligence gathering of civil rights and antiwar activists of the 1960s and 1970s, and alleged Communist movie figures in Hollywood in the McCarthy era?

There will be inevitable victims of investigative abuses in trying times, to be sure. No one questioned the deceptions and spying we and our allies performed during World War II in the war against fascism; indeed we romanticize what the OSS accomplished at Bletchley and elsewhere to bring down our fascist enemies by any means or tactics. The government's specific rationale for the particular practices Snowden has questioned is classified, and therefore impossible to assess. Presumably the rationale is that after 9/11 extreme precautions were prudent, necessary.

The policing of government at its highest precincts is a tricky but vital assignment. The late New York University law professor Edmond Cahn argued, in *The Predicament of Democratic Man* (1961), that misconduct by the government is more pernicious than that of individuals. We are all morally involved in the wrongs of government. Undermining the rule of law, which is the bedrock of democracy, is the ultimate crime, Professor Cahn posited, because it leads to anarchy and the police state.

That notion is the premise of Snowden defenders, that whatever his offense may have been, the official misconduct he revealed is worse. When James Clapper, our Director of National Intelligence, was asked at a Senate inquiry—pre-Snowden disclosures—if NSA collected data on Americans, he said under oath, "No, not wittingly," a perjury in the view of some critics, though no one has called for his indictment. Nor has there been criminal action taken against CIA employees who reportedly improperly surveilled U.S. Senate personnel and records. Senator Ron Wyden reportedly knew Clapper's remarks were false, but prevailing confidentiality rules forbade his challenging them publicly. "If the American people knew what I knew," he was quoted as saying, "they would be angry and they would be shocked."[14]

The efficacy of congressional oversight of the executive actions of seventeen separate agencies in national security matters became a matter of heightened public interest in the wake of Snowden's actions. How effective can congressional oversight be? For there to be synchronicity between branches of government, there needs to be trust between the congressional committees performing oversight and the executive agencies they oversee. Legislators have full plates of responsibilities. They rely on special committees and on their staffs and experts, some with more expertise and longevity and time than the members they serve. But they can probe only so far without the risk of spoiling the relations they depend on. Trust, but verify, works only insofar as one can verify.[15]

Dealings are not always collegial between the overseers and the overseen. The CIA inspector general reported that, in July 2014, CIA Director John Brennan apologized to Senator Dianne Feinstein for "spying on the senator's activities," in regards to her investigation of the CIA's torture practices in this instance.[16] No surprise, Senator Feinstein, a chief senatorial watchdog of executive surveillance practices, expressed pique at the interference with her committee staff by agents of those executive officials her committee was authorized to oversee.

Historically, some managers of congressional oversight didn't want to know what was going on and gave security agencies carte blanche. When he was Armed Services Committee Chairman, the late Senator John Stennis told CIA Director James Schlesinger in 1973 concerning the CIA's activities abroad, "No, no, my boy, don't tell me, just go ahead and do it but I don't want to know," according to Loch Johnson's history of intelligence oversight.[17,18]

In the 1970s, this attitude changed, but after 9/11 the national security apparatus ramped up, understandably. In the follow-up of the Snowden affair, congressional experts and critics are reexamining the effectiveness of Congress acting as proxies for the American public in overseeing the intelligence community, and legislation is pending to rein in NSA's surveillance practices.

If there was greater professionalism by Congress in exercising its oversight responsibility—for example, a joint select committee and super staff for national security matters—as the 9/11 Commission recommended, would that improve the status quo? The 9/11 Commission stated:

> *Of all our recommendations, strengthening congressional oversight may be among the most difficult and important. So long as oversight is governed by current congressional rules and resolutions, we believe the American people will not get the security they want and need. The United States needs a strong, stable, and capable congressional com-*

mittee structure to give America's national intelligence agencies over-sight, support, and leadership.[19]

A 2006 report by the Center for American Progress, *No Mere Oversight,* prepared by national security veterans, concluded that congressional oversight has been dysfunctional: "Congress has all of the tools it needs; it is simply not using them." The process has become "paralyzingly partisan," needs to be prodded by the press to deal with abuses, and is hampered by lack of cooperation "all but non-existent today" between congressional committees with different responsibilities. Congress largely defers to the executive, the report states. Congress is in an awkward position because there is a difference between what its members can say in public and in classified briefings.[20]

How does Congress know about what intelligence agencies are doing? The CIA and NSA require a written finding from the uppermost echelons of the executive branch before it carries out its surveillance programs. Congress knows that, and the budget breakdowns report the funding of these programs, even if code words are used in describing sensitive areas. Therefore, it appears unlikely that at least the top congressional intelligence members did not know about the surveillance programs Snowden revealed. Or that the private companies the PRISM data-mining program exploited did not go to those congressional officials to complain. We, the public, can't know the answer, of course.

A former congressional official told me that, even if it is counterintuitive, considering the scale of the surveillance procedures now in question, it is possible no one in our Congress was aware of them.[21]

However, a knowledgeable, retired CIA and Senate intelligence official advised me that the law requires committees to be "fully and currently informed," and that the intelligence agencies are required to inform the committees about covert action. They fail to do so "at their own peril," he concludes. In his experience, both on the committee and in the intelligence agencies, ". . . the agencies generally make a good-faith effort to tell the committees what they are doing, *especially* if it appears to be problematic to them. They don't want something to blow up in their faces and have the committees pissed off that they were never notified. They want buy-in from the committees because it protects them."

Nevertheless, the 9/11 Commission concluded that legal oversight for intelligence and counterintelligence is now dysfunctional. It interviewed members of Congress and staff and reported that "dissatisfaction with congressional oversight remains widespread." Few members have the necessary knowledge of intelligence work, the Commission concluded.

This criticism does not mean that Congress has failed to act to improve its oversight practices in recent years, one experienced insider advised me. It has required an array of additional oversight measures: notification of executive intelligence activities, added financial oversight and improved appropriations and authorization processes, and created the position of inspector general in intelligence agencies. These inspectors are authorized to work with whistleblowers, respond to press pressures, and oversee the minimization of excessive practices.

Another former intelligence official suggested that as a practical matter, the controversial programs Snowden disclosed may be curtailed for economic reasons, especially if their utility is of dubious value. Further, he speculates, there may be worse incursions of privacy by local and state police officials whose gathering and collating of their terrorism surveillance are likely to be available to federal intelligence agencies.

Still another expert suggested that one of the problems with the post-9/11 national security process is that the NSA hired many contractors to do what its employees did in the past. That led to hires, like Snowden, who had access to highly sensitive materials. The agencies were not as careful about hiring outside employees as they had been in the past, this former high CIA and Senate official told me. And further, he added, political polarizing has hurt the oversight function, adding mistrust and uncertainty to the process of synchronization of congressional and executive branch officials in this sensitive field.

New Yorker political analyst Ryan Lizza spelled out the background politics of congressional oversight in detail in "State of Deception" (December 16, 2013). While the Intelligence Committee was created in the 1970s to provide "vigilant oversight of the intelligence community," he noted, there have been and still are differences in congressional members' views of their responsibility. Currently there are those who believe the Committee is too beholden to the officials they oversee. Congressman Jim Sensenbrenner, one author of the Patriot Act, wrote in August 2013, "I did not know the administration was using the Patriot Act (Section 215) for bulk collection and neither did a majority of my colleagues." Others, the majority, are deemed by critics to be solicitous, sometimes deferential to the expertise of executive officials in the intelligence community.

Lizza's behind-the-scenes depiction of how, up to the present, the Department of Justice, the White House, and even the Foreign Intelligence Surveillance Act (FISA) courts have gone along with intelligence excesses, even when some had criticisms of them, is daunting. He concludes his analysis: ". . . given the history of abuse . . . it's right to ask questions about surveillance— particularly as technology is reshaping every aspect of our lives."

James Risen's *Pay Any Price* describes a revealing incident that demonstrates the weakness of congressional oversight. A NSA official advised Diane Roark, a staff member of the House Permanent Select Committee on Intelligence, that a domestic surveillance program was potentially unconstitutional and he couldn't persuade his colleagues of its danger. Roark agreed and questioned NSA Director Michael Hayden about this, and he resisted her entreaties, stating that high congressional officials and lawyers "from three branches" had been informed of and approved the program. She raised the question with her Committee colleagues and was told to drop the matter. She called a FISA judge, who didn't talk to her but reported her call to the Department of Justice. Everyone she called seemed to accept the executive decision that the program was legal. Roark was told by Hayden that if challenged they "have the majority of nine votes," the Supreme Court, presumably. Risen wrote: "She had gone to all three branches of government . . . and had discovered that there was a conspiracy of silence . . . to protect an unconstitutional operation." Roark resigned her job and moved to Oregon.[22]

Bottom line, it is unfair to criticize national security agencies alone for these now controversial programs. The public elects representatives in Congress to oversee the executive. Periodically, the question whether the constitutional tripartite function of our government is working as it should be is up for consideration. One history of intelligence oversight concluded that it has gone through five phases—eras of trust, uneasy partnerships, distrust, partisan advocacy, and congressional acquiescence. Historically, and to this day, the pendulum swings favoring different demands, different emphases, as events change. Where will it—should it—go after Snowden?

There is a fundamental quandary separating those who favor erring in favor of national security and those concerned about invasions of personal privacy in times of conflict. Everyone sensibly favors national security *and* personal privacy. National security specialists argue there is no proof that their practices damaged anyone; and civil libertarians argue that the mere fact of the incursions alone *is* the damage.

Florida Senator Bob Graham, now retired, chaired the Senate Intelligence Committee for a decade at the end of the last century and the beginning of the present one. He wrote about congressional oversight in *Intelligence Matters* in 2004. Graham chaired the post-9/11 joint congressional committee inquiry into intelligence activities. Until the mid-1970s, he wrote, "Congress interfered as little as possible and trusted our intelligence agencies as much as possible." The CIA and the FBI failed to communicate with each other, and the executive branch had a blank check after 9/11, Graham wrote, as the intelligence process was politicized. Information was overclassified, he complained, and as a result "the public had its vision shrouded."

Graham pointed out that the Bush administration practiced "incestuous amplification," where people sharing the same point of view were making decisions. Graham believes that congressional oversight requires more expertise in Congress and avoiding too close an association with agencies it oversees. The December 2002 Joint Inquiry recommended, among other specifics, "the need to enhance national security while fully protecting civil liberties." It also pointed out that classification can impair congressional oversight, as it may shield self-interest.

The lessons Graham advocates are relevant today. Complaining about excessive secrecy, Graham pointed out, "The public can't respond to things it isn't told, or seek reforms to problems it is kept from seeing." Prophetically, he added, "America must decide how much domestic security they will accept and the inevitable intrusion that it will cause on our individual civil liberties. The debate on that balance has yet to begin."

I asked Senator Graham how congressional oversight might be improved in the wake of the Snowden affair. He doesn't think, as the 9/11 Commission suggested, that structural change is needed. He believes improvement will come with more qualified and aggressive members and a unified nonpolitical professional staff. As much as politics can be taken out of the mix, the better; though that is unlikely in such an essentially political institution. Graham is critical of the insularity and competitiveness of the executive agencies managing surveillance, which can result in missed opportunities to prevent terrorism, as has happened. In the final judgment, however, Graham agrees that there is a fundamental problem in oversight when, as is the case, the overseer must rely on the overseen: "You don't know what you don't know."

Congress does not seek to and ought not manage national security, so oversight is reduced to watchdogging and reforms after the fact. Congress can do something about Snowden's revelations now if it wants to, but can it ever prevent excesses from happening before they happen? Or must Congress ultimately defer to executive branch practices, relying on its expertise and on the courts to perform judicial oversight? Professor Barry Siegel's "Judging State Secrets" suggests that relying on judicial oversight is illusory, or has been in modern times. Judiciary Committee Chairman Senator Patrick Leahy has noted, "The press is doing our work for us and we should be ashamed of it."

Critics of Snowden argue that if every rogue government employee was free to decide when and whether to violate his duties and commitments, we would have nihilistic anarchy. If our government cannot insure domestic tranquility and provide for the common defense, as the Constitution declares in its opening passage, there will be no democracy, no surviving society, no "perfect union," and ultimately, no Constitution. Snowden admits he signed an agreement, Standard Form 312, subjecting him to civil sanctions and the risk of jail, when he took his job.

How did our country's defenders become the accused offenders in performing their important work, and Snowden suddenly a hero, to some, for what others claim was treacherous malfeasance?

For one reason, as Professor Mills points out, the national security apparatus decided, in the frightening aftermath of 9/11, to go after our enemies, even if it meant "collecting the haystack" in search of the dangerous needles within it. At times of threats like this, the public understandably defers to its government to do whatever is necessary to defend us, no-holds-barred.

But secrets rarely remain secrets, and inevitably there is exposure and pushback. In his recent novel, *The Director*, David Ignatius's antihero, reminiscent of Edward Snowden, is a fugitive in Caracas who has leaked secret U.S. government records. His credo is not unlike some real-life, new-generation geek hackers and rogue patriots—or pseudo-patriots, in some eyes—who decide for themselves what is good and evil, moral and immoral, and take pride in doing it:

> *"I didn't kill anyone. I didn't torture anyone. I didn't listen to people's telephone calls or steal their secrets. They claim that I broke the laws of the United States, but I didn't break any of the laws of humanity. I left the CIA as an act of conscience. I revealed its secrets to give liberty to others."* [23]

The question, as we see it, is not whether the executive branch of our government should take all proper steps to guard the security of the nation—of course it should. But what are the proper bounds of those steps? And who gets to say so? And how should that be accomplished and monitored in the public's interest?

The NSA was created by President Harry Truman in 1952 to coordinate government surveillance after WWII. It is a military agency that reports to the Director of National Intelligence. In response to congressional disclosures of intelligence gathering excesses (the Church Committee) in 1978, Congress enacted FISA to oversee domestic surveillance practices by a special secret court. The effectiveness and fairness of this method of judicial review of executive activities (rarely denying government requests for warrants, or hearing an opposing argument) has been questioned, as bordering on ministerial rather than judicial. The failure of judicial review in national security cases is demonstrated in Professor Siegel's chapter.

Professor Mills's chapter details how after 9/11, the Patriot Act widened the scope of prior authorized government surveillance practices. Under Section 505, National Security Letters (NSLs) were issued by the FBI to communications providers, banks, phone companies, and Internet companies, demanding their data and forbidding them from revealing that fact. In effect, they are administrative subpoenas, needing no prior judicial approval, though they later can be and have been challenged in courts. Section 215 of the Patriot Act was the basis of a FISA ruling that Verizon data could be collected, procedures which the President's Oversight Board called an "impermissible" interpretation.

Litigation questioning the constitutionality of these NSLs disclosed the FBI had issued 56,000 of them, *Frontline* reported. The gag order provision of the NSLs under the Patriot Act has been challenged in federal courts as a violation of the Fourth Amendment. A bill reforming this practice as it pertains to U.S. citizens was proposed by President Obama and passed by the House. It is pending in the Senate.

A distinction has been made between the collection of metadata and content, suggesting that the former is less invasive of personal privacy than the latter, and doesn't necessarily require warrants. But critics, even the former general counsel to the NSA, point out, "If you have enough meta data, you don't really need content." One commentator cited a hypothetical example. If a husband calls his wife to say he is working late, his remarks to her are the content. But the metadata might show that the call came from a motel, following an earlier call to an escort agency (ZDNet, September 16, 2014).[24]

The Bush administration acted on the theory that presidential power under Article II, Section 2, of the Constitution itself allowed additional means of collecting information in time of "war." Executive Order 12333, issued in 1981 by President Reagan, expanded the essentially secret collection of intelligence overseas on foreigners. The reach of this surveillance practice is vast, and includes data not reviewed by courts or Congress because it targets foreigners, though it dragnets American citizens in the process under FISA, Section 702, which became the basis for the collection of data of U.S. citizens, too. The evolution of all these laws is analyzed by Professor Jon Mills in his chapter.

An additional wrinkle was reported by former State Department official John Napier Tye in a *Washington Post* article in July 2014.[25] His article, "reviewed and cleared" by the State Department and the NSA, states that Section 215 of the Patriot Act authorizing the government to obtain court orders to compel private telecommunications companies to turn over phone data is not the whole story. It does not include the collecting and storing of U.S. communications, which is covered by Executive Order 12333. That order, not a law and not subject to judicial review or congressional oversight, allows collection of content, not only the gathering of metadata, of U.S. citizens, even if it is "incidentally" collected overseas. That "loophole," Tye pointed out, "can be stretched very wide."

Since U.S. communications travel across U.S. borders routinely, the NSA can collect and store the content of communications between U.S. citizens gathered outside the United States as part of a foreign intelligence investigation, without a warrant or court order and without Congress knowing about it. Senator Dianne Feinstein, chairman of the Senate Select Committee on Intelligence, stated that her committee cannot oversee conduct covered by Executive Order 12333. Nor does the NSA need to advise the private companies collecting this data that it is doing so.

Tye reports that he advised the State Department inspector general, NSA's inspector general, and House and Senate intelligence committees that he thought 12333 violates the Fourth Amendment's unreasonable search and seizure prohibition. He discussed his view with a member of the President's review group appointed after the Snowden disclosures and was advised that it had recommended (Rec. 12) that all data of U.S. citizens incidentally collected be "purged unless it has foreign intelligence value or is necessary to prevent serious harm." Tye was told by White House staffers there were "no plans to make such changes."

Tye argues that it makes no sense that U.S. citizens should have weak privacy protection when their communications are collected by their government outside the United States. In words reminiscent of Snowden's (who, unlike Tye, did not try first to go through all available official channels with his complaints), Tye protested:

I am coming forward because I think Americans deserve an honest answer to the simple question: What kind of data is NSA collecting on millions, or hundreds of millions, of Americans?

The USA Freedom Act, passed by the House and pending in the Senate, would reform FISA practices and end bulk collection of phone records, as the President and intelligence chief James Clapper proposed after Snowden's disclosures of PRISM became public. Microsoft's general counsel Bradford Smith recently told a Harvard Law School audience that the FISA court should be reformed. However, that act hasn't been passed, and proponents fear that, given the current reemergence of worldwide terrorist activities, the public pressure for limiting intelligence gathering will fade.

How did all this happen? There was understandably "a profound shift in national security priorities" after 9/11, which combined with a "tectonic shift" caused by advances in technology. We now know that in addition to its own surveillance, the NSA appropriated data from nine private Internet companies, capturing "enormous flows of data at the speed of light from fiber optic cables that carried Internet and telephone traffic over continents and under seas," Pulitzer Prize–winning journalist Barton Gellman reported, based on his interviews with Snowden.

Those private Internet companies, like Microsoft, acknowledge their duty to comply with legal orders and judicial dictates, but were outraged by being seen as "candy stores for U.S. intelligence," Gellman noted. Where there is probable cause to target people for proper intelligence purposes, doing so is legitimate. Yet *The Wall Street Journal* reported that roughly 75 percent of all U.S. Internet traffic is vacuumed by the U.S. surveillance programs, including private communications of both U.S. and foreign citizens. Intelligence Committee member Senator Ron Wyden told Silicon Valley executives that the government's "digital dragnet" created a clear and present danger for the Internet economy without making the country safer.[26]

Microsoft's general counsel Bradford Smith and his otherwise competitive legal counterparts at Google, Facebook, Twitter, Apple, and LinkedIn recently formed a coalition, Reform Government Surveillance, to push for government changes to its appropriation of online social media data. Those companies, along with Yahoo, Microsoft, and Dropbox, signed an open *New York Times* letter calling for stronger congressional controls. Private companies are concerned about their image, and the economic impact of these surveillance practices on their business, as well as the constitutional implications. Their awareness has heightened as a result of the Snowden disclosures. For example, Yahoo has improved its security practices and other companies are taking more care of data security through encryption. New companies in Switzerland and Germany are developing NSA-proof encryption products to exploit this new market.

Government officials have expressed fears that encryption devices developed by Apple and Google in the wake of Snowden's disclosures will adversely affect law enforcement. As a result of Snowden's exposure of the PRISM program, Google and Apple (96.4 percent of the smartphones in the world) have developed encryption techniques to avoid intrusions. The new head of Government Communications Headquarters (GCHQ) in Britain, along with the FBI and the New York City district attorney, complain that this will preempt search warrants and thus impair necessary law enforcement. Snowden says that, after a warrant is issued, encrypted material and geo-location data can be accessed from the cloud. And he told Harvard law professor Lawrence Lessig that backdoors in any system can be accessed by savvy intruders, not only law enforcement officials. Snowden advocates an international Magna Carta for the Internet governing digital rights worldwide.

The Communications Assistance for Law Enforcement Act of 1994 (CALEA) requires traditional phone companies to include lawful intercept capabilities. The FBI is seeking its expansion to other companies as a law enforcement necessity. Civil liberties organizations and software manufacturers argue that weakening encryption makes citizens vulnerable to hacking by criminals and foreign governments. That seesaw debate will continue until a balanced compromise is found.

Economic considerations merge here with ethical ones. Bloomberg News reported that technology companies fear losing $35 billion in the next three years from foreign customers who choose not to buy U.S. products because these companies cooperated with spy programs (July 2014). However, a *Forbes* magazine report suggested these private companies "don't look to be suffering from any kind of mass exodus" (April 15, 2014). *Politico* added,

"Nations and companies have too much invested in the global Internet to let it balkanize," as different countries are motivated to apply rigorous safeguards to prevent excessive surveillance protection (June 5, 2014).

The release in September 2014 of 1,500 pages of formerly classified sealed documents made headlines because they showed that the government had ordered Yahoo to make its customer records accessible, and threatened to fine the company $250,000 *a day* if it refused to comply. It would have bankrupted the company to dispute the government's demands. The government acted under the earlier Protect America Act of 2007 and later FISA 2008 Amendments. Yahoo argued unsuccessfully before trial and appellate FISA courts that doing so violated its customers' Fourth Amendment rights. As a result of this defeat, other tech companies capitulated to the PRISM program providing for warrantless orders.

While Google, Yahoo, Microsoft, LinkedIn, and Facebook have settled with the government, Twitter is suing in the Ninth Circuit (Northern District, California), challenging the nondisclosure provision of the NSLs on First Amendment grounds. Twitter argues that it has been subjected to prior restraint, in effect a gag order, which requires preapproval of its company reports, or refraining from any comments at all to its customers about government surveillance of its reports. The government contends that this information is classified.

The irony is, as a recent *Frontline* documentary on PBS described,[27] the private sector companies who surveilled their subscribers for advertising and economic purposes learned that the government was accessing their stored data for national security purposes through advanced tracking techniques.

Snowden advocates that there should be no constitutional "distinction between digital information and printed information." Yahoo's new security consultant reports that "[p]rivacy is much more effective as a selling point than it used to be." Professor Mills's chapter traces the law of privacy from the ideas of the progressive Justice Louis Brandeis of an earlier era to that of the current conservative Chief Justice John Roberts, demonstrating that the Constitution, then and now, protects personal privacy.

Resort to the Espionage Act for disclosures in the press, as is threatened in the Snowden matter, is rare. During World War II, *The Chicago Tribune* was investigated, but not indicted, for reporting secret government naval intelligence. It ran antiwar stories mentioning our breaking encrypted Japanese messages about its armada at Midway in 1942, and an account on December 6, 1941, of U.S. military plans in Europe. The government threatened, but backed off, indicting *The Tribune* under the Espionage Act of 1917. One can hardly imagine a situation more warranting of prosecution than the disclosure of secret wartime maneuvers. The only example of a successful prosecution for press behavior involved Samuel Morison's publication in *Jane's Defence Weekly* of three classified photos of a Soviet nuclear submarine. He was convicted under the Espionage Act, served two years in prison, and was pardoned by President Clinton. In other cases involving the Espionage Act, such as the notorious Rosenberg and Pollard cases, disclosures had been made to foreign countries (one hostile, the other friendly), but that was not the case here.

The press usually prevails in comparable clashes with the government, more so than lone individuals. When the notorious Pentagon Papers were leaked and published by *The New York Times* and *The Washington Post*, despite government arguments that this endangered America's interests, the U.S. Supreme Court refused to enjoin publication of that Vietnam War history. It was a cause célèbre and became a landmark victory for freedom of the press.

The role of the press is critical when intragovernment checks and balances don't work. The digital press changes and speeds up this process. In the Snowden case there was an ironic element. Snowden distrusted the establishment press and sought out Greenwald, Poitras, and Gellman for that reason, but they all realized that without the resources of the establishment press their story would lack the impact they sought. First, they reached out to *The Guardian*. While it broke the story, *The Guardian* was pressured by United Kingdom government officials who actually came to their offices and destroyed *Guardian* computers. *The Guardian* then made a deal with *The New York Times* (we have the thumb drives, they said to their new press partners, but you have the First Amendment, which protects us better than British law). Barton Gellman and *The Washington Post* also were brought in, and Gellman's stories have been prominent.

Even then, Glenn Greenwald complained in his book that the establishment media was timid, risk averse, not as adversarial with the government as he thought it should be, and that some of its members treated him and his extraordinary stories with cynicism while others seemed protective of the government. Hodding Carter, a former newspaper editor and later government spokesman for the State Department, discusses the role and responsibilities of the press in tense situations like Snowden's in his chapter, "The Press."

Snowden's revelations have caused a furor abroad, as well as in the United States. Brazilian President Dilma Rousseff protested after learning that her personal conversations were monitored, along with other officials in the world, whether they be foreign allies or enemies (i.e., Iran, Turkey, Venezuela, Cuba, China, Russia). Australia and Indonesia formed a new agreement on their spying practices. Former Israeli Prime Minister Ehud Olmert learned his phones and e-mails were tapped, though Israel and the United

States, however close their relations, are known to spy on and share information with each other.

Chancellor Angela Merkel complained to the German Parliament after learning that her cell phone records had been "monitored" by the NSA program (those of thirty-five other foreign leaders were, too, the AP reported). Her charge has been disputed by a later study, but, at the time, Merkel warned that the ethics of security in democratic states must be a model to the undemocratic states around the world.

There is a *Casablanca* element here: "There is gambling in Rick's place." Hark, nasty surveillance practices are going on! *Washington Post* columnist David Ignatius noted that the United States and Germany had cooperated for years in secret surveillance activities. NSA also works with GCHQ, its British counterpart, in surveillance practices, and the United States has arrangements with Australia, Canada, and New Zealand for sharing intelligence. Josef Joffe, the editor of *Die Zeit* in Hamburg, noted in *The Wall Street Journal* that friends do spy on friends, pointing out examples of Germany doing so, and he refers to Germany and America "as comrades-in-snooping." He added, referring to a dated adage, "This world of power, politics and terror is not run by gentlemen" as gentlemen "don't read each other's mail."[28]

Snowden has won several German prizes for his disclosures. *The Wall Street Journal* reported (September 24, 2014) that Snowden has become a cult hero in Germany, portrayed in graffiti, posters, T-shirts, pop performances, and advertisements.[29] Sweden has proposed Snowden for its Humanitarian Award, and he was nominated for the 2014 Nobel Peace Prize.[30]

In an interview with *The Guardian* (July 2014), Edward Snowden sarcastically pointed out that the fact that the NSA spying on millions of German citizens wasn't considered a scandal, but when Merkel's cell phone allegedly was invaded, it became one. "[T]he priorities of governments seem to be very distinct from the desires of the public," he pointed out, ". . . the search for truth has been subordinated to political priorities." That other countries do versions of what Snowden exposed the United States as doing doesn't make it right, but it does add perspective to the current international uproar.

The sheer volume of current surveillance practices is mind-boggling. Glenn Greenwald reported that the NSA "was processing more than 20 billion communications from around the world each day," including Internet and phone records, of Americans and foreigners. The recent post-Snowden presidential review board reported that collecting this information did not prevent attacks on the United States, and the NSA was instructed to cease monitoring world leaders.

President Obama demanded that the Director of National Intelligence make public information about U.S. surveillance programs in the wake of the Snowden revelations. A year later a list of almost 90,000 foreign persons and organizations who were surveilled through U.S. companies was disclosed. The names of U.S. citizens whose phone calls or e-mails were gathered up accidentally or because they were in contact with foreign contacts were not listed. Privacy advocates complained. However, a federal court in Portland, Oregon, ruled that the Section 702 orders under 2008 FISA amendments allowing intercepts without court orders are constitutional. There is no public record of Executive Order 12333 authorizing intelligence collection overseas on foreigners.[31]

Among many responsible observers—from the left and the right of the political spectrum—there is a deep concern over the implications of Snowden's revelations. They exposed "an all-out assault on the Constitution" (Rand Paul), and they revealed practices that are "obscenely outrageous" (Al Gore). As an ACLU counsel argued to a Brookings Institution conference: "you don't have to think the NSA is malevolent in order to conclude that it's unwise to concentrate so much information, so much power in its hands."

Nevertheless, critics are concerned about the fallout from Snowden's actions. Sir Iain Lobban, retired GCHQ director, said Snowden's revelations made his agency's work more cumbersome, and his country less safe. There have been concerns in the United States, too. At a Brookings Institution conference in 2014, law critic Stuart Taylor Jr. reported: "America's diplomacy has been hobbled, its image abroad tarnished, its alliances strained, its government's standing in the eyes of its own people damaged, its policies challenged in court . . ." Princeton University professor Sean Wilentz wrote in *The New Republic* that while we are right to be concerned about the information Snowden disclosed about government secret practices, that concern goes too far if as a result we come to distrust democratic governments: "Surveillance and secrecy will never be attractive features of a democratic government, but they are not inimical to it, either."

NSA defenders point out that Congress passed our security laws, that in recent decades the chief executives of Republican and Democratic administrations employed them, and about forty federal judges approved their exercise. Why should rogue employees or contractors be trusted more than our government agencies? Clemency for Snowden would send the wrong message, his critics claim. Laura Poitrus and Glenn Greenwald recently reported there is a second leaker at NSA, senior to Snowden, who is being investigated for leaking details of the government's watch list.

As time passes, the initial strong widespread public criticism of Snowden's actions has been tempered and some public sympathy has evolved. The debate continues in the cloud. Snowden spoke for an hour to NBC's Brian Williams from Russia in May 2014, as he had earlier on German television and Skype, defending his actions. Snowden claimed he has not given any records to Russia or any other country (more than what he made available to the public worldwide). He argued that the U.S. government has offered no explanation of how his revelations prejudiced our national security or caused harm to anyone. In October 2014 he told a *New Yorker* audience over the Internet that there is no evidence that as a result of his revelations agencies hostile to the United States have hurt communities we want to protect, that sources have gone "dark," or disinformation resulted, or that his acts caused damage to our national security, as his critics have claimed. He spoke to a UK audience in a virtual, live video link explaining how GCHQ agency has been collecting citizens' data unchecked.

In the only case dealing with the question of whether Snowden's acts caused damage to our national security, *Klayman v. Obama,* federal trial judge Richard Leon wrote in December 2013 that the government asserted that NSA's surveillance program prevented fifty-four terrorist attacks, but would offer no proof of that, even to the judge *in camera.* The judge concluded that he was not convinced "that the NSA's database has ever truly served the purpose of rapidly identifying terrorists in time sensitive investigations."

Poitras claimed that information about the 9/11 suicide bombers was available to our intelligence authorities, but not used. Snowden stated that while the FBI had been warned that the Boston marathon bombers had ties to Islamic terrorist groups, our mass surveillance was unable to prevent their terrorist acts. Here were instances that might justify mass surveillance, but which were of no use to the government. In Thomas Blanton's chapter, "Secrecy, Surveillance, and the Snowden Effect," he points out how "the 9/11 attacks themselves were enabled by excessive secrecy," and agencies' failure to share materials made surveillance practices "counterproductive." Needles in the haystack can be missed because too much data has been accumulated by too many collectors.

The judicial verdict on the value of our surveillance practices is inconclusive. While the *Klayman* judge viewed NSA's actions harshly, in December 2013 a federal court in New York City ruled that collecting phone metadata was protected by Section 215 of the Patriot Act. And a federal trial court in California, which initially restrained NSA from destroying evidence of dragnet surveillance, revoked its order when the federal government argued maintaining Section 702 evidence would freeze NSA's system. These cases, this subject, will be in play after the publication of this book.

Admiral Michael Rogers, now in charge of the NSA's cyber operations, told David Sanger of *The New York Times* that he doesn't believe "the sky is falling" as a result of Snowden's disclosures, though terrorist groups are making changes as a result of Snowden's revelations. Working relations with American telecommunications, tech, and social media firms are changing. When the President's commission reviewed the practices Snowden exposed, "it could not find a case in which a program lead definitively halted a potential terrorist attack."

There is a central point in any evaluation of Snowden's conduct. While he stole secret government documents, and absconded with them, he did not dump a mass of raw information onto public screens. He says he retained nothing, posted nothing, turned all his misappropriated data over to a few trusted journalists he considered responsible, with instructions to publish only information that they thought would *not* endanger public safety but would reveal misconduct. Barton Gellman reported that Snowden "has not tried in any way to tell me what to write, what not to write, or when."

Gellman was questioned in a *Frontline* interview about his relationship with Snowden, who, he says, "turned out to be among the very most reliable sources I've ever had." After extensive questioning of Snowden, Gellman became convinced he was "the real thing," his revelations "a jaw dropper." Everything Gellman printed was authenticated and verified independently. Gellman was unable to rebut information Snowden provided him. Snowden did not ask to be protected through anonymity, preferring to unmask himself, knowing that in doing so he risked his freedom and perhaps his life. Gellman describes Snowden as ascetic, introspective, "almost Zen-like in his serenity," a "classic sort of digital native." On a recent Internet broadcast, looking like a gentle version of tennis star Novak Djokovic, Snowden said he was appalled by what he discovered were NSA's intelligence gathering practices. Claiming that they were illegal, he determined he had to document his claims in order to "provoke a public debate." He surely succeeded in that respect!

Snowden relied on the journalistic judgment of the three people to whom he gave his collected information to publish only the documents whose revelations wouldn't harm innocent people. He did not publicize en masse all the records he purloined, as Julian Assange and Bradley, now Chelsea, Manning did. Rather, he relied on his press contacts to curate what was published.

That is what they did. Gellman, along with *Washington Post* colleagues who are analyzing the Snowden material, quoted Snowden's instructions to them: "I know that you and *The Post* have enough sense of civic duty to consult with the government to ensure that the reporting on and handling of this material cause no harm." In fact, before the reporters published excerpts from Snowden's materials, which they considered of important public interest, they determined not to publish revelations concerning ongoing intelligence operations, which would have been prejudicial to our national interests if disclosed. Of course, Gellman's remark confirms that Snowden did reveal information that even his admirers admit should have remained secret could be offered as proof of the recklessness of his revelations, and confirms his critics' contention that he caused problems to our country's intelligence and diplomatic missions. In *Slate*, critic Fred Kaplan takes the position that a mass misappropriation should not be rationalized by relying on others to curate the publication of parts of it. The fundamental underlying question is whether it is the individual's or the press's role, or should it remain solely the government's responsibility, to make these decisions.

The curating of Snowden's material and the independent determinations by responsible journalists of what not to publish did make all the more powerful their embarrassing disclosures. The public was shocked to learn that "startlingly intimate, even voyeuristic . . . stories of love and heartbreak, illicit sexual liaisons, mental health crises, political and religious conversions, financial anxieties and disappointed hopes" were found in the records of "10,000 account holders who were not targeted." Snowden told *The Guardian* that it was the culture of NSA to pass around nude photographs of people in sexually compromising situations.

The *Post* reporters "reviewed roughly 160,000 intercepted email and instant message conversations, some of them hundreds of pages long, and 7,900 documents taken from more than 11,000 online accounts." According to Gellman's report, only 11 percent of those targeted by the NSA were legitimate targets; nine out of ten were "snagged in the NSA's net," which had been cast to entrap others, but were found on online accounts of digital networks. These captured records, gathered without warrants, may be kept for five years. A 2014 study in *Washington Lawyer* magazine reported that NSA "gathered about 250 million Internet communications each year without a warrant." *The New York Times* reported (August 2014) that "20,800 U.S. citizens and permanent residents are included in a federal government database of people suspected of having links to terrorism," over a million in total. Whatever the final number is, it is vast!

Breaching confidences of personal information collected by the NSA in its Internet sweeps raises a related but troubling legal issue. Communications between doctors and patients, attorneys and clients, priests and penitents, psychiatrists and people in analysis, are protected by law from disclosure. The privacy of these communications is widely accepted as fundamental to professional relationships. If they are swept up by the NSA, legally or illegally, intentionally or negligently, serious legal implications result. My book *In Confidence: When to Protect Secrecy and When to Require Disclosure* discusses these special relationships and the law governing them. All these professional communications are affected by any of the NSA's intrusions. In his interview (July 2014) in *The Guardian*, Snowden commented that he is researching the special problems of journalists and their sources in this regard. Poitras, too, has expressed concern that government surveillance could disclose journalists' sources.

Government officials have claimed that Snowden never protested the NSA's activities through proper channels before going public with them. Snowden's ACLU lawyer, Ben Wizner, told a conference that "[t]here was no one to report to who had not been part of the system of approval." Snowden told the European Parliament in March that he reported his concerns "to more than ten distinct officials, none of whom took any action to address them." He did not name those former colleagues, management, and senior leadership team members, though he identified them as two superiors in the NSA's Technology Directorate, and two in the NSA's Ops Center in Hawaii. He noted that as a private contractor he had no statutory whistleblower protection. The government denies he made these attempts to operate within intramural regulations for complaints. This matter is relevant in assessing Snowden's actions and can be resolved by a good faith, impartial investigation of the facts in dispute, and should be.

A May 2014 *Frontline* special, "United States of Secrets," reported the frightful treatment of several recent whistleblowers, no doubt daunting to others contemplating such action. Professor Edward Wasserman's chapter, "Protecting News in the Era of Disruptive Sources," reminds readers how some former whistleblowers have been cruelly mistreated, and he offers interesting ideas for reform. Law professor David Cole analyzes the problems of leakers as well. No surprise Snowden shied away from that course.

James Clapper admitted to security specialist David Ignatius that the impact of Snowden's disclosures may be less than once feared; he thinks Snowden took less than he originally thought. But the exact volume—whether Snowden purloined 1.5 million rather than 1.7 million documents—is not the issue. In Clapper's view, volume aside, the danger Snowden caused was "profound."

Clapper's comments are reminiscent of former Solicitor General Erwin Griswold's statements in the Pentagon Papers case where he argued to the Supreme Court on behalf of the United States that Daniel Ellsberg's release of the Pentagon Papers endangered the national security. Years later he wrote in *The Washington Post* that he had exaggerated the dangers and was wrong to have argued so. The government's position at the time was a cover-up of its misconduct, he admitted. Professor Siegel's chapter on judicial review of executive action presents a line of cases where the claims of state secrets in fact shielded government misconduct. Ellsberg argues that Snowden's acts were heroic, that he did what he had to do, and acted appropriately when faced with a moral dilemma.

In Snowden's case, there are moral, as well as legal, questions to be considered. In doing what he did, for the reason he said he did it, Snowden aligned himself (in his eyes, detractors would say) with the classic positions of civil disobedience taken throughout history. In the Bible's Exodus, in Sophocles' play *Antigone*, in the writings of Shelley and Thoreau, and the actions of Gandhi and Martin Luther King Jr., martyrs have faced and endured condemnation and punishment for their acts taken against their state to seek morality, justice, or changed policies.

Looking back, many of those figures—real or fictional—were pilloried and punished at the time of their acts, only to be honored retroactively when their points of view later were accepted. Snowden's remarks to his allies and collaborators indicate he viewed his actions in the historic light of civil disobedience. Snowden's acts were themselves nonviolent, though critics claim they might have caused violence. Snowden's acts of electronic disobedience are a product of our new age, rationalized as acts of conscience in the public's interest. One academic observer called Snowden "a conscientious objector to the war on privacy."[32]

Is punishment a critical part of civil disobedience? Law violators understand—or ought to—that they risk punishment, whether the laws they disobey are fair or just. Snowden says he expected punitive reactions, as happened to his models. He told *The Guardian* in 2014 that he was prepared to go to Guantánamo if that sanction was adjudged, though he thought that if he was tried by a jury, the moral element of his acts would hold some weight.

Professor Wasserman's chapter urges that the modern whistleblower should be judged by the public interest served by his disclosures, and that any sanctions for his conduct must take that matter into consideration, as is the case in other countries. The public interest defense is not recognized in the United States. It is akin to jury nullification in cases where technical rules warrant conviction but moral ones suggest otherwise. Snowden has said he isn't interested in being deemed a hero or celebrity, only in being tried and judged by a jury of his peers, and allowed to present a public interest defense. He told *The Nation* editors that the label whistleblower "otherizes us" and excuses the public from exercising its civic duty to speak out against abuse of power.[33] Wassserman argues that the press, which distributes whistleblower information, in addition to seeking its own glorification for having done so, also has an obligation to defend its sources after exploiting their information.

Law professor John Yoo, who when in government championed strong measures of national defense after 9/11, argued that the press's prizes do not vindicate Snowden's crimes. "Awarding a prize to a newspaper that covered a hurricane does not somehow vindicate the hurricane," Yoo argued. Thus, he continues, prizing the leaked reports "was by no means an endorsement of the leaker or the leaks." Hodding Carter's chapter (and Professor Coles's) describes the editor's dilemma and professional duty in balancing legitimate government requests to honor national security claims and their obligation to publicize information in the public's interest.

A *Harvard Law and Policy Review* article by Professor Yochai Benkler in 2014 advocated passage of a law providing a defense to leakers who challenge abusive systemic practices that threaten democracy and avoid public accountability. All organizations are subject to imperfections, error, malfeasance, Professor Benkler states, and those which deal with issues of war and peace "require public understanding." "Checks and balances become corroded and subverted over time," Professor Benkler wrote in *The Atlantic,* so whistleblowing "is a central pillar of the way American law deals with these dynamics of error, incompetence, and malfeasance in large organizations." Leaks in these cases, the author argues, "serve both democracy and security," and the powerful national security establishment doesn't merit a "magical exemption," based on its mystique.

Professor Benkler's rationale for his proposal is that "where a person takes a substantial personal risk reasonably calculated to inform the public about substantial abuses of government power, the state should correct itself, not the person who blew the whistle." Professor Benkler lists cases in our country's history where whistleblowers like Snowden were not prosecuted, suggesting that his proposal is consistent with past practices. He also proposes a civil cause of action for abuse of powers when leakers are harassed but not prosecuted.

Underlying all the questions about Snowden's mass disclosures is the systemic question whether all or some of the data our government keeps secret should have been classified in the first instance. That issue is not confined to the Snowden disclosures; it pertains to all secret government documents. Perhaps one good result in the fallout of the Snowden disclosures would be a reform of our classification system.

As I reported in my book *In Confidence*, and as the Director of the National Security Archive, Thomas Blanton, develops further in his chapter, our government's classification system excessively blankets much government information that ought to be available to the public.

Secrecy raises the potential for mischief and abuse, so it should not prevail unless there are clear and strong reasons for it. Many classified records do not have a redeeming public purpose for their classification as confidential, but bureaucrats in government agencies have the proclivity to hide behind classified claims. Philosopher Sissela Bok suggested in her book *Secrets* that there is a primordial tendency in government to hide information. If wrongdoing can be shielded by the very wrongdoers' shield of secrecy, citizens have no redress of their legitimate grievances. On a more innocent level, there is a self-protective inclination to err on the side of being careful with disclosing government records.

The government-wide system of executive classification of sensitive records began with good reasons during wartime under President Franklin D. Roosevelt, but it has been expanded under later administrations during the Cold War. In recent history, the prevailing policies have varied. The Clinton administration attempted to contain the growing trend toward classification of government records (and to accelerate declassification). But since September 11, 2001, classification has expanded (and declassification has been reduced) under Presidents George W. Bush and Barack Obama. Few would deny the justification for classifying some selective government information, but recent history has demonstrated that the process is far too expansive and has been abused.

Classified information falls into three categories: "top secret," "secret," and "confidential"—the latter defined as "information, the disclosure of which reasonably could be expected to cause damage to the national security."

Seven blue-ribbon committee examinations of the classification system over the years have criticized its application, expansion, and costs. In 1956, the Coolidge Committee reported that the classification system had "vague standards, failed to punish overclassification," which had reached "serious proportions," and had lost public confidence. In 1957, the Wright Commission also criticized overclassification and recommended abolishing the "confidential" category. In 1958, the Moss subcommittee called for punishing overclassification. In 1970, the Seitz Task Force called for "major surgery" of the system that would eliminate 90 percent of classified technical and scientific information. In 1985, the Stilwell Commission criticized the "implementation" of existing classification policies. In 1994, the Joint Security Commission criticized "unacceptable levels of inefficiency, inequity and cost."

Despite these critical analyses by prestigious independent experts, the problematic classification system remains, and in the words of the most recent (1997) commission headed by the late Senator Daniel Patrick Moynihan, the system "simply will not let go." The Moynihan Commission concluded that the classification system has proliferated; it is conducted by millions of self-interested people administering complex regulations so that "secrets in the federal government are whatever anyone with a stamp decides to stamp secret. . . . Such a system inevitably degrades." We have become "a nation of secrets," a 2007 book concluded.[34] Jack Goldsmith, Harvard law professor and former Justice Department official in the second Bush administration, calls it "a secrecy bureaucracy" of about 1.5 million people having top security clearance.

The steady stream of studies of the classification system for government records has uniformly described both an increase in the volume of classified documents and a decrease in declassification, both exacerbated dramatically since September 11, 2001. Indeed, there has been a rise in the reclassification of declassified documents in this recent period. During the first four years of the Bush administration (2001–2004), classifications rose from 8 million to 23 million; declassifications dropped from 100 million a year to 29 million a year. Derivative classifications occur by the millions (over 14 million in 2005) as a result of a secret appearing in a document, which said document then is derivatively classified and becomes a secondary market in secrets.

This secrecy machinery costs over $7 billion to run; at an incalculable cost to litigants, historians, common sense, and notions of democracy. Andrew Bacevich, a retired general and now a professor at Boston University, reminds that "insiders' control of secrets . . . insulates them from accountability and renders them impervious to criticism."

Government agencies classify thousands of documents every day, millions of documents every year. So many documents are now classified that the term has no meaning, *Time* magazine executive Norman Pearlstine has noted, and "much of what is classified is of dubious value to anyone."

Despite the evolution of sunshine laws aimed at opening the operations of government, and despite a consensus among experts that the classification system is too pervasive and expansive, and that there is a major need to declassify documents, these critical findings have been ignored. In fact, the trend of controlling the secrecy of government information has expanded. As one newspaper editor remarked, "Labeling something 'classified' or important to 'national security' does not make it so. The government overclassifies with abandon. And the definition of 'national security' is elusive."

Recent assessments put the number of people with top secret

clearance in the millions, not an exclusive club. The Snowden revelations led to a bizarre government directive instructing military employees *not* to read Greenwald's *The Intercept,* even those having top secret security clearance, because it might contain classified information. So government insiders now cannot read public Web site stories while Web site readers can read leaked insider stories?

Over 1,000 government agents and 2,000 private companies work on super-secret intelligence matters in 17,000 locations and 33 buildings in Washington, D.C., alone, according to Dana Priest of *The Washington Post* and William Arkin in *Top Secret America.* Our "bottomless well" of official secrets, as Priest and Arkin call it, costs the public $10 billion annually, only part of an $81 billion national intelligence network. There are also about 4,000 federal, state, and local organizations who are involved in counterterrorism work. NSA is building a data center in Utah "five times the size of the US Capitol Building, with its own power plant that will reportedly burn $40 million a year in electricity," according to a recent report.

In August 29, 2013, Gellman and a *Washington Post* colleague described the $52.6 billion "black budget" for fiscal 2013 that funds 16 spy agencies with 107,035 employees, predominately the CIA.

When people think of state secrets they presume that military plans, clandestine spying, and back-channel diplomacy are involved. As Professor Siegel reported in *Claim of Privilege,* and he expands and updates in his chapter, many claims of state secrecy by the government arise in civil matters—tort claims, for example. The 1953 case *U.S. v. Reynolds* set the questionable precedent that courts essentially abide by and defer to the judgments of the executive about what should remain secret. More often than not, the claim of state secrets has been a pretext to hide government misconduct, and since 9/11 the practice has increased remarkably, as the battles over disclosing information about our country's rendition practices demonstrate.

Making the secret mine of executive government information

accessible to the public was the goal of the 1966 Freedom of Information Act (FOIA) (amended in 1974 and 1986). FOIA was enacted to ensure transparency of government records. The Supreme Court stated that FOIA was designed "to ensure an informed citizenry," "check against corruption," and "hold the governors accountable to the governed." FOIA was supposed to "open agency action to the light of public scrutiny." Full disclosure is mandated unless clearly exempted by the statute. Lee Hamilton, who vice-chaired the House Intelligence Committee, and Thomas Kean, who chaired the 9/11 Commission, recently placed the burden of demonstrating the value of intelligence gathering on the government, not the American public.

The FOIA process is expensive and slow, and it can be daunting. It effectively puts the burden on citizens to pursue their interests in discovering information instead of on the government to justify its claim for confidentiality. A survey of FOIA practices in eighty-seven government agencies and departments disclosed that instead of responding to FOIA requests in the "timely manner" called for in the law, agencies took months and years to respond—in the extreme, fifteen to twenty years! That survey concluded that the system is "plagued by delay and backlogs." The trend is discouraging: FOIA requests have fallen 20 percent, personnel has been cut 10 percent, backlogs have tripled, and denials have increased 10 percent. One neighboring country handles such requests overnight, electronically.

Neither FOIA nor the regulations designed to permit declassification by interested agencies and officials have succeeded in adequately opening government records to the public. As a result, we are left with a "disturbing new culture of government secrecy."

The line between justifiable governmental claims of confidentiality and overly autocratic claims is elusive. It is easy to agree that openness and sunlight are good disinfectants and that the pitiless light of public glare is salutary, as civil libertarians historically have argued. But all three branches of government, like all private organizations, have a legitimate need to protect the confidentiality of some of their work. Military secrets like those pertaining to troop movements—the classic example—are obvious to defend. So, too, are diplomatic communiqués and sensitive national security records. The problem, however, is where to draw the line, by whom, and when and how to traverse it—how to balance self-preservation against appropriate transparency and public access. If the Snowden disclosures generate a national reform of our classification system, his questioned behavior will have served an important public service.

Outside of the government, we rely on the press as the public's institutional watchdog, and the Constitution provides the press with special protection. The clash of core values between self-government and self-defense, between the government's interest in protecting national security and the public's interest in knowing about its government's practices, was discussed by Barton Gellman in a Nieman Report in 2004, before Snowden. "If we are sovereign," Gellman argued, "we rule those who rule us. Secrecy corrodes self-government." The courts are disinclined to play the role of overseer, and Congress knows what the government officials tell it. Thus informal methods are required to keep equilibrium, and leakers to the press in effect perform a form of "arbitrage."

Journalism dean and professor Edward Wasserman and now university professor Hodding Carter deal with the apparent conflict between giving the press awards for revealing government malfeasance, as was the case with the journalists behind Snowden's disclosures, and indicting the source of that very content that won two reporters their Pulitzers for public service. Fears have been expressed by two senators (Ron Wyden and Chuck Grassley) that monitoring practices designed to prevent Snowden-like incidents may chill whistleblowers.

The fallout after the Snowden affair, as the following chapters make clear, deals with the fundamental question of how to protect public privacy without degrading our national security. There is general agreement with the notion that public participation is required in a democracy for state decisions to have moral legitimacy. The public relies on the courts and Congress and the press to protect against excessive executive actions. *The Economist* noted that there is a "maddening, vertiginous, spiraling quality" to the debate about deciding who should and how to decide right and wrong in these confounding circumstances. We hope the treatments of this issue in the following chapters will help the public with its decision. President Obama recently stated the profound issue simply:

> *We have to make some important decisions about how to protect ourselves and sustain our leadership in the world, while upholding the civil liberties and privacy protections that our ideals—and our Constitution—require (* Huffington Post, *June 5, 2014).*

The chapters that follow bring the decision-making quandaries to light and offer wise recommendations for reforms.

NOTES

1. Michael Winship, "Snowden's Legal Counsel: Forget About Orwell, Worry About Kafka," *Moyers & Company,* March 11, 2014, http://bill moyers.com/2014/03/11/our-chat-with-edward-snowdens-legal -counsel/.
2. Luke Harding, *The Snowden Files: The Inside Story of the World's Most Wanted Man* (New York: Vintage, 2014).

3. Glenn Greenwald, *No Place to Hide: Edward Snowden, the NSA, and the U.S. Surveillance State* (New York: Metropolitan Books, 2014).

4. Brian Brooks, "Laura Poitras Film about Snowden & Surveillance Added to 52nd NYFF," September 16, 2014, http://www.filmlinc.com /nyff2014/blog/laura-poitras-citizenfour-edward-snowden-nsa-nyff -world-premiere

5. Alan Rusbridger and Ewen MacAskill, "Edward Snowden interview— the edited transcript," *Guardian,* July 18, 2014.

6. George Packer, "The Holder of Secrets," *New Yorker,* October 20, 2014.

7. Daniel Byman and Benjamin Wittes, "Reforming the NSA: How to Spy After Snowden," *Foreign Affairs,* May/June 2014.

8. Benjamin Wittes, Jamil Jaffer, Julian Sanchez, John Inglis, and Carrie Cordero, "A Debate One Year After Snowden: The Future of U.S. Surveillance Authorities." Debate held at the Brookings Institution, June 5, 2014. Transcript available through http://www.brookings .edu/.

9. David Ignatius, "James Clapper: We underestimated the Islamic State's 'will to fight,'" *Washington Post,* September 18, 2014.

10. Linda Greenhouse, "The Nation; Suicide Pact," *New York Times,* September 22, 2002.

11. Charles J. Reid Jr., "Constitution is Not a Suicide Pact," *Huffington Post Politics Blog,* January 23, 2014, http://www.huffingtonpost.com /charles-j-reid-jr/constitution-is-not-a-sui_b_4073379.html.

12. James McCartney and Molly McCartney, *America's War Machine* (New York: Thomas Dunne Books, to be published 2015).

13. Glenn Greenwald and Murtaza Hussain, "Meet the Muslim-American Leaders the FBI and NSA Have Been Spying On," *Intercept,* July 9, 2014.

14. Winship, "Snowden's Legal Counsel."

15. Barton Gellman, "Edward Snowden, after months of NSA revelations, says his mission's accomplished," *Washington Post,* December 23, 2013.

16. Julian Hattem, "CIA admits to spying on Senate," *Hill,* July 31, 2014.

17. Loch K. Johnson, "Congress' Experiment Overseeing Spies," *New York Times,* July 9, 2002.

18. Loch K. Johnson, "Governing in the Absence of Angels: On the Practice of Intelligence Accountability in the United States." Paper

presented at the Geneva Centre for the Democratic Control of Armed Forces (DCAF), The Norwegian Parliamentary Intelligence Oversight Committee, Human Rights Centre, Department of Law, University of Durham. Oslo, Norway, September 2003.

19. Michael M. Castle (R-DE) to Speaker Nancy Pelosi (D-CA). Congressional Record—House, Vol. 153, Pt. 9, May 10, 2007.

20. Denis McDonough, Mara Rudman, and Peter Rundlet: "No Mere Oversight: Congressional Oversight of Intelligence Is Broken," Center for American Progress, June 2006, http://cdn.americanprogress.org /wp-content/uploads/kf/NOMEREOVERSIGHT.PDF.

21. References to congressional and executive officials and former officials noted in the following pages are based on extensive personal interviews and correspondence.

22. James Risen, *Pay Any Price: Greed, Power, and Endless War* (New York: Houghton Mifflin Harcourt, 2014), 232–63.

23. David Ignatius, *The Director* (New York: W.W. Norton & Company, Inc., 2014).

24. Stilgherrian, "Can Snowden Finally Kill the 'Harmless Metadata' Myth?" *Full Tilt Blog*, September 16, 2014, available through http:// www.zdnet.com (Australia).

25. John Napier Tye, "Meet Executive Order 12333: The Reagan Rule That Lets the NSA Spy on Americans," *Washington Post*, July 18, 2014.

26. Brandon Baily, "Senator Wyden: NSA Tech Spying Hurts Economy," Associated Press, October 8, 2014.

27. *Frontline*, "United States of Secrets (Part One): The Program," (May 13, 2014) and Part Two: Privacy Lost (May 20, 2014), available through http://www.pbs.org/.

28. Josef Joffe, "Of Spycraft and Statecraft," *Wall Street Journal*, July 17, 2014.

29. Harriet, Torry. "Edward Snowden Emerges as a Cult Hero in Germany," *Wall Street Journal*, September 24, 2014.

30. Karl Ritter, "Snowden Honored with 'Alternative Nobel,'" Associated Press, September 24, 2014.

31. David Cole, "'No Place to Hide' by Glenn Greenwald, on the NSA's Sweeping Efforts to 'Know It All,'" *Washington Post*, May 12, 2014.

32. David Bromwich, "The Question of Edward Snowden," *New York Review of Books*, December 4, 2014.

33. Katrina vanden Heuvel and Stephen F. Cohen, "Edward Snowden Speaks: A Sneak Peek at an Exclusive Interview," *Nation*, October 10, 2014.

34. Ted Gup, *Nation of Secrets: The Threat to Democracy and the American Way of Life* (New York: Anchor, reprint edition, 2008).

THE PRESS

Hodding Carter III

Hodding Carter III is Professor of Leadership and Public Policy at the University of North Carolina, Chapel Hill. He came to that post after nearly eight years as president and CEO of the John S. and James L. Knight Foundation, which has a major interest in media freedom and improvement. A longtime reporter and editor on his family's daily newspaper in Greenville, Mississippi, he joined the Jimmy Carter administration as Assistant Secretary of State for Public Affairs and Department Spokesman. In 1980, he left the State Department and was among the founders and anchor/ chief correspondent of *Inside Story*, a PBS program on media criticism. His PBS work won four national Emmys and an Edward R. Murrow Award. He is the author of (or contributor to) eleven books, and a contributor to many major newspapers at home and abroad. He has served on the boards of the Center for Public Integrity and the Reporters Committee for Freedom of the Press.

There gets to be a point when the question is, whose side are you on?
Now, I'm Secretary of State of the United States and I'm on our side.
—Secretary of State Dean Rusk

What follows is based on sixty years of experience in public life and journalism. It arises from deepening concern about the people's limited appreciation of the First Amendment and disgust with media waffling behind timidity's breastworks. It also arises from urgent unease about government overreach in the name of "homeland security," an overreach based on post-9/11 fear, political opportunism and an all but explicit assertion that a free people do not need to know and should not demand to know how they are being protected. There is no pretense here of carefully allocated balance, that briefly treasured convention of American journalism. Instead, this is an attempt to explain the evolution of today's media-government confrontations and to suggest answers to the hard questions that currently face the press when national security clashes with the Bill of Rights.

Unless informed consent is to be treated as a dangerous relic of more tranquil times, these questions should be answered on behalf of the American people as often as they arise. That means applying general principles to specific cases. Knowing the evolution of press freedom can be useful. Having an accurate picture of the chaotic realities of the murky present is crucial. Hard cases are inevitable; hard-and-fast rules are rarely available and too often inapplicable to current conditions. In the end, as always, it is up to each journalist and news organization to be willing to stand alone, to ask, and to answer individually:

"Whose side are you on?"

When Edward Snowden's breathtaking leap off the high board made its first splash, most public and media reactions featured shock and outrage, even among those appalled by the scope of the government's electronic eavesdropping that he revealed. A minority applauded. A smaller minority yawned. But public ambivalence all but vanished within a month. Consecutive polls showed growing numbers giving emphatic thumbs-down. "You weren't acting on my behalf," they seemed to roar.

Not much surprise there. It wasn't Pearl Harbor and it wasn't 9/11, but selective media use of Snowden's huge cache of stolen NSA files seemed to give obvious aid and comfort to America's enemies and a black eye to the nation. The images of the collapsing Twin Towers were still vivid. No surprise to friends and family, either, when my snap reaction was rage. The ex-Marine, "Gunboats Carter" persona was in full swing. Hang first, try later. It was self-evident that Snowden was a traitor.

Having worked for and with government officials from federal marshals to Presidents for over five decades, I knew that they and I were in lockstep solidarity. Contempt and consternation were near universal, both about Snowden's betrayal of the public trust and about media publication. They—we—saw both as flaunting a cavalier disregard of legal and moral obligations to safeguard vital national security secrets. As then-National Security Administration Director General Keith B. Alexander claimed, Snowden's revelations were causing "the greatest damage to our combined nations' intelligence systems that we have ever suffered."

The critics did not wear jackboots. Among them were former college classmates who had spent considerable time in the national intelligence enterprise, children of the mid-century who knew where their duty lay. They were vehemently certain that the electronic excavation of private as well as public records was as constitutional as it was vital. They were proud of their response in younger days to the call of duty, knowing the fragility of freedom and the ferocity of its enemies. The new world disorder seemed confirmation enough that questions about their mission were for academic seminars only.

And then I changed my mind, though God knows the generally uninspiring media reaction was not responsible. It is hard even now to fully appreciate how many press commentaries either saluted the official line or fell back on patronizing, snide dismissals of Snowden's character and intelligence. Those who supported him were few and far between, though vigorous in their support. Among them were *The New Yorker, The Guardian, The Washington Post, Vanity Fair,* McClatchy newspapers, and Knight Ridder. To others overlooked in that summary listing, my apologies. Those who decided to go forward with their coverage deserve sustained public applause. They took significant chances when they pressed the print button and revealed the NSA's dirty linen. Of no less importance, they sounded the alarm, warning the American people anew of how much further down the road to an all-intrusive garrison state Washington had ventured.

The number of major media organizations and figures who twitched at every government accusation was appalling. For the more pompous, Snowden and his media shepherds were unworthy intruders in the grand game of serious journalism and commentary. Planted in a self-referential clique, it was all but unnecessary for them to grapple with the meaning of a government that conceived, created, and operated a secret high-tech vacuum cleaner to suck the meaning out of the Fourth Amendment.

According to what the conventionalists wrote or said, Snowden was an immature, self-aggrandizing exhibitionist. He was no one with whom you might wish to have a conversation while supping in intimate dinners with Washington's powerful. Not of Le Carré's world, he was the distasteful new man of the onrushing technological dystopia, doing what he did because he could. Why he said he did it was secondary if not irrelevant; it was an irritating sideshow. Don't look at that man behind the curtain, they all but shouted. Look at the boogeyman.

As for the three reporters he entrusted with portions of the material, were they chosen because he trusted them to use it wisely? They were enablers of the unthinkable or traitors themselves. It was a hard position to maintain, since they were varied in background and outlook. Snowden apparently picked each because of what he saw as their unsparing coverage of government's rogue activities. They include Laura Poitras, a left-wing freelance television producer whose previous work had stirred waters, and Barton Gellman, a mainline journalist who had won two Pulitzer Prizes while working for *The Washington Post*. The most prolific was Snowden's tireless Boswell, Glenn Greenwald, a columnist for the British newspaper, *The Guardian*. He was, and is, unrestrained in his free-swinging indictment of what he considers to be mainstream media's absence without leave from the fray. Major press heavies returned the compliment, labeling him a radical nouveau whose rants outran reason. To reread their snide fulminations is to realize that the best antidotes to arrogance are looped replay or a long memory.

The great bulk of the print press ran wire service accounts, as usual, along with Washington-based and Washington-influenced commentary purchased on the cheap. Attention must be paid to the exceptional precursors to Snowden whose stories sparked threats of prosecution, smears from the far right, and outright denials from the President. Among them, *New York Times* reporters Eric Lichtblau and James Risen shared the 2006 Pulitzer Prize for national reporting for exposing President Bush's approval of warrantless domestic wiretaps. In the same year, Dana Priest of *The Washington Post* won the Pulitzer for stories revealing that the CIA ran foreign prisons where terrorists and those suspected of terrorism were tortured. It should also be noted that many secondhand accounts leaned heavily on Gellman, Greenwald, and Poitras.

The new world of the Internet was more diverse and more extensive, but of mixed quality. *Politico* and the Center for Public Integrity offered first-rate if sporadic work. To reread most of the blogs, our outliers of an inevitable future, is to weep for their strident ignorance. The networks and cable news at first ran all-out with the startling revelations, but then, as though exhausted by their close encounter with meaningful news, pulled over to concentrate on missing airliners and celebrity journalism. Public TV and radio did a more consistent job, *Frontline* most particularly, but some major figures admitted that Washington influenced the tone of their coverage as well.

The horde of talk show reactionaries came baying from their ideological kennels to snap and snarl across the land. Snowden's sympathizers were "useful idiots," to use the former Soviet phrase, just as Fox's propagandists had been saying all along. The terrorists had a fifth column within America. Debate over; gong-show commentary, interminable.

It is easy to understand their overwhelming nastiness. Whether they knew better or not, they knew their employers and they knew their audience. It is a defense unavailable to those segments of the establishment press who ducked when the hard balls came in high and close. Perhaps it was too much to expect that they would suddenly fall off their asses on the road to Damascus.

The relatively pallid media reaction stung. While government service and politics have consumed decades of my life, journalism, my first and last great love, has consumed even more. Short form, long form, television or print, and now the world of the Internet, I have seen them as the great bedrock and protector of American liberty and freedom. Small town and big city, reporter, anchor, editor, publisher, or columnist, all taught the same lesson. The Bill of Rights gave the press, like every citizen, previously unthinkable freedom to speak truth to power. As the Founders saw it, without the media, the public would be forever blinkered. Without it, government could do as it invariably prefers: conceive, organize, and implement policy decisions untrammeled by the opinions of those it is supposed to serve.

It sounds corny, like *Mr. Smith Goes to Washington,* but the Founders were right. Thomas Jefferson famously wrote: "Were it left to me to decide whether we should have a government without newspapers, or newspapers without a government, I should not hesitate a moment to prefer the latter."

However, Jefferson had different things to say after the vicissitudes of office, and it is easier to recite July Fourth rhetoric about the inexorable march of American liberty than to remember how frequently it has been called into question by the Founders and lesser men alike. Remarkable breakthroughs in press and individual rights have been met and leapfrogged by stunning expansions of government power. Seventy-five years of hot, cold, and open-ended war have taken their toll. "The first casualty of war is truth" is an aphorism that goes back over a hundred years and is validated anew in every conflict. The press has repeatedly crossed lines visible and invisible that the government thought sacrosanct. The government has repeatedly responded with measures that defied the Constitution.

The language on both sides has frequently been absolutist; the outcomes, less absolutist, but always recorded as victories or defeats. When the first encounter took place in America toward the end of the seventeenth century, there was no doubt. It ended in total victory for the side with the guns and padlocks. On September 25, 1690, the first edition of *Publick Occurrences Both Foreign and Domestic* was published in Boston as America's first newspaper. Publisher Benjamin Harris promised to provide as many accurate accounts of domestic and foreign happenings as he could obtain. On September 29, his first press run became the last. The governor and council of Massachusetts "suppressed and called in" as many copies as it could. The authorities asserted that Harris's four-page sheet, one left blank to allow space for subscribers to use as they wished, had contained "reflections of a very high order" (gossip about the French king's sexual dalliances) and "sundry doubtful and uncertain reports" (i.e., accounts of the slaughter of French prisoners by Britain's Mohawk allies). Both stories were widely understood to be true. Thereafter, not only did Massachusetts newspapers have to pay for the privilege of publishing, nothing could be published without prior approval.

Much has changed in the written and unwritten laws about press freedom in the intervening 425 years. Much has not. "Fraught" is the right word to describe the ups and downs of press-government encounters ever since. If journalists do not know that most public officials think of them as the Europeans long thought of the Germans, as either at your feet or at your throat, then they are willfully blind. Personal friendships can have little to do with it; professional responsibilities, everything. Veteran government officials know that each relationship with the press must be negotiated and renegotiated; good reporters know that permanent alliances with sources lead to captivity, the kennel dog instead of the hunting dog. A press that cares about its responsibilities to a free, self-governing people and a government elected to safeguard the security of the state are bound to clash.

So the question posed earlier becomes encrusted in unavoidable complexity. How far should media push the envelope? Preceding Snowden, a decade of cases ranging from Abu Ghraib to Wiki-Leaks, from CIA torture camps to NSA snooping on Americans, left the envelope hanging off the edge. A succession of court decisions based on government's assertions of national security pulled it back. And then the seriatim publication of carefully selected top secret information, a fraction of the total under Snowden's control, shoved it off the table and onto the public thoroughfares.

Snowden's decision was illegal and would have been if only one document had been at issue rather than hundreds of thousands. Many highly professional journals found the theft and its predecessors a cause for concern. *The New York Times* squelched a report in 2005 that won its team a Pulitzer in 2006. No less professional, those who disagreed felt their primary duty was to the free flow of information. Their chief client was the public, rather than the temporary custodians of the state.

That can sound self-righteously pretentious. It may be monumentally wrong. But error is a frequent companion of choice, and most people, whether in public service or the media, do not strap on their shields in order to weep in the face of tough choices. Presumably they do it to serve a nation, its people and the principles that undergird both. And also presumably, they were hired or elected not as gods or mandarins, but as imperfect human beings who usually must decide long before certainty emerges. In the meantime, they must call it as they see it.

Right or wrong ethically, wasn't the decision to accept top secret material and then to publish it illegal on its face, or at the very least, unacceptable? Many in the media felt that question had been answered forty-four years earlier with the Pentagon Papers. That case was widely celebrated by free press advocates, but far more narrowly decided on the core issues than memory allows. Supreme Court Justice Hugo Black gave the absolutist answer for the press, as he always did:

In the First Amendment, the Founding Fathers gave the free press the protection it must have to fulfill its essential role in our democracy. The press was to serve the governed, not the governors. The Government's power to censor the press was abolished so that the press would remain forever free to censure the government. The press was protected so it could bare the secrets of government and inform the people. To find that the President has "inherent power" to halt the publication of news . . . would wipe out the First Amendment and destroy the fundamental liberty and security of the very people the Government hopes to make "secure."

Writing for the Justice Department's Internal Security Division, Robert Mardian laid out the government's basic contention and demand:

I have been advised by the Secretary of Defense that the material published in The New York Times *on July 13, 14, 1971, captioned "Key Texts from Pentagon's Vietnam Study" contains information relating to the national defense of the United States and bears a top-secret classification. As such, publication of this information is directly prohibited by the provisions of the Espionage Law, Title 18, United States Code, Section 793. Moreover, further publication of information of this character will cause irreparable injury to the defense interests of the United States. Accordingly, I respectfully request you publish no further information of this character and advise me that you have made arrangements for the return of those documents to the Department of Defense.*

Though the press won, Richard Nixon never went gently into that good night. In an interview with David Frost a few years later, the former President restated his losing case in terms that the second Bush administration's inner circle were to make their own: "When the President does it, that means that it is not illegal."

On the day after the split court decision on the Pentagon Papers, Assistant Attorney General Richard Kleindienst warned a *Washington Post* reporter that if the press didn't back off, "The President is going to pick up a stick and start fighting back. I know he would go to the people on this. If he does, the big issues of the 1972 campaign may not be Vietnam or the economic situation, but whether an arrogant press is free to undermine the security of this country without check." Sic Snowden. No matter how the individual case presents itself, the language on both sides deviates very little. ("The stick," inter alios, included my old TV debating partner, Pat Buchanan, and Vice President Spiro Agnew, the latter turning out to be too rotten even for this rotten assignment.)

It has been a long time since I had responsibility for news choices and somewhat longer since I handled top secret and other classified material while State Department spokesman. However long ago, my ruminations on both subjects march forward today preceded by former Secretary of State Dean Rusk's exasperated challenge to the press a half century ago that opens this chapter: "Whose side are you on?"

The question is a sneering restatement of that older bit of mindless chauvinism, "America, love it or leave it." For me the acceptable—the necessary—alternative refrain has always been, "America, love it or change it."

For rank upon rank of civilian and military officials, there is only one correct answer to Rusk's question. They are dead wrong, not because their obsessive/compulsive desire to make reporters salute every classification stamp is always wrong, but because the classification system is ludicrous in its assumptions and practices. Five post–World War II presidential commissions, the most recent one chaired by Senator Daniel Patrick Moynihan of New York, came to similar and remarkably consistent findings. Too much government material is classified. Too much that is classified is classified at too high a level. As Supreme Court Justice Potter Stewart wrote over forty years ago, "When everything is classified, then nothing is classified. And the system becomes one to be disregarded by the cynical or the careless, and to be manipulated by those intent on self-protection or self-promotion."

The roots of the current classification go back to the early 1950s, though there were much earlier government attempts to protect national security information. (Much of what immediately follows is based on *The Papers and the Papers*, an invaluable book by Sanford Ungar, a man of many press hats who recently retired as president of Goucher College.)

President Eisenhower issued Executive Order 10501 on November 5, 1953. It gave permanent status to some existing wartime rules and emergency regulations, proclaimed its purpose to be "Safeguarding Official Information in the Interest of the Defense of the United States," and established the categories of "top secret," "secret," and "confidential," each of which is defined and detailed. In the category of "Who Are You Kidding?," the order urged that "unnecessary classification and over classification shall be scrupulously avoided." That earnest admonition was then followed by decades of promiscuous expansion in the number of departments, agencies, and individuals allowed to control classification. The Tennessee Valley Authority, the FCC, the Peace Corps—name the office, guess the number of papers classified by each over time. What you do not have to guess is that the growth of classified files has been exponential. Several Presidents, the latest being Mr. Obama, have issued executive orders on classification aiming for "clarity" and common sense. All were followed by more classified pages.

It is important to note how little Congress has had to do with any of it outside the small select oversight committees, which tend to be enablers rather than the public's ombudsman, and had been sporadic in their oversight until 9/11. (Irony was redefined with added emphasis when the CIA was caught rifling the files of a congressional oversight committee whose chair was one of its chief defenders. The agency's director first angrily denied the allegation, then grudgingly coughed up an apology. The chair was not amused. The President, who should have fired the director, also coughed.)

A final indictment by a man who knew firsthand what he was talking about. Going much further than I feel competent to venture, former Air Force security official William C. Florence, in testifying to the House Foreign Operations and Government Information subcommittee in the midst of the Pentagon Papers controversy, said:

> *I sincerely believe that less than one-half of one percent of the different documents which bear currently assigned classification markings actually contain information qualifying even for the lowest defense classification under Executive Order 10501. In other words, the disclosure of 99.5 percent of those classified documents could not be prejudicial to the defense interests of the nation.*

A few facts add weight to skepticism about the seriousness, security, and efficacy of today's classification system. According to the June 10, 2014, *USA Today*, 4.9 million people have some form of security clearance; 1.4 million of them have top secret clearance. *Top Secret America* reported that 850,000 Americans have top secret clearance, including 250,000 private contractors. The figures clearly are not precise and vary from source to source, but the conclusion is the same. It should not be a surprise that in 2004, 15 million new pages were classified.

The Intercept, an online magazine, reported that some 26,800 U.S. citizens and permanent residents are on a federal database of those having alleged links to terrorism or who are terrorists. The Directorate of Terrorist Identities listed among its accomplishments in 2013 the construction of a database of over 1 million suspected or actual terrorists. Command and control may be possible with such numbers, but there is little public evidence available to assess its probability. What is available are the examples of breakdown and impermissible excess.

I was a small-town editor in Mississippi, far from Washington, when Rusk spat out his rancorous query, but I recognized what he was saying when I read it. As with the racist refrains of my time and place, it was a naked proposition: Our side is the side of America, of our way of life. Questioning what we say and do gives aid and comfort to the enemy. You are either a patriot or a traitor, you are either for us or against us. You either accept the most troubling ramifications of current American policy, or you are an enemy of the state, an ally of international _____. (Fill in the blank, but do so quickly. The axis of evil tends to change overnight these days: see the Middle East.)

Not everyone in the press was offended. Rusk gave a speech to the American Society of Newspaper Editors in Atlanta in which he assailed *The New York Times* and other antiwar newspapers as irresponsible, error-laden, and unpatriotic. He was given a rousing, roaring vote of approval by most of the crowd, who were cheering and clapping at length as though they were defense contractors rather than newsfolk. I grabbed a floor mic to protest angrily that the *Times* record on truth and error, as opposed to the government's, was as day to night, and that he knew it. Loud boos. One of my fellow believers in free speech, a Scripps Howard man, told me I was anti-American scum.

While the press and government are both products of a Constitution designed to safeguard liberty, they are not the same. Their roles and responsibilities differ mightily and carry within them inherent conflict. To paraphrase the great Yale law professor Alexander Bickel, it is presumably in the conflict that the public interest and the truth will be best served.

Like Secretary Rusk, at the end of day I know which side I'm on, though I'm proud to say I've worked on both sides of a couple of streets. For several years in the late 1970s I was State Department Spokesman and Assistant Secretary of State for Public Affairs. The job was well worth its frustrations if for no other reason than the education of Hodding Carter. It sorely perplexed a number of friends and critics who felt that going over to "the dark side" would destroy my integrity and my reputation. Perhaps some felt vindicated from time to time when I got it wrong, but there was no professional blackball when I left State to work as a press critic for public television. Being on the government side did not make me feel any more soiled than working the press side. As a journalist, I represented what I took to be the public interest. As spokesman, I felt I was doing no less. I was never asked to lie, and never did. Vigorously articulating the government's position did not fall in the Constitution's shadow any more than vigorously pushing for more information than the government wanted to provide.

In daily press briefings as spokesman I tried to wrestle the press and public's view of the travails and triumphs of U.S. foreign policy into approval at best and indifference at worst. As assistant secretary, I was responsible for supervising the creation and dissemination of a wide range of information outside the briefing cycle. We put out country reports, speeches by various department officials, FBIS (Foreign Broadcast Information Service) texts of foreign policy pronouncements by friends and foes, and, not incidentally, answered the mail. Some of this was propaganda, some was the relay of information from other sources, some were straightforward attempts to keep Americans and foreign nations up-to-date on where U.S. policy stood. Some of this openness came as the result of congressional demands.

Wearing the same hat, I ostensibly ran the department's freedom of information process. That is, I ran it until someone in authority belatedly noticed that as an editorial writer I had previously been an open government nut. Whoever he was, he squeaked loudly and maneuvered the FOI office out of my hands and into the more constipated bowels of the Administration Bureau. For the record, FOI is a remarkably useful tool for prying information out of a reluctant government, but even more remarkably, it is an underutilized tool. Business interests use it far more often than reporters and news organizations. It can take forever and frequent requests to get an answer, but the materials set free are often of real importance—not least because they expose official lies of major significance. Lyndon Johnson, who tried hard and often to restrict or manipulate the flow of public information, was the man responsible for passage of the FOI act, for which credit is due.

The office of the historian was my responsibility, too, which made it impossible not to notice that the official history of the nation's foreign policy was so behind its required publication mark that the last volume published on my watch dealt with Woodrow Wilson's attempts to keep us out of war. Congress has mandated that publication of the annual reports should be no later than twenty-five years old. There is and was no way to exaggerate the intelligence community's mulish role in repeatedly blocking timely declassification of material necessary to meet the mandate. They were bureaucratically sincere in worrying that premature publication could turn off allies, endanger agents, and reveal too much about intelligences sources and methods, but their specific justifications often made no sense at all. It didn't matter. Alleged national security interests repeatedly trumped; emphatic assertions too often passed for evidence.

In both roles, I had frequent access to highly classified materials, few of them of the highest order, but close enough to give me adequate evidence for a judgment about their worth. Once I stopped being dazzled by access, I came to the lasting conclusion that you could throw at least 90 percent of all classified material onto the street and whistle for the press and spies to come get it—and nothing of any real consequence would result. A little embarrassment here, a compromised initiative there, a bit of time for official blood pressure to subside, and the sun would rise again in the East. Google can attest to how many others, similarly situated over the years, agree with my estimate. They are legion. (See William Florence above.)

Then and now the best way to guarantee that classified material will be given heavy press play is to pitch it over a news organization's transom and wait for the front page lead story that begins, "*The Herald-Times* has learned . . ." Leaking is the preferred Washington sport, ahead of the beleaguered Redskins or the remarkable Nationals. The most prolific leakers sit in the highest offices, starting with the Oval and its immediate satellites. Preferred media conduits include both legitimate news outlets like *The Wall Street Journal* and *The New York Times*, and blatantly dishonest propaganda organs such as Fox News. But men and women who work in the midlevel offices have been prime players, too, and the axes they grind are at least as likely to be sharpened for the public good as a President's. In my experience some of the leaks most useful to public understanding have come from these sources.

Leaking, like prostitution, will forever be with us because it is beneficial to all participants. Its chief drawback is that it is primarily a Washington insider's game, a tribal telegraph system as well as a backstabber's delight whose players and signals are hard for the general public to comprehend.

Barry Schweid, AP's longtime diplomatic correspondent and one of the funniest and most cynical men I have ever known, would look up from one of those so-and-so has learned pieces (more often than not in *The New York Times*) and snarl, " 'The *Times* has learned.' 'The *Times* has learned'? Does that mean that one of your guys threw it through the window or just handed it over at lunch?" Jealous competitors were much given to calling the *Times* America's *Pravda*; some still do with a somewhat different meaning.

Of course, there is leaking and then there is leaking. There is a difference between the Manhattan Project and Cabinet arguments about the future of food labeling. So here goes another slightly overstated assertion drawn from personal experience: The ratio of leaks that are harmful to national security as opposed to those whose chief results are embarrassment or temporary advantage for an inside warrior come in at roughly 1-to-10,000. There hasn't been a President in my lifetime who has not used them; there is not a President in my lifetime who has not cursed them. There has not been a President who didn't order his staff to shut them down or find the culprits, with President Obama high on the list. There has never been a President, no matter how disciplined his inner circle, who has succeeded except at the margins. And there has never been a White House press corps that sooner or later did not complain about each administration's "unprecedented clampdown," all the while giggling behind their hands.

Every so often the press also professes outrage when it is discovered that a presidential administration has ordered lie detectors be used to squeeze out the identity of leakers. It's also fun to be able to say you are "shocked, shocked" by such high-handed tactics. Very infrequently the lie detector gambit works and some poor devil has to walk the plank. Mostly it is a waste of time, either because the leaker knows how to game the exercise or, more often, because the wrong people are examined. I leaked frequently, occasionally at the behest of the President's men, more often to fire back in the ceaseless conflict between the State Department and the National Security Adviser's office. Since my boss, Secretary of State Cyrus Vance, did not approve of what he considered a schoolboy's game while the National Security Adviser loved it, it was usually a losing exercise for "our" side. Every now and then I'd lob a big one over the White House fence, and it was immensely gratifying to hear of Mr. Brzezinski's screams as he demanded the culprit's scalp. Since I refused as a matter of principle to submit to a lie detector test, I don't know what the consequences might have been. I can only say no one I knew was ever weeded out because the graph went crazy.

There were despicable leaks, of course. Robert Novak's column blew the cover off CIA Officer Valerie Plame, whose offense was that her husband had written a report contradicting claims of bomb-useful material in Niger. As I told Ronald Goldfarb in his book *In Confidence,* "The dirty little secret of that incestuous closed circle of beat reporters, well-placed columnists and official sources who do their horse-trading out of sight is that officials get their propaganda and reporters get their hot story." Of course, Plame lost her job, and the leaker never lost his. More recently, a number of NSA employees or officers were run out of their jobs and one run into jail, because of alleged misuse of classified material. It more than occasionally appears that in high governance and politics, the only standard is the double standard.

Which returns me to Snowden and the post-Snowden era. Almost every commentary on Snowden's appropriation of masses of classified information and his decision to release a fraction of them overlooks a very large elephant. What he did was all but inevitable. If not him and not then, another Snowden would have come along shortly. The dike holding America's ocean of secrets has been spilling over the top for a long time. With WikiLeaks and Chelsea/Bradley Manning and Julian Assange, it crumbled. The flow of secrets became the flood of the century. The only meaningful debate was about how much damage had been done to U.S. security interests, individuals, policies, and allies. Snowden would later argue that he was no Manning, and that he had been carefully selective in what he released and how it was curated. A distinction without a difference, the government replied with considerable force. As of this writing, the public still does not have a clue as to approximately how much material Snowden whisked away, a question that is certain to have concerned the government more than the people.

The point is that Snowden's appropriation and then release of a portion of the NSA's crown jewels only confirmed rather than established that we live in a world in which tidy lines between those who "own" information and those who toil with it, like Snowden, between labor and management, have blurred. To repeat what was said during the Pentagon Papers showdown, give too many people security clearance and classify too much information, and normal government is incapable of plugging the holes in the security dike. The biggest of Big Brothers might be able to do it, but aside from the constitutional issues, free men make bad slaves. Snowden's wholesale theft and the subsequent press coverage illustrate how a half century of dramatic technological change, near perpetual conflict, and governmental abuse of power have overturned old media conventions and subverted old assumptions about unqualified support of a government in wartime. The king is larger and infinitely stronger than he has ever been, but the cats who care— alley to parlor—are warier and faster than ever and multiplying exponentially, far beyond the bounds of traditional media. Eye to eye, from issue to issue, there is no safe bet on who blinks first. The safe bet is that there will be a number of cats jumping the line.

Like Presidents before him, President Obama came into office pledging that there would be more transparency and that he intended to tighten and lighten the classification rules and procedures. What emerged in 2009 was Executive Order 13526. The record of its effect is mixed and the language both more rigid and more permissive than that of its predecessors. The categories remain the same, but declassification is at least formally encouraged. The President, meanwhile, like other would-be reformer Presidents, seems increasingly in thrall to the panic-driven instincts that produced the Patriot Act and the Homeland Security Act. He has wielded an iron fist despite his softer language. Of the eleven attempts to prosecute journalists under the Espionage Act of 1917, contrary to legislative understanding and precedent, seven have come since he was elected. More have been threatened.

There can be no argument that terrorism, red of fang and claw, is not a real threat to American interests and to Americans at home and abroad. It is an even more lethal threat to those who live in or near its perpetrators' homelands. As real as the old Soviet menace? Not a chance. As real as the Axis powers when they seemed on the verge of taking control of Europe and the Pacific? To ask is to answer. The dead at the Twin Towers cry out for retaliation and revenge, at least in my ears, and they have been given it several fold over. Do they also cry out for the curtailment of liberty and the use of domestic police state tactics?

That there are too many people entitled to classify information is a given. That too many people of all sorts of backgrounds have relatively easy access to highly classified information is equally true and calls into question the evolving structure of the secrecy state. Privatization of military and security functions is a danger by definition. Any free market theologian should be quick to admit that the point of the enterprise system is to make money. Among other things, that means controlling costs. The point of the military enterprise is to protect the nation, and cost-cutting is not or should not be among its top priorities. A man in uniform or direct government employ is one kind of entity; a person who comes aboard for the money and the game is another. There are 60,000 civilian contractors in the NSA. There are 30,000 civilian employees.

The first leak is lost in the mists of unrecorded history. There are, however, plenty of pertinent examples. Benjamin Franklin, tucked comfortably in a London sinecure in the run-up to the Revolution, leaked a story to a Boston newspaper, which got him run out of town. George Washington, worried about the press obtaining the deliberations at the Constitutional Convention, told delegates, "I must entreat gentlemen to be more careful lest our deliberations get into the newspaper." Some president between

Teddy Roosevelt and Barack Obama may have never leaked, but it is hard to know who it could be. Even Calvin Coolidge used a nom de plume to release the news he wanted out.

Leaks aside, experience in the newsroom and in the public sector convinced me that government more often than not tells the truth. That said, it is a conviction that must be paired with Ronald Reagan's famous saying, "Trust, but verify." It must also be paired with the sobering history of direct lies and misstatements aimed at misleading the public.

The most egregious recent one was President Obama's on the *Tonight Show with Jay Leno* on August 2013: "We don't have a domestic spying program. What we do have is some mechanisms that can trace a phone number or an e-mail address that is connected to a terrorist attack." A National Security Adviser here, a CIA Director there, and an administration spokesman across town, and the list begins to add up. As Snowden observed, you don't know what you don't know, and press and public haven't known enough of what is being done in America's name to demand accountability.

For the super patriotic son of a super patriotic father, the fact that government lies and misuses its power has been a hard proposition to swallow. I was the kid who felt frequently impelled to recite from Sir Walter Scott's "The Lay of the Last Minstrel":

> *Breathes there the man, with soul so dead,*
> *Who never to himself hath said,*
> *This is my own, my native land!*

I could let go almost simultaneously with Emerson's "Concord Hymn" and Lincoln's Gettysburg Address. I joined the Marines to serve and protect, and the "Gunboats" nickname was tagged during a one-year journalism fellowship at Harvard, because I repeatedly argued that the Munich analogy fit Vietnam exactly. Over the years I was a member of the board of Radio Liberty, that erstwhile CIA broadcasting service aimed at the Soviet Union, and a clutch of other Cold War–related enterprises, about all of which I have no regrets. In other words, I am an American who might be expected to accept the case for all-out war on terrorism with whatever curbs on freedom that entails, but I can't and won't.

The main reason is that virtually all of my experience in press and government has led me to the conclusion that good people in a good system can still do stupid things, as noted above, and that officials driven by ideological demons can do terrible things. To pick a name at random, there is and was Vice President Dick Cheney, who never met a self-serving lie that he didn't like or a war he couldn't justify.

The absurdities of the security system itself were an early drag on my enthusiastic cheerleading for the official line. The person responsible for vetting officers for top secret clearance at Second Marine Division let it be widely known I'd never make it, that my father was a "known nigger-loving Communist." I got the clearance, but I never had a chance to get at him. Many of the classified messages I decoded on the antique crypto machines in the Communications Center were rewrites of that morning's press reports about the Marines' Lebanese venture of 1958. Some of my Basic School classmates were serving there, having gone ashore to be met by the friendly fire of sweet young things selling iced Cokes. Ike had ordered the amphibious show of force as an answer to the overthrow of Britain's puppet regime in Iraq. He hoped to protect the pro-Western Lebanese government from the effects of Iraq's contagion. If that sounds familiar, it should. It was the U.S.'s fateful introduction to the Middle Eastern tar baby.

They taught me in Basic School that you couldn't win a down-and-dirty local war with high-altitude bombing. It would take boots on the ground, grinding it out. (Not then the phrase of the moment. We talked about troops then.) Basic was right, American intelligence and the official line were wrong, but until the bombing began in the mid-1960s, I held fast to the faith: We either had to beat them in Vietnam or we would have to meet them in California. Then, as the big bombers began to dump their loads, I bailed out. Much as I would like to pretend otherwise, it was not a moral decision. Marine doctrine, and the evidence on the ground, outweighed the Kennedy-Johnson doctrine and their administrations' claims of success in the battle for hearts and minds through the bomb blasts. The reporting from Vietnam also played a huge part. By the mid-1960s, a press corps unhampered by the censorship was able to send out informed firsthand accounts calling the official line into question.

Later, the abuses of government surveillance cut directly across my grain. Cochairman of a biracial delegation from Mississippi that was seated in place of the all-white regulars at the 1968 Democratic Convention in Chicago, I savored the unprecedented victory. Others did not. It was much later we learned that J. Edgar Hoover had apparently decided that our mix of radicals and all-out integrationists, Young Democrats and labor, was by definition a threat to American values. As part of his COINTELPRO program to infiltrate black organizations in particular, but left-wing ones in general, he had convinced a white member of our delegation to play snitch, snoop, and agent provocateur. His code name was "Captain Magnolia" and he was as smooth a lying bastard as you could want. The Lord knows there was a lot of incendiary talk coming from our delegation, but luckily, no incendiary action. It doesn't really matter. What matters is that Washington thought it appropriate and necessary to spy on private citizens exercising their right to free assembly and free speech.

How did we find out? Because a tiny group of antiwar pacifists broke into an FBI office in Pennsylvania and stole bushels of material. Some of it detailed the COINTELPRO operation. Law breaking uncovered law breaking, proving that old adage that "it takes a thief to catch a thief" has more than one application. Their justification was Snowden's.

From the past comes the present. Taking their cues from the feds, state and local governments are also in the surveillance game these days, some at a sophisticated level. Mississippi, then a leader in black shirt innovation, was at it in the 1950s and 1960s with its own secret police, the State Sovereignty Commission. The Commission's stated task was to protect "our way of life," which meant defending de jure segregation and white supremacy.

Its tools ranged from placing misinformation in the region's most rabidly racist news outlets, to working with segregationist organizations to force nonconforming professors and students to get in line or get out, to planting informants in the integrationist groups, wiretapping, and the occasional bit of goon work.

In other words, emulating the professional practices of their federal betters.

The Commission supported boycotts that cost our paper subscribers and advertisers all across the Delta, and a legislative hearing featuring a professional anti-Communist who testified that Dad was a member of Communist-front organizations. Yet labels to the contrary, we were white moderates and it was neither easy to sell the smears to our neighbors nor easy to overlook the well-known fact that all Carters carried guns all the time. Black folks were much easier targets. It was no secret that Mississippi was a closed society in which the Constitution need not apply.

Seeing the Sovereignty Commission record laid out in neat lines of type was a special kind of shock all the same. The import of the Snowden files was equally shocking for many of his fellow citizens, even for Americans who had long assumed that their government was tapping more than it was telling and were glad that it was. Its enormous appetite for information about private citizens with no record or accusation of terrorist sympathies was as unexpected as it was nauseating. You could almost hear people saying,

"This is America, for God's sake," even as they called for Snowden's scalp.

Why this retelling of old tales? To help explain how I would react as an editor if confronted by government demands that I withhold classified information from print. I would expect that the first questions would be, "Who elected you declassifier in chief? Are you confusing yourself with the President? Stop the presses." (If you think that is exaggerated, read the record of the Pentagon Papers drama.)

To which I hope my response would be: "Back off and push the restart button. We stand on a playing field leveled by the Constitution. You can ask, but not demand. I don't automatically salute. And speaking of unilateral, who gives you and your superiors the right to do in the dark what has long been considered un-American activity? We may come to eventual agreement, but not without much more conversation. Why have you and yours lied so frequently about this activity, activity your bosses don't even bother to deny anymore? Don't patronize me and the American people by adding to the shameful record.

"I hope we can work out a mutually acceptable agreement, but automatic acquiescence is off the table. Here's what I think I know. Tell why it is U.S. policy. Tell me who authorized it. Explain its purposes and its potential consequences as well as its necessity. I want you to be right, but assertion is not enough. After the last fifty years, 'Trust me' isn't going to hack it."

To be clear, the decision to print would not be automatic. Having known SOBs in government and in the press, I would not begin the exercise believing truth and virtue are automatically on one side or the other. Most whistleblowers I have known have been truth-tellers as they see it. Some, however, have been aggrieved losers, looking for revenge, carrying a long knife long whetted by jealousy or the sense that their brilliance is not appreciated. Some of the fast-rising Washington wunderkinder, the Praetorian Guard intellectuals, impressive résumés in hand, use their shivs for self-promotion as well as the security of the state. When they come calling to push a point, the best response is a polite smile and a request that you meet with a decision maker. Others are exactly what you would hope of a public servant. They have a job to do, and they do it with civility and intelligence.

The conviction that the bad guys *are evil*, not victims, would also be sitting on my shoulder. They must be put out of business. That said, it must be done in ways that allow a nation to look at itself in the mirror each day without wincing. To violate the privacy of tens of millions of Americans in hopes of finding a hitherto unidentified possible terrorist is not acceptable. That is profiling to the extreme. You exist; therefore, you are a suspect.

To which the reader should now mutter impatiently, "Alright, alright. So what would you do? Quit meandering and get down to it." My answer would be the same as Gellman's and Greenwald's and Poitras's, not to mention the people to whom they answered. Put it through the sieve, decide what needs to go and what needs to be held back, and then let it rip.

Conservative Republican Congressman Jim Sensenbrenner of Wisconsin is a proud sponsor of the original Patriot Act. He believes it has been perverted by both President Bush and President Obama, "whose intelligence services took the limited power Congress intended and went rogue." Ignoring explicit requirements to the contrary, he wrote, the intelligence community has used the act to "justify vacuuming call records from millions of innocent Americans. . . . The bottom line is: bulk collection would never have been authorized." It is nice to believe and welcome news that he has been trying to put belief into action by leading an effort to rewrite and tighten the act.

The other bottom line still tastefully neglected in various quarters is that without Snowden, it might have been a cold day in hell before the record became the subject of public debate. Or, as suggested earlier, it might not have taken that long, given the number of secrets and the number of people who have access to them. That is conjecture on horseback. Snowden says he did what he did because the American people need to know what the government is doing to violate some of the nation's basic tenets. I agree with him, and they need to know now, not in that far distant future when the Archives finally get their hands on some of the most startling records in American history. If the people are going to regain meaningful control of their government, the first step is transparency. That was among the most important of the Founders' operating assumptions, built into the Bill of Rights and expanded thereafter.

Only the lunatic right believes Edward Snowden is a spy, a long-buried sleeper emerging to destroy the republic. Nor is he a Manning, or a Julian Assange, blowing everything loose on the Internet. He went the traditional route and gave the material to reporters he thought he could trust to do the right thing. They did, spending months to verify his near-unbelievable story and his bona fides. As journalism, it was a model of professionalism as well as a staggering scoop.

Just to close the circle, there is no evidence that Snowden was bought. There have been so many CIA and FBI agents who recently sold out their country for money as to make that a likely explanation. If it were true, or even partially believable, however, it would have made the leak circuit long ago. He does not believe in a radically different form of government from our own. What you see and what you hear is what you get. He believes so passionately in the American creed that he put his life and liberty on the line to expand its perimeter.

There is no question about whether he broke the law. By self-admission, he did. There is also no question in my mind about the man as person. From everything I read and see, he is a patriot.

Snowden is also the tip of a huge iceberg. Given the nature of our outsourced security (one contractor is reported to have cleared

15,000 people for classified access in one week) and our insatiable appetite for more and more classification, another *Titanic* looms ahead. You cannot lock a ton of cheese in a basement safe, put the keys on top, and come back expecting to find it still there. The temptation to crack down with a vengeance might be irresistible. Before it is too late, and it may already be too late, a fundamental rethinking of the security state/free press/free people matrix is required. It cannot arise by osmosis. As with the long "Great Debate" about the United States' proper role in the world after World War II that scuttled isolationism and ushered in the long era of internationalism, what is required is a structured national conversation in every venue available, from the grand buildings of government in Washington to local courthouses and the proverbial barbershop.

We have arrived at the cusp of a garrison state by fits and starts, on a long arc that bends steadily toward a far different America from the one the Founders envisioned or would have tolerated. Unlike Argentina under the junta, Russia under nearly everyone, and China forever, it is not too late to reverse course. It may ask too much of today's media to play as key a role in reviving the democratic experiment today as the far more primitive press played in birthing, nurturing, and cheering on what became that unprecedented creation—a democratic Republic with majority rule and a Bill of Rights. I think that is defeatist nonsense. The fire bell is ringing. There can be no certainty about final answers, but there is absolutely no excuse for allowing inertia to make the big ones. Edward Snowden has proved it.

EPILOGUE AS NIGHTMARE

But what of Snowden the person? He is a dead man walking. When Putin tires of toying with him, he will be dumped onto foreign soil to await his highly trained American rescuers. Unlike Bin Laden, he may make it off the pickup zone alive. He may survive the trip, though it is not hard to fall out of a helicopter door. He may be diverted into some rendition rendezvous where he can be tortured enough to make him confess that he is the Islamic State's number one man. He may even be given a jury trial by his peers, perhaps in Washington, though I would bet against it. Dangerous at large, he becomes even more dangerous when Big Media are shouting questions about Big Data and he is answering them. Since Gitmo is forever, I'd be least surprised to see him become our version of the man without a country, the permanent prisoner/exile. It would be unsettling, but not unlikely, that the man who knew too much would become the man no one remembers.

SELECTED BIBLIOGRAPHY

Getler, Michael. Assorted ombudsman columns. *Washington Post*, 2002–2004.

Goldfarb, Ronald. *In Confidence: When to Protect Secrecy and When to Require Disclosure*. New Haven, CT: Yale University Press, 2009.

Lichtblau, Eric. *Bush's Law: The Remaking of American Justice*. New York: Anchor Books, 2008.

Priest, Dana and William Arkin. *Top Secret America: The Rise of the New American Security State*. Boston: Little, Brown and Company, 2011.

Risen, James and Eric Lichtblau. "Bush Lets U.S. Spy on Callers Without Courts." *New York Times*, December 16, 2005.

Sigal, Leon V. *Reporters and Officials: The Organization and Politics of Newsmaking*. Lexington, MA: D. C. Heath and Co., 1973.

Unger, Sanford J. *The Papers and the Papers: An Account of the Legal and Political Battle over the Pentagon Papers*. New York: Columbia University Press, 1989.

PROTECTING NEWS IN THE ERA OF DISRUPTIVE SOURCES

Edward Wasserman

EDWARD WASSERMAN is dean of the Graduate School of Journalism at the University of California, Berkeley. After a twenty-five-year career as editor and publisher, he served a decade as the Knight Foundation Professor of Journalism Ethics at Washington and Lee University, where he taught courses in professional ethics, media ownership and control, and coverage of poverty in news and popular culture. He lectures widely on matters of media policy and practice, ranging from industry structure to plagiarism and privacy, and writes a biweekly op-ed column distributed nationally by the McClatchy-Tribune wire. Wasserman has degrees from Yale and the University of Paris, and received his PhD from the London School of Economics. His Web site, Unsocial Media, is at http://ewasserman.com.

As a practical matter the news media—whatever their sense of social mission, their standards, their market reach and industrial health, their legal shields or constitutional privileges—are first and foremost dependent on their sources. That dependency means the press can't be any better, stronger, braver, more richly informed, or more dedicated to broad public purpose than the people who swallow their misgivings, return the phone call, step forward, and risk embarrassment or reprisal to talk to a reporter. That dependency also means the press is susceptible to pressure and manipulation by sources whose collaboration is indispensable to the routine coverage of public policy and institutional performance, and who become an offstage constituency that the conscientious journalist must be ever mindful of when deciding what to report and how to report it.

Hence sources, a many-headed beast. The source dimension embraces the best and worst of contemporary journalism—the press as sanctuary and independent public servant, and the press as self-serving agency tilted toward the powerful, its journalists preoccupied with maintaining the working relationships on which their own careers depend. Those two poles of source relations have been apparent in marquee episodes of both courage and malfeasance since the dawn of the new century, from the Valerie Plame–Joseph Wilson matter a decade ago to the current spate of high-tech whistleblowers, exemplified in the ongoing Edward Snowden affair. The upshot of the discussion that will be offered here is that the whole subject of obligations to sources—a chronically neglected area of journalism ethics—is a richly convoluted and deeply perplexing matter: It telescopes the unavoidable incompatibilities reporters must negotiate between workplace necessities and public service; promotes compromises in which the reporter's signature duty—to unearth and bring to light publicly significant information in the service of a self-governing polity—may take a backseat to expediency and workplace calculation; and leads to a powerful institutional undertow that operates to deepen the vulnerability of a class of invaluable sources whose influence is truly disruptive. In some cases efforts by the news media to protect their sources worked against the public interest by shielding high-level wrongdoing from exposure.

Now, in the post-WikiLeaks era, we've seen a greater role played by what I call disruptive sources. Disruptive sources challenge and defy the routines of normal journalism. These sources—Chelsea (formerly Bradley) Manning, Julian Assange, and Edward Snowden are digital-era exemplars, Daniel Ellsberg their linear forebear—are disruptive in a number of ways: they're not on the newshound's roster of what sociologist Gaye Tuchman called "authorized knowers," don't drink with the beat reporters, aren't part of the approved social nexus out of which the standard coverage of their area of occupational knowledge normally flows. They may have no continuing benefits to bestow, no implied promise of a future flow of valued intelligence. (Indeed their value as informants may be self-liquidating, consisting of one-off affairs.) They are disruptive, too, because they have access to alternative channels through which to publish their information, and that access is an institutional threat to the centrality of the news media as the principal conduits of big news. The information they proffer is a disruption as well, because it's both credible and challenges, implicitly or explicitly, whatever it is that reporters had previously been told. Accordingly, it raises serious questions about the adequacy and trustworthiness of the information the media had been offering. (Consider how many years of Vietnam-era reporting were found deficient and credulous once the Pentagon Papers were made public.) And, of course, because the information challenges the received wisdom, it undermines confidence in the integrity and values of the dominant institutions that the media are supposed to be holding accountable—and challenges, for instance, the degree to which secrecy classifications serve any genuine national security interests or are, instead, fig leaves to ward off public exposure and bureaucratic embarrassment.

But because this source is an outsider, not a member of the usual social nexus of relied-upon informants, it isn't likely he or she will receive much in the way of protection or indulgence if the information provokes official displeasure. Instead, the recent spate of disruptive sources has been met with a disquieting ambivalence among the news media that have benefited from their information. Typically, the public value of the material the informants have disclosed is praised, even while their motives, psychological makeup, personal integrity, and the harm they might be doing to the legitimate security interests of the state are foregrounded in the coverage. The limits to any actual protection the media might offer are generally confined to the terms of reporter privilege, contained in various shield laws that enable journalists, under limited circumstances, to resist legal pressure to disclose the names of informants with whom they have confidentiality agreements. The reporter's silence, however, doesn't necessarily protect the source. In only one of the current crop of cases in which news sources were charged under the Espionage Act during the George W. Bush and

Barack Obama administrations—the case of former CIA operative Jeffrey Sterling—have prosecutors pushed aggressively to force a reporter to break a confidentiality pledge and identify a defendant.

The question is whether the media can or should generalize their social role, moving to something broader and more aggressive than simply keeping their reporters safe: facilitator and even guardian of the flow of newsworthy information, defender of the ability of individuals to go public with significant knowledge that deserves wide exposure. Accordingly, what's worth defending is the sources' right to speak, independently of the right of the news media to report what they say. It makes little sense for the media to confine their protective response to withholding the identities of valued sources when their identities can be readily learned by law enforcement and the only outstanding issue to debate is how harshly the sources themselves should suffer in reprisal.

WHO CARES ABOUT SOURCES ANYWAY?

The idea that reporters have some general duty to protect their sources is articulated only vaguely, but it's widely held. Jack Shafer, now media writer for Politico, referred to it in a 2005 column he wrote during the unraveling of the CIA leak investigation, which apparently drew evidence from a number of journalists, as we'll discuss below. "If protecting sources is paramount," Shafer wrote, "why don't more journalists go to jail?" It was a good question, but it rested on a shaky premise. The fact is that source protection is miles from being a paramount concern for journalists. Apart from the narrow matter of upholding confidentiality agreements, obligation to sources is a poorly developed area of press ethics. The well-being of informants, and the ways that the reporting they nourish may rebound on their lives, are things that journalists worry about rarely, if ever.

Indeed, perhaps the best-known—and probably the most jaundiced—formulation of the relationship between journalist and source suggests that the reporting enterprise is essentially predatory. This was the argument advanced by Janet Malcolm in her 1990 book, *The Journalist and the Murderer*: "Every journalist who is not too stupid or too full of himself to notice what is going on knows that what he does is morally indefensible."

Malcolm's book focused on the relationship between author Joe McGinniss and the Green Beret doctor Jeffrey MacDonald, who had been accused of slaughtering his wife and two small daughters in 1970. McGinniss befriended MacDonald, and remained privy to the inner workings of his defense team even after, by his account, he became privately convinced that MacDonald was guilty of the harrowing crimes. Eventually MacDonald was convicted, and then sued McGinniss, claiming the author had wronged him—essentially, by pretending to be his friend. (After a lengthy trial the jury was hung, and MacDonald received a $325,000 out-of-court settlement.) The journalist, Malcolm writes, "is a kind of confidence man, preying on people's vanity, ignorance or loneliness, gaining their trust and betraying them without remorse."

Even sophisticated sources are susceptible to the charms and blandishments of reporters, and may wrongly believe that because the journalist is friendly he or she is also a friend—that is, will act with the source's best interests in mind. In 2010 Army General Stanley McChrystal lost his job as commander of allied forces in Afghanistan after *Rolling Stone* magazine published a profile of McChrystal, titled "The Runaway General." In it, freelancer Michael Hastings, who had spent a month with the general and his staff, quoted McChrystal's top aides—who claimed to be reflecting his views—speaking scathingly about their civilian bosses, notably Vice President Joe Biden. Hastings later expressed surprise at their candor.

Garden-variety sources pose different problems. Often they are vulnerable and unsophisticated people with outsized expectations of what publicity will do to them. They may believe that talking to the press will make them celebrities and immunize them against payback, even when they say things that are certain to infuriate people who can harm them. Encouraged by the affable reporter, they may share observations that will make them look ridiculous— as the journalist knows. One case used in ethics classes involves a woman in a small New England town in the early 1980s who was the subject of one of those perennial "first baby of the year" stories in the local paper. As it happened, she was an unwed mother, welfare-dependent, who prattled on to the reporter about how happy she was that her toddler now had a sister, and how, since she could rely on the dole, she really had nothing better to do than have another baby. The happy-face story hit the wires, and the delighted mom became a calendar girl among Welfare Queens, vilified nationally on talk radio as a social parasite.

Should somebody have nudged her, midway through her idiotic—though revealing—reflections, and pointed out that she was soaking herself with gasoline in the presence of a professional with a lighted match? True, citizens have a right to know where their tax money is going. But if source protection were truly a journalistic duty, the answer would likely be that the reporter, assuming she understood better than the source did the possible impact of publishing the comments, had some obligation to her to offer some kind of heads-up. In a general sense, reporters might feel obliged to caution people they were interviewing when they were saying things that might well hurt them, that the story they were helping create was unlikely to cure the conditions they were eager to deplore, that they were taking part in a process whose consequences were unknowable—and, above all, that they were on their own.

If source protection were understood to be a duty, vulnerable informants wouldn't have to ask for anonymity, and reporters wouldn't be instructed to agree to confidentiality only when sources won't talk otherwise. Instead, reporters are admonished to name sources whenever possible. The reasoning is sensible: information from named people is more credible and verifiable, and identified sources can be held accountable for falsities. Yet when confidentiality is in the source's best interest, shouldn't the reporter suggest it? True, concealment isn't the reporter's job, and finding information is hard enough, but it's reasonable to ask whether the superior knowledge the reporter has of the likely consequences of the source's comments confers any obligation on the journalist. Isn't minimizing harm an important value?

The fact is, source protection generally becomes an issue only with canny, high-level officials who use the press as another lever of influence and who insist on confidentiality. Their actual need for protection from reprisal may be dubious, but their continuing cooperation is of great value to the journalist. So in a turnabout of Marx's principle, they get protection based not on their needs, but on their abilities. True, a thoroughgoing concern for the welfare of sources could constrain reporting in ways that would be paralyzing, and journalists can't be both zealous reporters and PR consultants. But it's deeply ironic that a profession that's supposed to have special sensitivity to the underdog routinely follows practices that ignore—if they don't aggravate—the plight of the most vulnerable people who seek its help.

In fact, the lore of journalism doesn't have much room for sources. Instead it extols the plucky reporters, sometimes their grumpy editors, on occasion even their publishers. The fact that the overwhelming majority of sources are well-placed officials who feed the media because it's their job makes them unlikely heroes. Yet beyond the rituals of normal news, the ability of the news media to act freely and independently of governmental or private power—when it's doing what we most fervently demand of a free press—is meaningful only in an environment where sources have information and are willing to disclose it. Press freedom, in that respect, is nothing more than source freedom one step removed. The right of a news organization to tell what it learns is a hollow abstraction without the willingness of news sources to tell what they know. No political regime, no matter how authoritarian, would need to censor a news organization that had no independent sources, and was doing nothing but publishing reports that were officially sanctioned.

Considering how indispensable knowledgeable sources are, it's remarkable how little affection they get and how flimsy the protections are that anybody claims for them, apart from the disputed right of reporters to keep source identities from the gaze of law enforcement. The rash of prosecutions that began toward the end of the Bush administration and intensified under the Obama White House has been conducted under the 1917 Espionage Act, but has been an assault on sources, not spies, targeting individuals because they provided newsworthy information destined for public consumption, not priceless secrets intended for foreign adversaries. Still, their plight has triggered little more than intermittent pleas for leniency rather than principled opposition based on the public benefit the leakers intended or, indeed, created. That, in spite of the undisputed reality that the informants gave news reporters secret information about governmental improprieties and illegalities that made headline news worldwide.

The media's reticence has several causes. One is that the assault on leakers has left the press itself largely untouched. As a matter of policy rather than law, the Espionage Act hasn't been used against the media organizations that make the leakers' secrets public—even though it's the publication, not the handover of information to a reporter, that irreversibly annihilates the secrecy of the information, and it's the media's willingness to accept and publish leaks that is the necessary precondition for the disclosures. Still, prosecutors, for the most part, are quite happy to leave the media alone. They, too, embrace the idea that even if an informant belongs in prison for handing over secrets for publication, the media organizations that actually publish them need not be taken to task. And as a matter of prosecutorial politics, as long as government agents can identify the informants through wiretaps and snooping they'd just as soon not hassle reporters. As mentioned, only in the case of former CIA operative Jeffrey Sterling has a journalist, *New York Times* national security reporter James Risen, faced government demands—and the threat of a contempt sentence—over his refusal to say whether Sterling was a source for a chapter in Risen's 2006 book about a blown U.S. intelligence operation in Iran.

The forbearance of prosecutors reflects a cozy entente between government and big media: the government avoids stirring the rancor of editorialists and averts long-winded litigation full of talk about sacred rights, while the media buy themselves a KEEP OUT OF JAIL card, even if it means disregarding their sources' safety. Moreover, it reflects the evidentiary realities of the ramped-up digital-era surveillance capabilities of post-9/11 America. As an unnamed administration official told Lucy Dalglish, then head of the Reporters Committee for Freedom of the Press, in 2011: "We're not going to subpoena reporters in the future. We don't need to. We know who you're talking to."

Again, it's worth pointing out that as a matter of moral logic—which asks that responsibility be assigned where it belongs—ignoring what the media do with the leaked information is absurd. Whatever the current dictates of First Amendment jurisprudence, if publishing government secrets actually causes harm, rational public policy would demand that those responsible be called to account—whether they're a former military intelligence worker or a mighty news organization. That would seem to be precisely what laws protecting national security are for. And by the same reasoning, if the publication in dispute produces, on balance, a public benefit, *nobody* should be punished—neither the publisher nor its source, even if classification stamps were ignored and secrecy rules violated.

But disruptive sources have rarely been able to rely on the media for support and protection. The whistleblower who gave *The Cincinnati Enquirer* access to Chiquita Brands voice mails for the newspaper's 1998 exposé of company wrongdoing in Central America was identified by the *Enquirer's* parent, Gannett Co., fired, prosecuted, and lost his license to practice law. Former Brown & Williamson scientist Jeffrey Wigand was portrayed as a brave and tortured man of principle determined to expose the lethal lies of cigarette makers in Michael Mann's movie *The Insider* in 1999, but he had been sold out by the media organization, CBS News *60 Minutes,* that he was trying to help. In the Pentagon Papers case, after *The New York Times* prevailed before the Supreme Court on the narrow issue of prior restraint, its source, former RAND Corporation analyst Daniel Ellsberg, was left to his own devices to fight the federal prosecution that continued another two years. In the private sector sources face enhanced surveillance and the proliferation of so-called nondisparagement clauses, which prohibit that most reliable of potential informants—the disgruntled ex-employee—from sharing critical observations to the press. Even after legislation such as the Sarbanes-Oxley financial reforms foregrounded enhanced protections for whistleblowers, the results were meager. In 2011, investigative business reporter Michael Hudson found sixty-three ex-employees at twenty financial houses who said they were fired or demoted for reporting fraud or refusing to commit fraud; only four had been reported in the news media.

The practical realities of serving as an unauthorized source have changed, too, generally for the worse. Looking at digital-era news practices, it's apparent the overall environment for sources has deteriorated, and potential informants have better reason than ever to keep silent. Consider the channels through which reporters and informants communicate. News organizations routinely post e-mail addresses for their reporters, but who believes an e-mail to a journalist is private, in the way a phone conversation was a decade ago? Can reporters even safeguard their own electronic correspondence and keep it from their bosses? And how many proprietors would pay to fight to block an outside litigant's attempt to see that correspondence—even one revealing major illegalities— if the source had violated a gag agreement he or she was pressured to sign on his or her way out the company door?

To be sure, not all sources are created equal, as we will see in a moment in the discussion of signature cases of source defense that exceeded the bounds of clear public benefit. Many informants are essentially professional conduits, sophisticated in using, managing, and gulling journalists. They're seasoned public relations pros who understand the rewards and risks of media interactions. Often they're officials who are in the game, who know how to negotiate terms beforehand, and who know that their continuing value to the reporter will usually guarantee they'll be handled with consideration. As they are.

The source who's imperiled isn't the special ops commando, it's the citizen soldier, the average Joe or Jane who has significant information the public should hear, but whose collaboration is a one-off thing; this person won't ever be on any reporter's speed dial. This is the source who steps from obscurity off a cliff into public notoriety, hoping the landing will be soft, maybe expecting that publicity will confer protection, believing that speaking out is the right thing to do. Often these sources are vulnerable and unsophisticated people with outsized expectations of what publicity will do to their lives. They may believe that talking to the press will make them celebrities and immunize them against revenge, even when they say things that are certain to infuriate people they probably shouldn't anger. These sources aren't honored in the press ethics books, and sociologists don't bother studying how often they get hurt. The absence of empirical data about the experiences of different categories of news sources is remarkable, since journalists routinely make judgments based in part on how they imagine their editorial decisions will affect the individuals whose collaboration they've relied on. Yet reporters know almost nothing about the aftermath, and neither the media nor the academy cares enough to find out.

Still, heedless of that indifference and of the risks they run, sources continue to come forward. Many, no doubt, are motivated by the wish to settle scores, and hope that the coverage they're spurring will rally support for their causes. But some understand that talking to the press is what a responsible, thinking, caring person does. It's an action that belongs among the irreducible elements of being a citizen, alongside the right to vote and the duty to give evidence in court. For all that, it's not anything that's included in civics books—at best, textbooks will mention how important it is to read the news, not participate in creating it—and whatever training in the rudiments of citizenship our educational system offers almost certainly omits any mention of it at all. Instead we're left with the media presenting the news as something they produce unaided so they can continue to brandish the First Amendment as if it's a private license issued for their benefit, ignoring the fact that without sources the press freedom clause is a dead letter.

SOURCES AND BEATS

That said, the untutored civilian who steps forward to disclose headline-grabbing revelations of great public import is the exception to the normal rituals of reporter-source interaction from which routine news flows. Those interactions, more often than not, take place in the context of beats. And the logic of beats encourages a troubling codependency in which the journalist must make tradeoffs between news values and the demands of the network of source relationships that is indispensable to the production of normal news. The upshot is that reporters develop powerful reasons of self-interest to be excessively protective of valued sources. Hence the paradox: The lack of concern for source welfare is a problem when it comes to ordinary citizens and whistleblowers, but excessive concern for the well-being of professional sources is corrupting.

Some years back a reporter with a small news organizations who was posting to an ethics site I took part in wrote in with a dilemma that in its essentials will be familiar to many reporters: a colleague of hers on the police beat had learned of minor wrongdoing involving the town's cops, but publishing a story on it would come at the cost of the reporter's continued access to useful sources within the police department. Worse, she said, her state's laws allowed police to withhold practically all information about investigations that haven't brought arrests. "This means that reporters have to keep up a good relationship with officers in order to get anything on unsolved crimes, no matter how small or how serious," she wrote. So the colleague had to choose between sitting on a perfectly newsworthy story that would embarrass the sources she relies on and destroying her effectiveness on the police beat.

That conundrum is more than an occasional problem for a small-town reporter. It has been institutionalized into a routine reality traditional journalists face, thanks to the still-robust reliance on beats to cover the country's most powerful institutions, private and public. The upside of the beat system is clear. It encourages journalists to develop a depth of expertise so they can report knowledgeably on topics that require focus and specialization to understand and explain. But the beat system also requires reporters to get to know the people who control the information their coverage depends on, so they can call on those sources and secure the necessary information from them. And that's where the problems begin. The reporter's success in covering his or her beat depends on the cooperation of the people being covered—and not just their knowledge, but their goodwill, too.

If you deliberately set out to devise an arrangement less conducive to tough, adversarial reporting, it would be hard to beat beats. And, indeed, bird-dogging the powerful wasn't the reason the beat system arose in the late nineteenth century. Instead, beats solved two problems: ensuring reliable conduits for official information to flow from leading institutions of government and business, and establishing consistent, low-cost sources of raw news for the burgeoning mass-circulation press. Under the beat system, reporters turned up at appointed times and received the news of the day. The notion that good coverage required deep understanding and specialized expertise came only later. What came first was the wish for a stable network of cooperative relationships, which would work to the advantage of the subjects of coverage, news organizations, and, to some degree, the public.

Of all the improper influences on the flow of publicly significant news—from commercialism to deliberate disinformation—one that is rarely mentioned for its corrupting effect is the beat system. The wisdom of beats rests on the idea that journalism can flourish in a setting where professional success utterly depends on the continuing cooperation of the same people that the journalist is supposed to badger, provoke, expose, and, in sum, hold accountable on the public's behalf. And that is, of course, illogical. Seen from that perspective, we shouldn't be surprised that journalism is so often timid and reverential to sources; the miracle is that journalists are ever tough and courageous, that beat reporters do defy their sources. However, that's a mark of their own guts and ethical maturity, and of the presence of determined informants within the institutions they cover. It's not testimony to the wisdom of the system within which reporters operate. Beats encourage a workplace in which asking frontline reporters the question—"What is the best story you know about that you cannot write?"—would likely bring embarrassing answers.

Would journalism suffer if beats were abandoned? Running a staff would be harder, but life could get interesting. Time and again great stories have been broken by outsiders with clear eyes, who owed nothing to the informants who feed and water the beat reporters. Watergate didn't come out of *The Washington Post*'s political staff, the My Lai massacre wasn't uncovered by a Pentagon correspondent, and the White House press corps was complicit in the disinformation campaign leading up to the Iraq invasion.

As a source of powerful conflicts of interest for reporters, beats achieved an apotheosis during the 1992 Gulf War when the Pentagon enforced, and the news media largely accepted, a requirement that correspondents be not just accredited but "embedded" in designated military units. That took source dependency to a new level, in which the reporters were literally reliant on the troops they were covering for their physical safety. By the time of the 2003 invasion of Iraq, embedding had become the norm for U.S. correspondents. The coverage that resulted, in my view, had a triumphalist glow, paid little attention to civilian suffering, and did little to anticipate the subsequent collapse of the postwar regime into chaos and internecine war.

Solicitude for sources and its power to corrupt reporting reached a different high point in 2012 during a flap over quote approval, exposed in a disturbing *New York Times* report about a newly clamorous insistence among top politicos on having the last word over what was actually published from interviews they gave. "Now, with a millisecond Twitter news cycle and an unforgiving, gaffe-obsessed media culture, politicians and their advisers are routinely demanding that reporters allow them final editing power over any published quotations," the *Times* reported. Officials were mentioned who red-penciled obscenities, squeezed back long-winded comments, and insisted on deletions, not because they had been misquoted, but because the remarks were deemed ill-timed or tactically unwise. "Organizations like Bloomberg, *The Washington Post, Vanity Fair,* Reuters and *The New York Times* have all consented to interviews under such terms," reporter Jeremy Peters wrote.

To be sure, there's something to be said for source consent, if the alternative is a practice under which interview subjects completely surrender any and all control of their words the moment they utter them. This might be called the Mouse Trap Model: The lid slams shut, and even if moments later the source has speaker's remorse—or has unwittingly uttered nonsense—the words pretty much belong to the reporter. As a source, you're of course grateful when reporters read back what they're going to use from your interviews. Sometimes you've been misheard, and sometimes your comments—once stripped of tone and inflection—don't really say what you were trying to say, so you suggest changes. The objective of an interview, after all, isn't to record stenographically whatever you say, but to convey what you mean. That's a slippery proposition, but usually the point is to learn somebody's views, not to catch him or her sounding foolish. Because few people speak in well-turned prose and most people grope and fumble, the idea of a reporter's treating an interview as a collaboration toward a common goal—clarity—isn't a terrible thing. Seeking source feedback beforehand is an excellent way to avoid both factual errors and, worse, the mistakes of context and meaning that routinely make even accurate reports misleading and infuriating. (Indeed, different media have long given sources greater regard than the traditional Mouse Trap Model suggests. Magazines employ fact checkers, who read back comments and characterizations to unearth substantive and interpretive problems. Some documentary filmmakers explicitly invite collaboration from their subjects: If the producer is telling "their" story, shouldn't they have a hand in shaping it?)

This controversy, however, wasn't about clarity. It was about strengthening official control over news to where the idea of an independent, adversarial press becomes yet another fairy tale beloved by civics teachers and retired editors. Not only were these prized sources deciding when they would talk, what they would say and to whom; not only might they agree to talk only if certain topics were off-limits and they were allowed to set conditions on how they could be identified—now they were getting yet another concession: They were permitted to meditate over their comments, consult with advisers, and change any they disliked, regardless of how unintentionally illuminating the original remarks might have been. The controversy took another turn when it was disclosed that a *Washington Post* reporter had sent drafts of a lengthy article on higher education in Texas to certain of his sources, and then incorporated some of their suggested changes into the version that was published.

Naturally, the value of source feedback can't be discounted. The concern, however, is over relinquishing a vital area of editorial independence and knuckling under to the already vast power of well-placed sources. There's a huge danger of compromise and corruption, once certain people who figure in coverage are given a seat at the editor's desk and invited to negotiate details of that coverage. And the fairness question looms: which sources are invited and which are left out? Won't this practice become another avenue for the already influential to wield yet greater influence? At a minimum, it would seem readers need a heads-up. If interviews are filtered through a post-facto, external editorial review in which comments that will appear as impromptu were actually little more than prepared statements, the public should know. Likewise, if people who figure in a story have a backstage role in critiquing and reshaping that story, their input should be signposted. A more collaborative model may have its strengths, but none of them matter if it's introduced furtively to a public that would be shocked to learn that's how the game is being played.

THE CIA LEAK AFFAIR

Hence, unlike the case in the current wave of Espionage Act prosecutions, it's a problematic solicitude for the well-being of sources—certain sources, anyway—that has been the hallmark of the most noteworthy affairs of recent years involving journalists and their informants. We're going to look at three such cases. In two of them, the news media served as conduits for disclosures that though unauthorized and possibly illegal, came from official sources and were intended to harm relatively powerless adversaries. The first of those cases involved CIA operative Valerie Plame Wilson and her husband, former ambassador Joseph C. Wilson IV; the second, nuclear scientist Wen Ho Lee. A third high-profile case concerned leaks from the BALCO (Bay Area Laboratory Co-Operative) grand jury investigating doping in professional sports. It didn't involve shielding public officials, but still foregrounds one of the underlying issues in source protection: whether journalists should weigh their own responsibility if they knowingly help sources pursue problematic aims.

The Plame Wilson affair began in February 2002, when Wilson, a retired career diplomat, was sent to West Africa by the U.S. Central Intelligence Agency to investigate rumors that Iraqi ruler Saddam Hussein's regime had been trying to buy yellowcake uranium from Niger for a nuclear weapons program. Wilson reported back that he found no evidence of such an effort. Nevertheless, President Bush in his State of the Union speech in January 2003 specifically cited Iraqi attempts to buy uranium in Africa as evidence of Saddam's hunger for strategic weapons, a principal justification for the preemptive war that followed in March. In July, as the nonexistence of such an Iraqi weapons program was becoming glaringly obvious, Wilson wrote an op-ed column in *The New York Times* wondering aloud why the administration had advanced claims that he, as its designated investigator, had months before determined were baseless. "I have little choice but to conclude that some intelligence related to Iraq's nuclear weapons program was twisted to exaggerate the Iraqi threat," Wilson wrote. A week later syndicated columnist Robert Novak, apparently trying to cast doubt on Wilson's bona fides, wrote that the ex-ambassador got the assignment to Niger only thanks to his wife, Valerie Plame. Novak described her as "an Agency operative on weapons of mass destruction." In fact, she was a veteran intelligence agent with extensive experience in foreign postings under nondiplomatic cover. In short, she was a U.S. spy.

After Novak's column ran, Wilson and others charged that Plame's cover was deliberately blown to discredit her husband's uranium allegations and to depict him as the thinly qualified beneficiary of her backroom influence-peddling. This suggests that Plame was exposed as a political action calculated to dampen dissent within the government, that Novak was the instrument by which that action was taken, and that his confidentiality pledge to his source was an element essential to the success of the action, since it enabled the question of whether Plame's cover was blown as part of a calculated, high-level administration scheme to go unanswered.

Depending on the circumstances, exposing an undercover U.S. intelligence agent can be illegal under the Intelligence Identities Protection Act of 1982, and anger over Plame's outing compelled the White House to name a special prosecutor to investigate the leak. The investigator ultimately concluded the law hadn't been broken. Before then, however, prominent members of the Washington press corps were subpoenaed to testify as the prosecutor attempted to determine which official first told of Plame's job, since Novak was apparently not the only journalist to whom that information was disclosed.

Ultimately, *New York Times* reporter Judith Miller, who never wrote about Plame, went to jail for eighty-five days for refusing to identify the origin of notes she had taken that suggested she had been told of Plame's identity, and I. Lewis "Scooter" Libby, chief of staff to Vice President Dick Cheney, was found guilty of lying to investigators looking into the leak. The full ensuing spectacle involved a number of troubling episodes, including the editorial chief of Time Inc., Norman Pearlstine, overriding the objections of *Time* magazine reporter Matthew Cooper and handing over Cooper's notes to prosecutors; *Washington Post* reporter Bob Woodward testifying about how and when he learned of Plame's identity; and stories of reporters pleading with their sources to be released from promises to keep their identities private. The upshot was a shabby affair in which source confidentiality was exposed not as a solemn pledge to enable public illumination, but as a cozy background condition for routine interaction among chums at the highest levels of government and media. Reporters flirted with jail time to safeguard the right of senior government officials to endanger a blameless CIA agent whose husband embarrassed the administration by telling the truth. Lost was the question of whether a source was deserving of the same reporter solicitude irrespective of the purposes for which the protection was being used. In this case, the leaker wasn't a whistleblower, seeking safety from reprisal for exposing official wrongdoing; it was the reprisal itself that was being protected, and the actual source of the initial leak was never exposed.

WEN HO LEE

A second case in which source protection was brandished as a cornerstone principle of press ethics, but was used to conceal behavior by government officials that was illegal and unconscionable, involved a Los Alamos National Laboratory nuclear scientist named Wen Ho Lee. He was charged with espionage in 1999 for stealing secrets on behalf of China in the early 1980s. Lee was never tried.

In 2000 he ended up pleading guilty to a single charge of wrongly downloading classified documents; the fifty-eight other charges were dropped, and the federal judge in the case apologized to Lee in open court for his treatment, which included 278 days in solitary confinement. (President Clinton said he was "troubled" by the handling of Lee.) Lee then sued the government for illegally leaking private information from his personnel files to reporters and tried to find out from reporters which officials had lavished them with material meant to damage him. The reporters refused to say.

In 2006, after seven months of negotiation, the U.S. government and five news organizations agreed to pay Lee $1.64 million to settle the suit. The cash settlement was funded half by the government, and half by the outfits that made use of the leaked information: ABC News (The Walt Disney Co.), Associated Press, *The Los Angeles Times* (The Tribune Co.), *The New York Times*, and *The Washington Post*. The news organizations weren't defendants in the suit, but faced the likelihood that they would be pressured to disclose their sources if it went to trial. In a joint statement, the organizations said they settled "to protect our confidential sources, to protect our journalists from further sanction and possible imprisonment and to protect our news organizations from potential exposure." Protecting innocent defendants wasn't mentioned. Instead the media organizations used the case to editorialize in favor of statutory protections that would enable reporters to keep confidential sources secret. "Media sources need a shield," declared *The Los Angeles Times*. To the editorialist, the most troubling issue in the entire affair was the fact that the news media lacked firm ground on which to claim the right to convey defamatory information about a private individual against an overmatched defendant in a groundless national security case.

Here was an instance where the media coverage of a federal prosecution was enough to end the defendant's career and destroy his reputation, long before the merits of the case could be fairly weighed. Lee couldn't sue for his good name and he wasn't likely to get his job back, so he sued over the violation of his privacy rights constituted by the leaks against him, which apparently were fueled by anti-Chinese animus and promoted by political operatives who believed the Clinton administration was impeding the case against him because it feared displeasing the Chinese government. The media organizations said they paid him only to keep their ability to protect confidential sources from being eroded. That was a familiar line, and much of the commentary about the affair focused on whether the media would henceforth be vulnerable to payoff demands from other plaintiffs who subpoenaed reporters to get at their sources and were willing to settle for money in exchange for withdrawing their demands. (*The New York Times,* for its part, was eager to say that its participation in the payment arrangement did not mean it was retreating from its long-standing policy of never settling libel suits.) But circling the wagons around the principle of source protection gave the media an easy, if formulaic, out. It enabled them to avoid considering whether there might be anybody else in this affair who deserved protecting, namely the hapless Dr. Lee. It also shelved the more prickly question of whether there might be times when cooperative, truthful sources turn out not to deserve protection, perhaps because of the harm that they're trying to do, which may warrant not concealment but exposure.

It's a perplexing question, but what about the plight of individuals whose lives and livelihoods are in the hands of powerful public servants who may be headstrong, vindictive, mendacious, and wicked, and who are supposed to be held in check—not shielded—by a vigilant and dedicated press? When the media decide that predatory bureaucrats with a good enough story to tell are entitled to professionally, and even constitutionally, sanctioned protection, regardless of their motives and their recklessness, where does that leave the citizenry? And what happens to that core principle of accountability—supposedly a mainstay value of public service, whether in government or media? Confidentiality promises are powerful and complex things. Sometimes brave and desperate people take great risks to expose important wrongdoing, and the reporters who shield them accept legal jeopardy. But it would be morally obtuse to fail to distinguish that from the more common scenario where the powerful use the press first as pack animals and then as guard dogs.

The Wen Ho Lee affair ended in a settlement, but it was far from settled. The intrigues that destroyed his career may never be exposed, because the media organizations that are best qualified to uncover those undertakings were instead parties to them, hopelessly compromised. Nurturing a source may be a professional necessity, protecting the source may sometimes be a public boon, but there are other duties, such as exposing the truth, that may be even more imperative, and which don't vanish in the glare of a self-serving agreement to keep an undeserving source secret.

WHEN THE SOURCE IS TRUTHFUL BUT EVIL

A third case that suggests the moral limits of source protection doesn't involve an especially well-placed public official but instead showcases an issue underlying all of these cases: whether reporters take on any responsibility for the stratagems their sources use them to further. In December 2004, *San Francisco Chronicle* reporters Mark Fainaru-Wada and Lance Williams broke a sensational story based on secret grand jury testimony that Fainaru-Wada later described as "a game-changer." There, Barry Bonds, one of the most accomplished players in the history of baseball, admitted to using two drugs that were at the heart of a years-long federal probe into the Bay Area Laboratory Co-Operative. Bonds also insisted he didn't quite know what the drugs were, and it's that claim that later got him convicted of perjury. The two reporters' December 2004 *Chronicle* story recounting Bonds's admission blew the doors off the sports establishment. It led to congressional hearings and a sweeping national effort to address the abuse of drugs by athletes at all levels, from high school on up. It also led to a two-year federal investigation into how the supposedly secret testimony found its way to the *Chronicle* reporters in the first place. The reporters refused to say. In 2006 they were subpoenaed to testify about their sources, but they held firm with the support of the newspaper's owners, the Hearst Corp., which spent more than $1 million defending their silence. Finally, in February 2007 the FBI found the source without their help and arrested a Sacramento lawyer named Troy Ellerman. He admitted letting Fainaru-Wada review and copy from transcripts of grand jury testimony by Bonds and three other athletes in June and November 2004. The government then dropped its efforts to get the *Chronicle* reporters to testify, and the threat of an eighteen-month sentence for contempt of court vanished. Of course, the newspaper was jubilant, and said as much in a lead editorial, "They stood tall for a free press." The reporters' determination to honor their confidentiality agreement with their source was generally praised, and the months of judicial pressure were cited as further reason to enact a federal shield law to insulate journalists from naming sources to whom they had pledged secrecy.

However, beyond the illegality of the leak, the *Chronicle* reporters' dealings with their prized source contained disquieting elements. Ellerman, it turns out, represented BALCO's founder and another executive—in other words, he defended clients who were targets of the grand jury investigation. Why would a defense attorney break the law to publicize highly incriminating testimony that couldn't help but reflect badly on his own clients? After all, the leak indicated that the grand jury had struck pay dirt and unearthed evidence of serious wrongdoing that was very likely traceable to them.

The reason? He was trying to sabotage the investigation. As the *Chronicle* reported: "While he was secretly leaking the transcripts, Ellerman acknowledged . . . he was publicly complaining to a federal judge about the leaks, and he even filed a motion in October 2004 to dismiss charges, arguing that the disclosures made a fair trial 'practically impossible.'" Ellerman initially leaked transcripts in June 2004 not because he wanted the facts made public, but because he hoped that the leak would be blamed on a "vendetta" among prosecutors and would thereby constitute legal grounds for scuttling the grand jury investigation.

He went public with his denunciation of the prosecution several weeks before he allowed Fainaru-Wada to see the grand jury transcripts that produced the explosive December 2004 article focused on Barry Bonds and other top ballplayers. Hence, Ellerman's purposes were clear at the time he provided access to the Bonds testimony for the December story. While the refusal of the *Chronicle* reporters to identify their source was generally acclaimed, this darker backstory brought serious criticism. "A defense attorney leaking grand jury testimony is suspicious, but one filing motions to dismiss based on his own leaks is absolutely dangerous," columnist Jack Shafer wrote. In *The Los Angeles Times*, Tim Rutten wrote: "Conspiring with somebody you know is actively perverting the administration of justice to your mutual advantage is a betrayal of the public interest whose protection is the only basis on which journalistic privilege of any sort has a right to assert itself."

At its core, this affair raises a question of professional conduct that makes journalists wince: Are reporters on solid ground when they focus exclusively on doing their job properly—ensuring that their published work is accurate, fair, and has the requisite public significance? Or are they morally responsible for unsavory stratagems that their source advances through their journalism, especially when they are fully aware of the stratagem, and, as in the BALCO case, are indispensable instruments of it?

This is the Dilemma of the Evil but Truthful Source, and it resonates through all three of these cases: The journalist is given solid information of public importance, and understands the reason for the gift is to further a private purpose that, from the perspective of public policy, fairness, or basic morality, is problematic. Does the journalist's professional obligation to put that information before the public entitle him or her to ignore that private agenda? It's fair to say that reporting is hard enough without taking on a further obligation to interrogate sources about their intentions. Said Mark Feldstein, a veteran broadcast news reporter, author, and professor at the University of Maryland: "The public is the poorer if reporters get high-and-mighty and say, 'We accept only leaks with pure motives.'" And, for that matter, what would constitute the requisite purity of motive? Would the Capitol Hill staffer qualify if she leaked information to discredit her boss's chief rival for a congressional leadership position? To be sure, that's sleazy. And which of numerous motivations are we interested in? Doesn't any source act routinely from a number of motives, ranging from self-promotion and settling old scores to saving the world? Which of them needs to be ethically permissible to entitle the reporter to use the information with a clear conscience? And which would argue for declining the highly newsworthy information—and leaving the public uninformed?

And yet the dilemma remains. We don't normally allow the explanation "I'm just doing my job" to erase responsibility if the routine performance of duties knowingly causes harm. Suppose a shop owner sold a knife to a man who declared he intended to kill his landlady. In his defense the proprietor says he has a business to run and a payroll to meet; his work serves the higher purpose of maintaining a robust market economy; he can't be bothered by speculation about his customers' motives; and besides, for the most part one can safely ignore most of what people say anyway. Still, there's good reason to find the shop owner's narrow focus on his job questionable and conclude—as a matter of ethics if not of law—that if the landlady died he would have some explaining to do.

The difficulty of ascertaining motive is real, and sometimes motives are elusive, sometimes they are concealed, often they are manifold. However, the BALCO case hinges on motivation not as a topic of abstract psychological inquiry, but as a source's deliberate pursuit of a plausible and highly questionable consequence—derailing an apparently meritorious investigation, a consequence that the attorney concluded might be accomplished with the help of the reporters. He secured that help by offering them irresistibly newsworthy information of broad public appeal. So the dilemma doesn't vanish because motives may be unknowable or hard to ascertain. Sometimes that's true, but much of the time, reporters know quite enough. And they hold their nose and proceed anyway, because they believe it is their duty to do so. This is morally questionable. Journalists are not free to act as if the private stratagem they are furthering did not exist. They may do their story anyway, and that may be the right thing to do, but they must accept that by doing so they will be complicit in that stratagem. This suggests that they must be satisfied that the wrongness of their complicity is redeemed by the wider public benefit of the secrets it unlocks.

Did BALCO meet that test? Hard to say. The *Chronicle* stories triggered outrage and reform. Fainaru-Wada argues that the investigation was shaping up like a conventional drug case, with lower-level wrongdoers—the drug users—granted leniency and, in this instance, anonymity in exchange for turning in the suppliers. The fear was that here the users were the star athletes, the most newsworthy and most publicly significant malefactors, and if they escaped exposure sports might well go unreformed. But it is hard to see how that concern justified actions that might have sabotaged an apparently determined investigation. If indeed the grand jury later handed up indictments that amounted to a whitewash, the testimony leaked by Ellerman would have been even more news-worthy then, and could have been published without obstructing the inquiry. The Dilemma of the Evil but Truthful Source recasts a problem familiar to many reporters: how to reconcile their broader ethical responsibilities with the duties that journalism de-mands. The journalist who can justify his or her actions only by ignoring wider obligations those actions seem to defy is likely to be acting ethically neither as a journalist nor as a person.

SOURCE PROTECTION IN THE DIGITAL ERA

The upshot of the foregoing discussion is that the normal dynamics of reporter-source relations are fraught with complexity and incon-sistencies. The picture that emerges is of sharply divided practices within the news media when it comes to the rights and privi-leges of sources. The notion that source protection has core stand-ing among the tenets of journalism ethics is an appealing one, but crumbles on closer inspection. Informants whose once and future value as news sources is deemed great can expect forbearance, editorial flexibility, and, if tracking back the information to them might cause discomfort, a determination to keep their identities secret. Such practices as quote approval, embedding, and even routine beat-tending exemplify an unavoidable tendency for jour-nalists, whose most fundamental nutritional need is information, to nurture the sources of that nourishment. When it comes to the one-off sources, the ones who are momentarily indispensable, there's little to suggest a comparable duty of care among reporters. The understandable journalistic preference for full attributions will incline the reporter to identify them by name unless they demand concealment as a condition for talking. Possible downstream consequences will be soft-pedaled, while possible benefits to such sources are likely to be scrutinized critically. (It's notable that the recurrent dustups over whether sources should be paid invariably concern largesse shown to ordinary people caught up in fleeting scandals. These are people who have no way to cash in on their media exposure the way that professional sources do, through enhanced prestige or name recognition or by having their interests advanced—benefits that constitute valuable compensation but are rarely seen as corrupting.)

In 2010, with its release of the classified 2007 gunsite footage of a U.S. helicopter killing civilians on a Baghdad street, WikiLeaks inaugurated a new era of relations between journalists and sources. For the first time global news organizations were confronted with an independent information provider of immense scope that was without ties to or dependency on existing national governments and which had no corresponding incentives to nurture relations with official news sources. The marquee sources of the WikiLeaks era—namely Chelsea Manning, Julian Assange, and Edward Snowden—constitute an influence on journalism that is profoundly disruptive to the patterns of source-reporter interaction discussed earlier:

- As sources, they're not on any conventional reporter's roster of people whose collaboration is a steady and predictable part of beat coverage, and they play no role in the informational network out of which routine news arises.
- They hold out no promise of a continuing flow of significant information; instead, their future as informants of any kind is under a cloud.
- The information they offer challenges what had been known publicly on a given matter.

- Their disclosures may therefore constitute a rebuke to the integrity and competence of the journalism establishment that had nourished and tended the inventory of discredited public understandings.
- They may have access to distribution channels of their own, which compete with and undermine the authority of existing news media channels.
- And because the sources emerge from outside the usual social nexus of information providers, they're unlikely candidates for media protection if the information causes official displeasure.

Before WikiLeaks, the exemplar of pre-digital era disruption was the defense analyst Daniel Ellsberg, who leaked the Defense Department's secret in-house history of the Vietnam War (1945–1967). Before he approached *The New York Times* in early 1971, Ellsberg tried to get sympathetic members of Congress to make the Pentagon Papers public on the floor of the Senate, hoping to take advantage of lawmakers' legislative immunities. Although the Supreme Court later barred the government from stopping the *Times* from publishing the material, in a widely heralded First Amendment case, the legality of Ellsberg's leaks was never adjudicated. Ellsberg himself wasn't treated especially kindly by the media, even by his beneficiary, *The New York Times,* and was left to his own devices to defend himself in the Espionage Act prosecution that publication of the history provoked. He recalls ruefully *Times* coverage of his personal life that he says impeded his ability to raise money for his defense. The case against him fell apart nearly two years after the 1971 Supreme Court ruling only because of disclosures about illegal wiretaps and the burglary of his psychiatrist's office by White House operatives.

The current spate of federal prosecutions of news sources began in the waning days of the Bush administration and intensified under Obama's, and now stands at seven, including the pending complaint against Edward Snowden, who remains in de facto exile in Russia. It's evidence of an approach to official secrecy that, by the standards of other countries, is ferocious.

Chelsea (then Bradley) Manning was arrested in May 2010 for downloading secret U.S. military and diplomatic documents to WikiLeaks, which became headline news worldwide. He was then held for nine months in a Marine brig in Quantico, Virginia, in what the American Civil Liberties Union called "prolonged isolated confinement and forced idleness," spending twenty-three hours a day in a six-by-twelve-foot cell, and allowed to exercise—shackled—for one hour in another windowless room. He was often stripped and forced to stand naked outside his cell to be inspected, had his sleep interrupted frequently, was periodically deprived of his reading glasses, and generally was subjected to treatment meant to "degrade, humiliate, and traumatize . . ." Why this former intelligence clerk without terrorist connections or secrets to hide should be treated with a cruelty that no dog pound would tolerate remains a mystery. (It's worth pointing out that Ellsberg spent no time in jail in connection with the Pentagon Papers case.) Ultimately Manning was tried before a court-martial and sentenced to thirty-five years. WikiLeaks founder Julian Assange has been under de facto house arrest in the Ecuadorean embassy in London since 2012; he has said he fears extradition to the United States, and has refused to travel to Sweden to answer complaints from two women about sexual misconduct. As for Snowden, the zeal with which the United States has pursued him was such that the plane carrying Bolivia's President was diverted from the airspace of several European countries and forced to land in Austria in 2013 because it was believed Snowden might be aboard. If he returns to the United States to face trial he could be sentenced to life in prison.

Elsewhere, punishment for making official secrets public is less severe than penalties in the United States for driving drunk: at worst, two years in Britain and Denmark. In other Western countries, maximum punishments range from four years in Sweden and Spain, to five in Germany, Belgium, and Poland, and seven in France, according to an analysis of twenty European countries by Sandra Coliver, a legal expert with the Open Society Justice Initiative. The group has been leading a multiyear, international effort to formulate broad principles reconciling the legitimate need to keep government secrets with the no less legitimate need to hold governments publicly accountable.

Not only are penalties mild elsewhere, Coliver found, prosecutions are rare. In six countries, as of 2013 nobody in the previous decade had been convicted for disclosing state secrets. In Britain, since the 1989 Official Secrets Act took effect, only ten public employees had been prosecuted. The longest sentence, one year, was imposed on a naval petty officer who sold intelligence to a newspaper about a possible Iraqi anthrax attack. In fact, apart from the United States, the only country where prosecutions were common is Russia. There, ten government employees have been imprisoned in the past decade for four to fifteen years for making government information public. The study found that Europe's courts seem to be moving toward backing whistleblowers strongly, even when state security is breached. In a 1996 case, a military intelligence official in Romania was initially sentenced to two years for releasing the tapes of illicit wiretaps his agency had made of journalists and politicians. However, the European Court of Human Rights ruled that he was wrongly convicted, that he was acting in good faith in exposing illegalities to the public, and that the public's interest in learning about the wrongdoing outweighed the agency's interest in keeping its good name.

That approach is broadly consistent with the international effort that has taken the form of a new set of legal and policy recommendations. Grandly titled "Global Principles on National Security and the Right to Information," it's known informally as the Tshwane Principles, for the South African district where it was put in final form. Tshwane is the work of twenty-two international organizations and academic institutions that, through fourteen meetings in various venues throughout the world, wrestled with how to balance the public's right to significant information against their governments' needs for secrecy. It received relatively little attention in the United States, though it has gained support from the Council of Europe. The Europeans seem to like the idea that governments should be made to explain their secrecy policies—and when those policies are defied, demonstrate that the harm done by security breaches actually justifies reprisal.

Among Tshwane's cornerstone principles:

- The public has a right to government information, and the burden is on governments to show why they must restrict that right.
- Certain types of information are of such compelling public interest that they should be disclosed except in "the most exceptional circumstances."
- People who expose wrongdoing "should not face retaliation if the public interest in the information disclosed outweighs the public interest in secrecy."
- Whistleblowers should first try to address problems through official channels. And they should not disclose any more information than is necessary to bring attention to the wrongdoing—which, Coliver has suggested, is a standard that was exceeded by Manning's own release of 700,000 military and diplomatic documents.
- Most remarkably, though, even if a whistleblower violates those guidelines, Tshwane asserts that any penalty should be proportionate to the damage done. "Government authorities, in order to justify any punishment,

should undertake an investigation, and should explain publicly, in as complete detail as possible, the actual and specific harm caused," Coliver writes.

That absence of a showing of harm is a deeply disturbing element of the U.S. secrecy panic and the frenzied counterattack against the people behind the disclosures. For all the gnashing of teeth over the Manning leaks, for all the fevered denunciations of Snowden's exposing domestic surveillance, nobody has pointed to actual damage—to national security, to counterterrorism, to intelligence agents, to diplomatic initiatives, to the confidentiality of top-level parleys. Indeed, a reasonable case could be made that, say, the diplomatic cables that Manning and WikiLeaks made available to news organizations in 2010 were of considerable public benefit (and of particular benefit to the United Sates, in that they couldn't fail to insert U.S. policy priorities and perspectives into headlines worldwide). At issue were closely observed dispatches that had bearing on a trove of political questions with global impact, among them:

Did Arab leaders privately share Israel's fears of Iran?
Had Russia's Vladimir Putin squirreled away so much graft that he's the richest man in Europe?
Was Iran approaching Venezuela's then-President Hugo Chavez in hopes of finding uranium for an Iranian nuclear program?
Did the United States pressure Spain to derail an investigation into the Army's 2003 killing of a Spanish newsman in Baghdad?
Was the Mexican military a reliable ally in the war on drug traffickers?
Was Argentina coveting the Falklands/Malvinas islands again, this time with Antarctic oil in mind?

Might China prefer a Korea reunified under Seoul to the uncertainties of a volatile North Korea in perpetual collapse?

It's true that Manning violated oaths and broke laws in downloading the low-grade military and diplomatic secrets he provided to WikiLeaks. But the world's leading news organizations then evaluated that material and decided to make much of it public because of its "immense value," as then *New York Times* executive editor Bill Keller wrote. So, if these news media believe they were right to publish the material Manning gave them, how could they stand aside as he faced life in prison for giving it to them? If they did right and the world benefited, did he do wrong?

The news media's silence concerning Edward Snowden is even more disturbing, since his disclosures exposed the National Security Agency's monumental, undiscriminating, intrusive, and illegal monitoring of civilian communications in the United States and abroad. Under the program code-named PRISM, Snowden disclosed, the NSA and FBI linked to the central servers of nine major Internet companies, downloading extensive materials so that foreign targets could be tracked. After the PRISM leak, an even more disturbing portrait emerged of close coordination between Silicon Valley and the security apparatus. As a *New York Times* account reported, "both hunt for ways to collect, analyze and exploit large pools of data about millions of Americans"—one for intelligence, the other for money. No less important, Snowden's leaks also indicated the NSA had been sweeping up data for seven years on domestic U.S. phone traffic, something previously assumed to have been outside the agency's remit. Unlike the WikiLeaks files, the Snowden material did not, by and large, consist of sensitive information the spymasters had scraped up, but instead illuminated a much more serious matter—their breathtaking capacity to scrape. That capacity, it seems, is unimaginably broad and deep, and encompasses practically all public communication systems—from phones to e-mails, corporate intranets, social media, the world's mightiest search engines, "the cloud"—most anything digital. The picture that emerges is of a stupendously vast surveillance system, one that U.S. intelligence agencies have been so successful in fashioning that their capability has been woven into the infrastructure of the Internet itself.

This was big, and the public seems to have responded. Despite vigorous denunciations by U.S. leaders, a 2013 national survey of U.S. voters by Quinnipiac University found that by a huge margin—55 to 34 percent—respondents considered Snowden a whistleblower, not a traitor. The media's response has been less robust. An exception was an eloquent *Times* editorial, "Edward Snowden, Whistle-Blower," published on New Year's Day 2014, that urged the White House to show leniency toward Snowden and recounted the broad impact of Snowden's defiance, including widespread public outrage, critical court rulings, internal investigations, and even a grudging nod from the White House for his role in provoking domestic debate over surveillance. The *Times* argued that Snowden deserves either clemency or some minimum-punishment plea bargain, and concluded: "When someone reveals that government officials have routinely and deliberately broken the law, that person should not face life in prison at the hands of the same government." Now, this was some improvement over the sparse coverage of the Manning trial and the *Times*'s apparent distaste for WikiLeaks founder Assange, who was the subject of a scathing and borderline defamatory 2011 profile in the *New York Times Magazine*, written by Keller himself, which characterized Assange as peevish, contemptuous, disheveled, malodorous, paranoid, manipulative, and volatile, in almost those words.

So amid this practice of source abandonment, the *Times*'s editorial plea was welcome, But in several regards the media still haven't embraced the pro-Snowden case with appropriate vitality, and haven't gone nearly far enough toward ensuring a fair shake for whistleblowers with vital stories to tell. First, the idea that Snowden deserved a break because his "disclosures have inspired an overdue debate," as *The Los Angeles Times* suggested, is a curious notion. Inspiring a debate hardly seems worth rewarding, all by itself. Lots of terrible things provoke debate. After all, 9/11 triggered major conversations about Islamist terrorism, and school shootings provoked debate about guns. Neither deserved public applause. What Snowden did was put before the public information about major government misconduct that belonged in the public domain, misconduct that constitutes, arguably, the most dangerous and far-reaching power grab of the Information Age. And he embarrassed the administration into reluctantly addressing questionable and invasive practices, which officials had lied about. That's not inspiring a debate; that's calling government to account.

Second, it's troubling that the news media haven't owned up to their own complicity in the affair. Snowden could do nothing without them. The media don't just report on his leaks; they are the indispensable means by which his leaks reach the world, the whole reason his leaks matter. The media aren't observers; they are Snowden's instruments, enablers, and beneficiaries. If they truly want to defend him, they should start by acknowledging that they stand alongside Snowden as public servants, and by publishing the information he provided have affirmed his value in the most compelling way they can.

Finally, the thrust of the editorial appeal was to the conscience of the administration. That seems an obsequious position to take, the twenty-first-century equivalent of imploring the sovereign for clemency. The unstated premise of the editorial is that Snowden's fate was in the hands of the state's prosecutors. If true, that would only be because the United States had been emasculated by laws that prevent them from actually administering justice in cases like his. Elsewhere, if civil servants violate secrecy rules by disclosing information about what they believe is criminality by officialdom, they can argue in court that their breaches served a greater public benefit. And judges could then do exactly what they're supposed to do—exercise judgment, and decide whether to forgive or punish the offenders. Snowden deserves a sturdier and more muscular defense, something appropriate to the enormity of the wrongdoing he has exposed, something that helps make the country safe for others who have stories the public is entitled to hear.

Yet, in the final analysis, the argument for a public benefit defense is premised on a dispassionate assessment of consequence: What indeed were the effects of WikiLeaks' massive 2010 military and diplomatic disclosures? Did the leaks do harm or do good? As of mid-2014 nearly four years had passed; the U.S. military presence in Iraq had ended, and the dust had settled from the release of the State Department cables. The moment was more than ripe for an accounting. Did WikiLeaks demoralize dedicated officials and expose trusting intelligence assets to risk and reprisal? Or did it blow whistles that needed to be heard, embolden dissidents worldwide, fuel the Arab Spring, encourage lackluster news media to defy official controls, help chase despots from power? What's so alluring about these questions is first, that they are answerable, perhaps not definitively, but persuasively; second, that they should be front and center in the determination of what course justice should take in setting sensible limits on official secrecy and the free speech rights of sources; and lastly, that they are just the kinds of things that journalists are trained to ferret out and report. That final point can't be overstated. It's the news media, if they mobilized their resources, that have the skills and the capacity to recast the entire debate over official secrecy by examining, with care and journalistic precision, the impact that the most audacious and most reviled violations of official secrecy have had.

The digital age explosion of communicative capabilities has

created greater capacity than ever for both suppression and eman-
cipation. There are no guarantees that the proliferation of channels will mean a richer availability of information with genuine
public significance. That happens only if people who have that information believe it'll be heard and welcomed, and if they can
step forward with it without fear of punishment. That's why the
whole edifice of informational freedom in the digital age depends
on creating an environment in which sources can speak.

SELECTED BIBLIOGRAPHY

Beausoleil, Mary. "Betraying a Source: Our Story Wronged a Naive Subject." *Journalism Cases Online.* Hosted by the Indiana University School
of Journalism. http://journalism.indiana.edu/resources/ethics/hand
ling-sources/betraying-a-trust/.

Boehlert, Eric. "How the *New York Times* Helped Railroad Wen Ho
Lee." *Salon,* September 21, 2000. http://www.salon.com/2000/09/21
/nyt_6/.

Coliver, Sandra. "National Security Whistleblowers: The U.S. Response
to Manning and Snowden Examined." *Open Society Justice Initiative,*
June 12, 2013. http://www.opensocietyfoundations.org/voices/national
-security-whistleblowers-us-response-manning-and-snowden
-examined.

Dalglish, Lucy. "Lessons from Wye River." The News Media & The Law,
Reporters Committee for Freedom of the Press, Summer 2011, p 1.
http://www.rcfp.org/browse-media-law-resources/news-media-law
/news-media-and-law-summer-2011/lessons-wye-river.

Ellsberg, Daniel. *Secrets: A Memoir of Vietnam and the Pentagon Papers.* New
York: Viking Penguin, 2002.

Hastings, Michael. "The Runaway General." *Rolling Stone,* June 22, 2010.
http://www.rollingstone.com/politics/news/the-runaway-general
-20100622.

Keller, Bill. "The Boy Who Kicked the Hornet's Nest: Dealing with Assange and the Wikileaks Secrets." *New York Times Magazine,* January 26, 2011.

Malcolm, Janet. *The Journalist and the Murderer.* New York: Alfred A. Knopf/Random House, 1990.

Peters, Jeremy W. "Latest Word on the Trail? I Take It Back." *New York Times,* July 15, 2012. http://www.nytimes.com/2012/07/16/us/politics/latest-word-on-the-campaign-trail-i-take-it-back.html?_r=1&pagewanted=2&pagewanted=all.

Risen, James. *State of War: The Secret History of the CIA and the Bush Administration.* New York: Frcc Press, 2006.

Tuchman, Gaye. "Making News by Doing Work: Routinizing the Unexpected." *American Journal of Sociology* 79, no. 1 (1973): 110–31. http://www.jstor.org/stable/2776714.

Wasserman, Edward. "A Critique of Source Confidentiality." *Notre Dame Journal of Law, Ethics & Public Policy* 19, no. 2 (2005): 553–71. http://scholarship.law.nd.edu/ndjlepp/vol19/iss2/11.

Wasserman, Edward. "A Robust Future for Conflict of Interest," in *Journalism Ethics: A Philosophical Approach,* edited by Christopher Meyers. New York: Oxford University Press, 2010.

WHAT SHOULD WE DO ABOUT THE LEAKERS?[1]

DAVID COLE

DAVID COLE is the Hon. George J. Mitchell Professor in Law and Public Policy at Georgetown University Law Center, where he teaches constitutional law, national security, and criminal justice. He is also the legal affairs correspondent for *The Nation,* and a regular contributor to *The New York Review of Books.* He has been published widely in law journals and the popular press, including the *Yale Law Journal, California Law Review, Stanford Law Review, The New York Times, The Washington Post, The New Republic, The Atlantic, The Wall Street Journal,* and *The Los Angeles Times.* He is the author of seven books, including *Less Safe, Less Free; Why America Is Losing the War on Terror* (coauthored with Jules Lobel), winner of the 2007 Palmer Civil Liberties Prize; and *Enemy Aliens: Double Standards and Constitutional Freedoms in the War on Terrorism,* winner of the 2004 American Book Award. His most recent book is *The Torture Memos: Rationalizing the Unthinkable* (2009).

WHAT SHOULD WE make of Edward Snowden, Bradley (now Chelsea) Manning, and Julian Assange? Their names are known across the globe, yet the actions that made them famous have also driven them to lives of intense isolation—in hiding, in prison, or in a foreign embassy. They have been lionized as heroes and condemned as traitors. Snowden, a former contractor for the National Security Agency (NSA), and Manning, a low-level Army intelligence analyst, are responsible for the two largest unauthorized disclosures of classified information in the nation's history.

Manning released to Assange's Web site, WikiLeaks, about 720,000 secret documents from the State and Defense Departments, and Assange published them on the Internet. The NSA still doesn't know the full extent of the information Snowden stole and passed on to the journalists Glenn Greenwald, Laura Poitras, and Barton Gellman, but it estimates the number to be 1.7 million classified documents, concerning some of the U.S.'s most closely guarded secret surveillance programs.

The federal government views Manning and Snowden as criminals. It tried and convicted Manning for violating the Espionage Act and he was sentenced to thirty-five years in prison. (Manning subsequently announced that he was changing his gender, and hereafter would be known as Chelsea.) The government has charged Snowden with stealing government property and violating the Espionage Act, although he has thus far evaded trial by obtaining temporary asylum in Russia. And the Justice Department has empaneled a grand jury to investigate Assange, who is holed up in the Ecuadorean embassy in London seeking to evade extradition to Sweden for alleged sex crimes.

The prosecutors in Manning's trial repeatedly contended that Assange actively encouraged Manning's crimes. In November 2013, however, a Justice Department official told the *The Washington Post* that Assange would not likely be prosecuted for publishing Manning's documents. According to former Justice Department spokesman Matthew Miller, "if you are not going to prosecute journalists for publishing classified information, which the department is not, then there is no way to prosecute Assange."[2] Yet the grand jury investigation continues.

Some praise Manning, Snowden, and Assange for exposing our government's secret and legally dubious activities at home and abroad. Snowden's revelations about the scope of NSA electronic surveillance have touched off a much-needed national and global debate about privacy in the digital age. Indeed, because of his influence he was rumored to have been the runner-up to Pope Francis for *Time* magazine's "Person of the Year." Manning's and Assange's disclosures had much less dramatic effect, but they, too, revealed a host of potential abuses, including U.S. troops in Iraq killing civilians, the U.S. State Department spying on foreign UN officials, and a secret agreement between Yemen and the United States to permit U.S. drone strikes there on the condition that they not be publicly admitted.

These leaks, the most significant since Daniel Ellsberg made the Pentagon Papers available to *The New York Times* and *The Washington Post* in 1971, raise anew the question of when it is justified to disclose classified information to the public. Some advocates of transparency seem to treat any exposure of secrets as an unmitigated good; this appears to be the philosophy behind Assange's WikiLeaks. However, that position is morally untenable. There are undoubtedly good reasons for secrecy in many aspects of government, especially foreign relations, and particularly during wartime. And there are many legitimate bases for condemning disclosures, particularly when they reveal the identities of sources and methods of foreign intelligence.

Security hawks consider any unauthorized disclosure of classified information unacceptable, stressing that cleared employees take an oath not to disclose such information, and that no government can operate without some secret deliberations and covert actions. But, this, too, is an untenably extreme positions. History demonstrates that secrecy is used not only for legitimate purposes of national security, but too often to shield illegal or embarrassing activity from public scrutiny. Even the most ardent security proponent must concede that the benefits from revealing illegal abuses of authority will sometimes outweigh the costs of disclosing those secrets.

If neither extreme is acceptable, how should we distinguish legitimate from illegitimate leaks? The Intelligence Community Whistleblower Protection Act, passed in 1998, marks one effort at striking a balance.[3] It provides a way for individuals to disclose classified information regarding a "serious or flagrant problem, abuse, violation of law," but only to members of congressional intelligence committees, and only after initially presenting it to the NSA's inspector general and the attorney general. This law, however, provides no protection for revealing information to the public, and has been used only rarely. Whatever balance it struck in theory has proven largely irrelevant in practice.

To understand why, imagine if Snowden had gone to the NSA's inspector general with information that the agency was collecting large amounts of "metadata" on every American's phone calls— i.e., records of who they called, when, and for how long they talked—storing the data for five years, and searching through it. What would the inspector general have done? As the NSA's defenders repeatedly emphasize, the metadata program was blessed by all three branches. The Bush administration instituted it and Obama maintained it. Fifteen federal judges on the secret Foreign Intelligence Surveillance Court—or FISA court—declared it lawful. And Congress reauthorized the Patriot Act provision upon which the program was based, even after being informed of the program (albeit in a limited and anodyne manner designed not to raise any alarms).[4]

Given these circumstances, the inspector general surely would have responded that there was no basis for disclosing it. Yet even if Snowden had been given a green light to bring the NSA's activities to the attention of the intelligence committees, the problem was not that those committees were in the dark, but that the American people were. As Snowden put it in a videotaped interview from Hong Kong at the time of his initial leaks, "These things need to be determined, by the public, not by somebody who was simply hired by the government. . . . The public needs to decide whether these programs and policies are right or wrong."[5]

The reactions that Snowden's disclosures have sparked suggest that he was onto something. The only parties kept out of the "checks and balances" so often lauded by the NSA's defenders were the American and global publics—in other words, the people whose privacy was at stake. As long as the program was kept under wraps, all three branches of government were willing to tolerate it. But once it became public, that changed dramatically. On December 16, 2013, the first federal court to assess the legality of the NSA's telephony metadata program in a public, adversarial proceeding declared it likely unconstitutional. U.S. District Judge Richard Leon ruled that the mass collection and search of metadata invaded U.S. citizens' reasonable expectations of privacy, and could not be justified without a warrant and probable cause.[6] In December 2013, U.S. District Judge William Pauley III in Manhattan, disagreeing with Judge Leon, ruled that the NSA's program was constitutional. Judge Pauley reasoned that Americans have no legitimate expectation of privacy in the phone numbers they call, and therefore have no constitutional basis for objecting to the NSA's mass collection and searching of that data. Both cases are pending appeal.

Two days after Judge Leon's ruling, the President's own expert panel, which included a former acting director of the CIA, raised serious questions about the wisdom and propriety of the program, and recommended forty-six reforms to rein in the NSA, including an end to the NSA's bulk collection of telephone records, more judicial and legislative oversight, and a requirement of specific presidential approval for spying on foreign leaders. President Obama shortly thereafter agreed to implement several of the recommendations.

The Privacy and Civil Liberties Oversight Board, a federal body charged with monitoring privacy issues raised by federal programs, issued two detailed reports on the two principal programs revealed by Snowden's disclosure—the collection of telephone metadata on virtually every American's every phone call, and the collection of the contents of foreigners' electronic communications—including phone calls, Skypes, e-mails, and chat room discussions. The PCLOB, as it is known, was particularly scathing about the domestic metadata program, which it found to be unauthorized by statute and to have disrupted no terrorist plots nor identified any actual terrorists. The PCLOB was less critical of the program for collecting foreigners' communications, although here, too, it recommended reforms.

Members of Congress have also been spurred to reform. They introduced more than thirty bills to restrict the NSA. The most important bill, the USA Freedom Act, was initially cosponsored by Representative Jim Sensenbrenner, a Republican from Wisconsin in his thirty-fifth year in Congress, and Senator Patrick Leahy, the veteran Democrat from Vermont. Sensenbrenner, an architect of the original Patriot Act, says that he never imagined that it could authorize what the NSA has been doing. And Silicon Valley is also urging reforms, arguing that the NSA's practices have not only damaged privacy but undermined their businesses—and the U.S. economy—by eroding trust in the confidentiality of U.S.-based Internet services.

The USA Freedom Act passed the House with bipartisan support in May 2014, but at the last minute it was watered down in closed-door proceedings with representatives of the intelligence community. The bill was so weakened that some civil rights and privacy groups that had been supporting the bill retracted their support. The CEOs of America's leading tech companies, including Google, Apple, Facebook, Yahoo, Twitter, Microsoft, and Dropbox, published an open letter to the Senate in *The New York Times* and elsewhere called on the Senate to strengthen the bill that passed the House.

Senator Leahy's version of the bill responded to these concerns. It barred bulk collection of phone data or other business records and required the government to specify a "person, account, address, or personal device" that "narrowly limit[s] the scope of the tangible things sought to the greatest extent reasonably practicable." And it promoted transparency about government demands for phone calling records and other business records, by (1) authorizing the recipients of orders to turn over records to provide more information to the public about those orders, (2) requiring the government to make a specific showing of need to prohibit the disclosure of such orders, (3) requiring the Foreign Intelligence Surveillance Court to make more extensive declassification and public summaries of its decisions, and (4) expanding the information that the government must report to Congress and the public on an annual basis about the frequency, scope, and results of its use of these powers. Had these provisions been in place, and had we been told that the NSA was collecting records on hundreds of millions of Americans, Edward Snowden might not have felt compelled to leak the information, and the NSA program would likely have been reformed long before now.

In November 2014, during Congress's lame-duck session, the USA Freedom Act fell two votes short of the sixty needed to overcome a filibuster, killing the bill despite its bipartisan majority support in both houses of Congress. The new Congress will be more conservative. But the provision on which the NSA's domestic telephone metadata program rests is set to expire in June 2015, so reformers should be able to insist on significant improvements as the price for extending the law. The extent and specifics of ultimate reform are uncertain. What is clear, however, is that some reform has already been undertaken, and that there is substantial support for considerably more restrictions on NSA authority. More targeted surveillance, subject to closer judicial oversight, should replace the NSA's current dragnet approach. How the conflict ultimately will be resolved will not be known for some time. But none of this debate would have happened without Snowden's revelations.

Consider what we have learned from Snowden's leaks and the further government disclosures that they prompted:

1. Since 2006, the NSA has been systematically collecting records on virtually every phone call every American makes. It has done so on the basis of NSA lawyers' secret, strained interpretation of a Patriot Act provision that authorized the collection only of records "relevant" to an investigation of international terrorism. The NSA

argued that it can collect everyone's phone records, regardless of any connection to terrorism, on the theory that the records might in the future become "relevant" to a terrorism investigation. But on that theory, what records couldn't the NSA collect?

2. Director of National Intelligence James Clapper lied under oath about this program when asked in a congressional hearing whether the government was collecting any kind of data on millions of Americans. Clapper answered "no," but Snowden has shown that the NSA was doing precisely that.

3. Under another statute, the FISA Amendments Act of 2008, the NSA has engaged in far more intrusive surveillance—including reviewing the content of e-mails, Internet searches, and chat rooms—of persons it believes are foreign nationals overseas, even if they are communicating with U.S. citizens here. It may do so without any individualized suspicion that the target is engaged in criminal or terrorist activity. The agency has tapped the phones and e-mails of some of our closest allies' leaders, including German Chancellor Angela Merkel and former Israeli Prime Minister Ehud Olmert.

4. These NSA programs were authorized in secret by FISA judges, but have often violated the terms under which the courts authorized them. For example, in 2009 FISA Judge Reggie Walton castigated the NSA for illegally reviewing thousands of Americans' phone data over two years, and imposed a temporary requirement (later lifted) that all searches of the database be preceded by judicial approval.[7]

5. Within the United States, the NSA has been collecting records not just of Americans' phone calls but of their e-mails as well. E-mail data is often even more revealing

than phone data (identifying, for example, the e-mail groups and political and religious organizations with which one communicates).

6. The NSA has been collecting cell phone location data and e-mail address lists from outside the United States on a vast scale, data that tracks phone users' every move around the clock and reveals e-mailers' closest associations.

7. The NSA has not been satisfied even with all of these powers. It has hacked into the overseas links between Google's and Yahoo's data hubs, vacuuming up enormous amounts of data, subject to no statutory or judicial limits whatsoever. And it has inserted vulnerabilities into private industry's encryption codes to enable it to hack into them more easily.

8. Finally (at least for now), the NSA has been cooperating in potentially disturbing ways with its British counterpart, Government Communications Headquarters (GCHQ), apparently exploiting loopholes that allow the NSA to do things GCHQ could not, and vice versa.

In short, Snowden's disclosures portray an insatiable agency that has sought to collect as much information as it possibly can, most of it relying on secret interpretations of law, often exploiting the fact that the law has not caught up to technology.

Were Snowden's leaks justified? Rahul Sagar's *Secrets and Leaks* sheds important light on the question. In carefully argued and lucid prose,[8] Sagar, a professor of politics at Princeton, argues that secrets and leaks are both inevitable—and that leaks play an important if precarious part in checking secrecy abuse. The power to declare information secret, like many other authorities, is both essential and susceptible to misuse. In theory, formal legal checks on executive power to determine what should and should not be secret would be preferable to leaving abuse checking to leakers who take it upon themselves to break the law. But, Sagar contends, the two principal alternative candidates for implementing formal oversight—the courts and Congress—are each unlikely to perform the function effectively.

Courts, Sagar argues, are not well positioned to second-guess executive assessments that particular information must remain secret, save in the most egregious circumstances. Judicial practice bears him out; courts generally defer when the executive contends that national security requires secrecy. For its part, Congress is simply too large, porous, and partisan to be entrusted with the job. And whichever branch of government undertakes this checking function will have to do its work in secret, and thus will face some of the same temptations and credibility problems that the executive does.

Moreover, the question of when a leak is justified is not generally susceptible to resolution by clear rules set out in advance. The disclosure of a flagrant criminal act might seem to be an easy case, but most leaks don't involve flagrant criminality. Nothing disclosed by Snowden or Manning, for example, rises to that level. And it is conceivable that even in the case of a clear crime, the damage to national security from disclosure might outweigh the benefits—as where revealing a minor crime would blow the cover of important clandestine agents.

Sagar is not a naïve defender of leakers, however. He recognizes that there are real risks when unelected individuals transgress judgments of elected leaders on matters of the nation's security. They may act for personal or partisan reasons and expose information in one-sided and misleading ways that are difficult for the government to counter without spilling still more secrets. They often do not have the information or perspective to assess accurately the potential damage from their disclosures. And as self-appointed guardians, they lack democratic legitimacy.

Nonetheless, Sagar argues that disclosure of secrets by private leakers is morally justified when it (1) is based on clear and convincing evidence of abuse of public authority, (2) does not pose a disproportionate threat to public safety, and (3) is as limited in scope and scale as possible. Sagar has helpfully identified the right questions. But as he himself is the first to concede, the application of these principles in individual cases is extraordinarily difficult.

By Sagar's standards, Manning's and Assange's disclosures were for the most part not justified. While some specific war logs and cables may have revealed illegal conduct without disproportionate harm to public safety, Manning's dump of more than 700,000 documents was in no way narrowly tailored. The leaked State Department cables in particular "outed" many individuals who put themselves at considerable risk by confiding in embassy officials in countries with repressive regimes or internal strife.

Manning's disclosures forced the United States to devote vast resources and time attempting to identify persons at risk and help secure their safety. Manning's defenders object that the government has not named anyone who was actually killed as a result of the disclosures, but that may well be a combination of quick responses and sheer luck. And even if no one was killed, the disclosures reduced the reliability of U.S. diplomats' promises of confidentiality, and thereby almost certainly deterred others from coming forward. Much like journalism, diplomacy depends for its lifeblood on promises of confidentiality. In any event, there is no evidence that Manning or Assange made the kind of fine-tuned assessment that would have justified disclosures—or that they had the knowledge to do so.

The ethical and legal questions for Assange, as for journalists generally, are different. Manning was afforded access to classified information on the specific condition that he not disclose it. Assange, an Australian freelance journalist and publisher, was under no such obligation. Because of the protection given to journalists by the First Amendment, no member of the press has ever been prosecuted under the Espionage Act for publishing classified information. Thus, while Manning serves thirty-five years and Snowden faces even more serious penalties, the journalists who published their leaks are generally free from prosecution.

Still, while journalists who obtain classified information generally have no legal duty to keep it secret, they have an ethical obligation to consider the risks that their reporting may create. Contrary to some reports, WikiLeaks did initially take measures to "redact," or black out, the names of individuals who might be put at risk from its publication of Manning's documents. However, it also made the unredacted documents available to some journalists, subject to a not very carefully controlled password, and when a *Guardian* journalist published the password, WikiLeaks in turn published the cables in their unredacted entirety. The result is that thousands of cables were published that disclosed no violations of law, many of which put innocent individuals at risk of retaliation.

Snowden's is a more complicated case. Did he have "clear and convincing evidence" of an "abuse of public authority," as Sagar would demand?

The most significant abuse of authority that Snowden has revealed is not the illegality of any particular NSA action, but the fact that such an extensive spying program was authorized entirely in secret, without public input, assent, or even knowledge. While there must be room in a democracy for limited covert actions, surveillance of this scope—affecting every American and large swaths of the world's citizenry—should not be instituted without public acceptance and accountability. And in an increasingly globally interconnected world, the legitimacy of the NSA's actions cannot be determined solely by the American people. If the NSA is indeed collecting comprehensive data on the lives of millions of innocent foreign nationals, they, too, should have a voice in how they are being treated.

Snowden's disclosure put an end, in the most dramatic way possible, to the secrecy that was, for him and many others, the central abuse of the program. For that reason, he told *The Washington Post* in December 2013 that he considered his mission accomplished.[9] Thanks to Snowden, we can now have the debate that we should have had long ago, and that we will need to continue to have as advances in technology give the government greater power to track at low cost the most intimate details of all of our lives. That is a substantial benefit.

As for costs, disclosing the details of the NSA programs may give terrorists a better chance to evade detection. It's not clear, however, how much of a cost that really is: terrorists already had to assume that they could be under surveillance. Even under the government's long publicly acknowledged surveillance power, it could tap the phones and obtain business, phone, and Internet records about persons it suspected of involvement in international terrorism. A terrorist cannot know how much the government suspects about him, and therefore must assume he is being monitored.

Perhaps most important, it remains to be seen whether Snowden's disclosures were narrowly tailored to abuses. We don't yet know how many documents he has shared with the media. If in fact he took and disclosed 1.7 million documents, one would be hard-pressed to call his actions narrowly tailored. On the other hand, the various stories that have thus far been published have for the most part been carefully circumscribed; they are very different from the Manning-Assange undifferentiated dump.

The New York Times has called on the government to grant Snowden "a plea bargain or some form of clemency" in light of the substantial good his disclosures have done. Richard Ledgett, the NSA official in charge of assessing Snowden's disclosures, has also suggested a deal in exchange for Snowden returning the remainder of the documents. There is a strong case that many of Snowden's leaks to date have been justified. Future disclosures, however, may do more harm than good, so it would be in everyone's interest to reach a resolution that falls well short of the harsh punishment that most intelligence officials have thus far demanded. Snowden has committed serious crimes, but he has also performed a considerable public service.

The question of the legitimacy of leaks is not new, of course. Ellsberg's disclosure of the Pentagon Papers more than forty years ago prompted similar questions. James Goodale, who as general counsel for *The New York Times* courageously advised publication of the Pentagon Papers, has recently published a fascinating inside story of the *Times*'s legal battles against censorship, *Fighting for the Press*. In a coda, Goodale portrays Manning and WikiLeaks as modern-day counterparts to Ellsberg and the *Times*, and insists that freedom of the press has as much to fear from Obama as it did from Nixon. Some of Goodale's parallels are apt, but the differences between the cases are more telling.

First, unlike Nixon, Obama did not attempt to prohibit the publication of any of Snowden's or Manning's leaks. The Pentagon Papers case, thanks in part to Goodale's own arguments before the courts, established an extraordinarily high legal bar for enjoining publication, and that bar holds today. For many of the justices in the Pentagon Papers case, however, that bar applied only to "prior restraints"—requests to prohibit publication altogether—and would not apply to after-the-fact criminal prosecutions of leakers. While the *Times* was not prosecuted, Ellsberg was, and his case was dismissed not on First Amendment grounds but on the basis of prosecutorial misconduct.

Second, the digital age has profoundly altered the dynamics and stakes of leaks. Computers make stealing documents much more efficient. Ellsberg had to spend months manually photocopying the Pentagon Papers. Manning used his computer to download over 700,000 documents, and Snowden apparently stole even more. The Internet makes disclosures across national borders much easier. Manning uploaded his documents directly to WikiLeaks's Web site, hosted in Sweden, far beyond U.S. reach. Snowden gave access to his documents to journalists in Germany, Brazil, and the United States, and they have in turn published them in newspapers throughout the world.

Third, computers and the Internet have made it easier to identify and prosecute leakers. When someone leaked the fact that the United States had placed an agent inside an active al Qaeda cell in May 2012, an entirely unjustifiable disclosure, the Justice Department spent eight months investigating the old-fashioned way, interviewing over 550 people without success. However, when the prosecutors subpoenaed phone records of the Associated Press offices and reporters involved in publishing the story, they promptly identified the leaker, an FBI agent, and obtained a guilty plea.

Free press advocates complain that the Obama administration has brought more prosecutions under the Espionage Act for leaks (seven) than all previous administrations combined (three). The most telling fact, however, is not that Obama has been more active, but that these numbers are so low, in view of the almost daily leaks of classified information published by the press. The increased prosecutions under Obama more likely reflect the fact that it is much easier to pinpoint the source of a leak in the digital age than that President Obama cares little for press freedom.

One thing has not changed from the days of the Pentagon Papers. There is still no good systematic way to regulate government secrecy. As a result, secret abuses are an ever-present risk—as are leakers themselves. For precisely that reason, leakers perform a critical, if troubled, function in deterring secrecy's misuse. Executive officials must act with the knowledge that even their most secret conduct may someday be made public. President Obama's expert panel recommended a "front-page rule," by which the government would undertake in secret only those programs that it could defend if they appeared on the front pages of the nation's newspapers. They may well have no choice in the matter. If a low-level enlisted man and a private contractor can steal and disclose millions of secrets, no government official can be confident that he will be able to shield his actions from public scrutiny. And while irresponsible disclosures unquestionably undermine national security, responsible leaks are an important check on secrecy's abuse.

Snowden and Manning are only the most recent and dramatic examples. Virtually all of the most disturbing and illegal actions of the United States in its "war on terror" were authorized and carried out in secret, and only came to public attention because of leaks. Those actions included torture and cruel treatment of detainees, rendition to torture at the CIA's "black sites," and the NSA's warrantless wiretapping. All of these programs were curtailed in significant part because of public pressure prompted by their disclosure. And in most instances, the leakers have not been identified or prosecuted.

In the end, the leaker puts both himself and society in a difficult position. By disclosing secrets, he may well burn his career, lose his liberty, and alter his life forever. As Snowden has said, he could have simply gone on living in Hawaii, enjoying a handsome salary in an island paradise. Instead, with considerable courage, he chose to act on his conscience, leave his country, and become an international fugitive with a future that is at best uncertain. Manning, who acted on similar motives, but with less sophistication and possibly less justification, is serving a thirty-five-year sentence. Assange, who devoted himself and his Web site to promoting accountability through transparency, remains isolated and confined in a foreign embassy, unable to walk the streets of London (albeit, at least for the moment, for fear of facing charges of sex crimes, not prosecution for leaks).

And while we as members of the public have learned from each of these men about what our government has done behind closed doors in our name, they have also taken it upon themselves to reveal hundreds of thousands of secret documents, only some of which may have been justifiably disclosed. No one elected Snowden, Manning, or Assange to act as our conscience. But if they didn't act, who would?

NOTES

1. This chapter is adapted from an essay originally published in *The New York Review of Books*. David Cole, "The Three Leakers and What to Do About Them," *NYRB*, February 6, 2014.
2. Sari Horwitz, "Julian Assange Unlikely to Face U.S. Charges over Publishing Classified Documents," *Washington Post*, November 25, 2013.
3. Intelligence Community Whistleblower Protection Act, Pub. L. No. 105–272, Title VII, 112 Stat. 2413 (October 20, 1998).
4. The NSA notified members of the Senate and House intelligence committees of the program, and made some information available to other members of Congress. However, it did not disclose the questionable reasoning of the FISA courts upholding the program. The chairman of the House Intelligence Committee reportedly barred the program's disclosure to other House members. And while senators were allowed to examine a classified letter reporting on the program, they could not bring any staff members with them, and could not take notes or copy the letter. They could review the letter only for a limited period of time, and could not discuss it with their colleagues or the public.
5. Edward Snowden, "NSA Whistleblower Edward Snowden: 'I don't want to live in a society that does these sort of things'—video," *Guardian*, June 9, 2013, http://www.theguardian.com/world/video/2013/jun/09/nsa-whistleblower-edward-snowden-interview-video.
6. For a discussion of Judge Leon's ruling, see my article "The NSA on Trial," *NYRblog*, December 18, 2013.
7. Declassified Order of Foreign Intelligence Surveillance Court, March 2, 2009, at www.dni.gov/files/documents/section/pub_March%202%202009%20Order%20from%20 FISC.pdf.

8. Rahul Sagar, *Secrets and Leaks: The Dilemma of State Secrecy* (Princeton, NJ: Princeton University Press, 2013).

9. See Barton Gellman, "Edward Snowden, After Months of NSA Revelations, Says His Mission's Accomplished," *Washington Post*, December 23, 2013.

JUDGING STATE SECRETS: WHO DECIDES—AND HOW?*

BARRY SIEGEL

BARRY SIEGEL is a Professor of English at the University of California, Irvine, and the Director of the UC Irvine Literary Journalism Program. From 1980 to 2003 he worked as a national correspondent for *The Los Angeles Times* and won numerous journalistic accolades, including the Pulitzer Prize for Feature Writing, which he received for his 2002 article "A Father's Pain, a Judge's Duty, and a Justice Beyond Their Reach." He has written seven books, the most recent of which, *Manifest Injustice: The True Story of a Convicted Murderer and the Lawyers Who Fought for His Freedom,* was published in 2013. Additional information is available on his Web site: www.Barry-Siegel.com.

---

*The early pages of this chapter draw in part from my book *Claim of Privilege: A Mysterious Plane Crash, A Landmark Supreme Court Case, and the Rise of State Secrets* (Harper, 2008). See the Notes and Sources section, pp. 315–63, for credits, sources, and detailed references to cases.

ON AUGUST 15, 2007, before an overflow crowd at the federal courthouse at 7th and Mission in San Francisco, three judges from the U.S. Ninth Circuit Court of Appeals listened to lawyers argue whether the once obscure "state secrets privilege" gives the government an absolute right to withhold documents, bury evidence, and block lawsuits. The particular cases at hand involved challenges to the Bush administration's domestic surveillance programs, including the controversial warrantless wiretapping operation revealed by *The New York Times* in late 2005. For the government, Deputy Solicitor General Gregory Garre maintained that the cases must be dismissed instantly, no questions asked, because a trial would endanger national security. Presenting any evidence in a courtroom, he said, would put the country at "exceptionally grave harm."

After listening to such claims for awhile, the senior judge on the appellate panel, Harry Pregerson, asked Garre whether the state secrets privilege meant that the courts must simply "rubber stamp" the decisions of the executive. "The bottom line here is the government declares something is a state secret, that's the end of it . . ." Pregerson said. "The king can do no wrong."

"This seems to put us in the 'trust us' category," agreed Judge M. Margaret McKeown. "We don't do it. Trust us. And don't ask us about it."

That's more or less right, replied the government lawyer. Judges must give the executive branch "utmost deference."

Pregerson looked irritated, and for good reason. Since the 9/11 terrorist attacks, the Bush administration had been repeatedly asserting the privilege as grounds for immediate dismissal at the pleading stage, before discovery, of cases challenging the executive branch's wiretapping and extraordinary rendition programs. The government argued, almost always successfully, that the "very subject matter" of these lawsuits, rather than specific privileged documents, made them beyond judicial review. Such a stark expansion—transformation, really—of the state secrets privilege threatened to eliminate the judiciary's role as a check on executive action. "What does 'utmost deference' mean? Bow to it?" Pregerson asked. He wondered what roles judges were to play: "Who decides whether something is a state secret or not?"

Let your mind roam and it could be August 9, 1950. In the Washington, D.C., federal courthouse that humid day, others faced a similar issue during litigation over the crash of an Air Force B-29 near Waycross, Georgia. A lawyer for the widows of three civilian engineers who died in that crash wanted the Air Force's accident report, expecting it would shed light on the cause of the disaster. An Assistant U.S. Attorney balked, offering up Air Force affidavits that insisted the report "cannot be furnished without seriously hampering national security" because "the aircraft in question" was "engaged in a highly secret mission" and "carried confidential equipment." In response, a skeptical U.S. District Judge William Kirkpatrick said, "I only want to know where your argument leads." The Assistant U.S. Attorney made plain where it led: "We contend that the findings of the [executive branch] are binding . . .

upon the Judiciary. You cannot review it or interpret it. That is what it comes down to."

The state secrets privilege had long existed in common law, but here in Kirkpatrick's courtroom the executive branch was launching a concerted drive to formally gain its explicit recognition. The litigation over the crash of a B-29 had started as a familiar tort action, but it had evolved into a test case for establishing the privilege—a test case that would lead to the landmark 1953 Supreme Court decision. Harry Pregerson's question—*Who decides whether something is a state secret or not?*—has haunted judges ever since.

This is where it began: In early January 1949, the Air Force chief of staff's office, having received an advance copy of an internal inquiry into the Waycross B-29 crash, promptly upgraded it and all related documents from "Restricted" to "Secret"—the highest security classification. The chief of staff had a reason. This report offered an unflinching (if incomplete) account of what happened over Waycross on October 6, 1948. Among the causes of the crash: an irregular flight team, missing heat shields that led to an engine fire, noncompliance with technical orders, inadvertent shutdown of a functioning engine, inability to maintain air speed, "confusion" among the crew, and the failure to brief civilians on emergency procedures. Though the report made no reference at all to "a highly secret mission" involving "confidential equipment," this was not a document the Air Force wanted to share with civilian agencies or anyone else. "Due to the purpose and nature of the Accident Report," an Assistant Vice Chief of Staff advised in a memo, "it is impossible to furnish copies."

All the same, the lawyer for the three widows wanted that accident report. So the battle was joined before William Kirkpatrick, by then a legend to his fellow federal judges for his legal acuity. In downtown Philadelphia, he took his meals and played bridge at the Union League Club, a bastion of WASP Republicanism, but his opinions often reflected a concern for the protection of individual rights. He also believed in an independent, strong-minded judiciary. What he seemed to care about most was getting all the facts on the table. In any discovery dispute, it was a sure bet he'd rule to get the maximum out there.

That's how he ruled, in June 1950, concerning the B-29 case: "I conclude that good cause appears for the production of all documents which are subject to the motion." He wanted it known that the type of executive immunity asserted by the government "had been fully considered and held not sustainable."

Within days of Kirkpatrick's order, the Air Force informed the Justice Department it still would not produce the accident report— the Air Force would not hand it over even to the attorney general. What's more, the Air Force was now, for the first time in the litigation, formally invoking the common law state secrets privilege. It was this claim that Kirkpatrick had before him at the hearing on August 9 in the Washington, D.C., federal courthouse (where he was sitting during the summer months). He did not sound inclined to accept the government's position. "That claim has been made in other cases," he pointed out, "and it has been usually met by submission of the [documents] to the Court to determine whether or not it is data which would imperil the safety of the military position of the United States."

"That procedure was followed in two cases . . ." Assistant U.S. Attorney Thomas Curtin allowed. "[But] we do not believe that is good law. We contend that the findings of the head of the Department are binding, and the judiciary cannot waive it . . . The Executive is the person who must make that determination, not the Judiciary . . ."

Kirkpatrick was having none of that. Despite the new state secrets claim, he would not relinquish jurisdiction; he would not agree that the judiciary had no say in this matter. But rather than require the United States to hand over the disputed documents to the widows, he now ruled, in an amended order, that the government should hand them over to him—far from public disclosure—"so that this Court may determine whether or not all or parts of such documents contain matters of a confidential nature."

To no one's surprise, the government did not produce the documents as mandated on October 4. Eight days later, Kirkpatrick entered a default judgment in favor of the plaintiffs, finding that the B-29 crash and the resulting deaths of civilian engineers Al Palya, William Brauner, and Robert Reynolds were "caused solely and exclusively by the negligence and wrongful acts and omissions" of the United States of America.

In an appeal filed to the U.S. Third Circuit Court of Appeals in April 1951, the government did more than challenge Kirkpatrick's ruling: It challenged Kirkpatrick's very right to make a ruling. Most fundamentally, the government now questioned whether any judge could force the executive branch to hand over documents it considered privileged: "We believe that the determination of what documents should not be disclosed . . . is . . . necessarily within the discretion and distinctive knowledge of the executive branch."

At a hearing on October 19, 1951, that assertion received much attention from a three-judge appellate panel led by Judge Albert Maris. If Kirkpatrick was a legend among the federal judiciary in Philadelphia, Maris was an icon recognized as among the finest jurists in the country. For weeks after the hearing, the matter of three widows suing the United States of America occupied his mind, for it had been decided he would write the appellate panel's decision. Maris returned time and again to Kirkpatrick's opinion. He and Kirkpatrick could not have been more different in their origins or politics (Maris came from very modest means and a liberal Democratic perspective, Kirkpatrick from affluence and a crusty Republican outlook), but they shared a belief in the notion of three separate but equal branches of government. They also shared the context in which they lived: the dawn of the Cold War, with a seemingly apocalyptic threat from the Soviet Union, a newly emerged Red China and East Germany, and the growing wave of Red Scare McCarthyism. The Soviets now had the bomb, Truman was talking about a "wave of hysteria sweeping the nation," and government lawyers in courtrooms were implicitly suggesting the country might somehow expire if secrets weren't protected. Maris and Kirkpatrick, in other words, were facing frightful pressures equal to any felt by post-9/11 judges. Nonetheless, they remained insistent that judges not relinquish their role as custodians of the country's constitutional rights and protections.

On the morning of December 11, Judge Maris finally filed his panel's unanimous "Opinion of the Court." Ruling in favor of the three widows, he offered a resounding affirmation of Kirkpatrick's decision, yet he went even further than Kirkpatrick in addressing the critical underlying issues involving the role of the judiciary and the balance of powers. In words both prescient and eloquent—his opinion, which reads as if written today, is still studied by law students—he made plain that he saw dangers in what the government sought: "It is but a small step to assert a privilege against any disclosure of records merely because they might prove embarrassing to government officials. Indeed, it requires no great flight of imagination to realize that if the Government's contentions in these cases were affirmed, the privilege against disclosure might gradually be enlarged . . . until as is the case in some nations today, it embraced the whole range of government activities . . ."

What bothered Maris most was the government's assertion of unilateral executive power, free from judicial review, to decide what qualified as secret. Maris pointed out that Kirkpatrick had not ordered any documents to be disclosed publicly; he'd only directed that they be produced for private examination in his chambers.

> *The Government was thus adequately protected. . . . [But] the Government contends . . . that it is within the sole province of the Secretary of the Air Force to determine whether any privileged material is contained in the documents and that his determination of this question must be accepted by the district court without any independent consideration. . . . We cannot accede to this proposition. . . . [T]o hold that the head of an executive department of the Government in a [law]suit to which the United States is a party may conclusively determine the Government's claim of privilege is to abdicate the judicial function and permit the executive branch of the Government to infringe the independent province of the judiciary as laid down by the Constitution.*

This abdication seemed unimaginable to Maris: "[T]he Government of the United States is one of checks and balances. One of the principal checks is furnished by the independent judiciary which the Constitution established. Neither the executive nor the legislative branch of the Government may constitutionally encroach upon the field which the Constitution has reserved for the judiciary. . . .

"Since we find no error," Maris concluded, "the judgments entered in favor of the plaintiffs . . . will be affirmed."

The government appealed again, and the Supreme Court took just three weeks to decide it would hear *U.S. v. Reynolds* (though four of the nine justices initially wanted to affirm Maris and deny *certiorari*). The Court at this time included a number of luminous, powerful personalities, including William Douglas, Hugo Black, Robert Jackson, and Felix Frankfurter. However, it was headed by a patient, amiable and thoroughly unremarkable Kentucky politician named Fred Vinson, a poker and drinking buddy of President Harry Truman, who in his seven years on the Court displayed a pronounced inclination to support the government against any challenge to its power. Nowhere was this tendency more apparent than in cases involving matters of national security. Vinson favored giving the government unfettered power to defend against the many perils of the postwar world.

In *U.S. v. Reynolds,* his perspective prevailed. After hearing oral argument, the justices, by a vote of 6–3 (with Black, Jackson, and Frankfurter dissenting), decided to reverse Maris. On March 9, 1953, Fred Vinson, from the bench, announced and read from the decision he'd written. As usual, he had reached in this opinion for a conciliatory balancing act, but in the end he had, also as usual, deferred to the executive branch.

Yes, Vinson held, the government had made "a valid claim of privilege" against revealing military secrets, a privilege "well established in the law of evidence." By "well established" he meant mainly that the state secrets privilege was rooted in common law— the British system of doctrines, customs, and usages deriving from court decisions rather than from codified statutory law. However, it can't be said such cases specifically defined or established the state secrets privilege. In truth, only now was the Supreme Court formally recognizing the privilege. Most important, the Court was also—for the first time—spelling out how the privilege should be applied.

The privilege must be asserted by the government, Vinson declared, and it is not to be "lightly invoked." There must be a formal claim lodged by the head of a department "after actual personal consideration by that officer." The Court itself must determine "whether the circumstances are appropriate for the claim of privilege," and yet do so "without forcing disclosure of the very thing the privilege is designed to protect."

This last, of course, was the tricky, ambiguous part; Vinson acknowledged that "the latter requirement is the only one which presents real difficulty." To resolve it, Vinson presented a "formula of compromise" that essentially said the government shouldn't have absolute autonomy, but courts shouldn't always insist on seeing the documents. You can't abdicate control over the evidence "to the caprice of executive officers," Vinson instructed trial judges, but if the government can satisfy you that "a reasonable danger" to national security exists, you shouldn't insist upon examining the documents, even alone in chambers.

In each case, Vinson added, "the showing of necessity" for the documents will "determine how far the court should probe" in determining the validity of a privilege claim. Where there is a strong showing of need, "the claim of privilege should not be lightly accepted," but even the most compelling need "cannot overcome the claim of privilege if the court is ultimately satisfied that military secrets are at stake."

At best, Vinson's *Reynolds* opinion can be seen as a limited, fairly reasonable way to weigh competing legitimate interests. In theory, it did make a kind of sense. Except, of course, for the tricky final condition Vinson laid down—that the judge must evaluate the claim "without forcing a disclosure of the very thing the privilege is designed to protect." How to know if the disputed documents contain secrets without examining them? Why would a federal judge be "forcing a disclosure" if he read the document in the privacy of his chambers? In the years to come, Vinson's "formula of compromise" would increasingly make more sense on the page than in courtrooms. By instructing judges not to insist upon examining documents if the government can satisfy that "a reasonable danger" to national security exists, Vinson was asking jurists to fly blind.

Which is precisely what he had done in this case: "Certainly," he concluded, "there was a reasonable danger that the accident investigation would contain references to the secret electronic equipment which was the primary concern of the mission." However, Vinson couldn't truly know for "certain," because the Supreme Court justices never read—never asked to read—the disputed Air Force accident report. If they had, they would have seen that the report contained no references to secret electronic equipment. At bottom, Vinson's opinion represented an act of faith. We must believe the government, Vinson held, when it claims this B-29 accident report would reveal state secrets. We must trust that the government is telling us the truth.

The application of *Reynolds* started out slowly, with the government asserting the privilege only four times in the first twenty years, and prevailing only twice. Then came the case that sparked the state secrets trend: *United States v. Richard M. Nixon*, the 1974 dispute over whether Nixon had to produce tape recordings and documents related to White House conversations about the Watergate scandal. Oddly, this was a case where an invocation of *Reynolds* failed. In a legal brief, White House counsel maintained that "the principles announced in *Reynolds* have been applied by the lower courts to all claims of executive privilege, whether dealing with military secrets or with other kinds of information." The Supreme Court wouldn't accept that, but not because it rejected *Reynolds*. The justices made clear they were denying Nixon's claim because it was based "merely on the ground of a generalized interest in confidentiality" rather than on "military or diplomatic secrets." By drawing such a sharp distinction between the two, the *Nixon* opinion inspired Presidents and government agencies forever after to make state secrets claims rather than more general executive privilege claims. They now had a fairly clear reading from the Supreme Court that they'd prevail with state secrets.

This is certainly one reason for the sudden spike in use of the privilege during President Jimmy Carter's administration. With this increase in use, government lawyers could not avoid noticing a judicial willingness to accept the claims—and this willingness only fueled the trend. Scholars differ when calculating state secrets claims—they use varying definitions and criteria—but according to one count, in the twenty-three years between the *Reynolds* decision and Carter's election in 1976, there were five cases in which the government invoked privilege; between 1977 and 2001, there were sixty-two.

Along with the numbers, the scope of what constituted state secrets began to expand, as did the definition of the privilege. No cases played a bigger role than *Halkin v. Helms I,* decided in June 1978, and *Halkin v. Helms II,* decided in September 1982. These decisions arose from lawsuits filed by former Vietnam War protestors who'd been subjected—like millions of citizens in recent years— to intelligence agencies' surveillance and wiretapping. Saying judges "should accord utmost deference to executive assertions of privilege," the district and appellate courts soundly upheld a CIA state secrets claim, which in effect stopped the litigation, since the plaintiffs couldn't get the information needed to prove their case.

What made the *Halkin* opinions even more pivotal was their embrace of the so-called mosaic theory about what constituted state secrets. No longer did the state secret have to be momentous or, for that matter, entirely secret:

> It requires little reflection that the business of foreign intelligence gathering in this age of computer technology is more akin to the construction of a mosaic than it is to the management of a cloak and dagger affair. Thousands of bits and pieces of seemingly innocuous information can be analyzed and fitted into place to reveal with startling clarity how the unseen whole must operate. As the Fourth Circuit Court of Appeals has observed: The significance of one item of information may frequently depend upon knowledge of many other items of information.

What may seem trivial to the uninformed may appear of great moment to one who has a broad view of the scene and may put the questioned item of information in its proper context. The courts, of course, are ill equipped to become sufficiently steeped in foreign intelligence matters to serve effectively in the review of secrecy classifications in that area.

The retreat of the judiciary intensified as the years passed. In December 1980, in a lawsuit over a contractual relationship with the Navy, the Fourth U.S. Circuit not only honored the Navy's state secrets claim but also held—in a ruling that foreshadowed recent post-9/11 cases—that the plaintiff could make no further attempt to press his action, even with nonprivileged information. In May 1983, in another case involving warrantless electronic surveillance, the D.C. Court of Appeals again talked of the "mosaic theory" and of "factors that limit judicial competence" to evaluate claims. In November 1985, in a defamation action brought by a scientist accused of espionage, a federal court once more foreshadowed post-9/11 cases by stopping a lawsuit cold, this time within an hour of when the Navy intervened; there just was no way to try the case, the trial and appellate judges agreed, without compromising sensitive military secrets.

Then came two rulings, concerning an Iraqi missile attack on the U.S. Navy frigate USS *Stark*, that would provide particularly instructive models for deferential judges to follow in the post-9/11 world of wiretapping and extraordinary rendition. When the estate of a crewman killed in the May 1987 attack filed a wrongful death action against various military contractors, the Secretary of the Navy asserted the state secrets privilege, the government moved to dismiss, and a district court promptly complied because the factual issues "could not be resolved without access to classified information." Even without this reason, the court found, the case still must be dismissed because it presents a "political question" about military decision-making that's not subject to judicial review. An appellate panel, in affirming, would not send the case back to district court even for private *in camera* proceedings.

Following this first *Stark* case (*Zuckerman v. General Dynamics*), the second one (*Bareford v. General Dynamics*) made much the same claims, but presented a more complicated situation, since those suing submitted 2,500 pages of unclassified information. To no end: Even if the plaintiffs could make their case using this unprivileged information, the district court ruled, the state secrets doctrine barred the action because a trial would threaten disclosure of state secrets. Going further, an appellate court also noted that because "classified and unclassified information cannot always be separated," it was appropriate for courts to restrict access not only to evidence involving state secrets but also "those pieces of evidence . . . which press so closely upon highly sensitive material that they create a high risk of inadvertent or indirect disclosures."

By then, the progeny of *Reynolds*, so appreciably expanded and evolved, little resembled their parent. Just as Judge Maris had predicted, the impulse to protect military secrets had come to look more like the impulse to cover up mistakes, avoid embarrassment, and gain insulation from liability.

In February 1989, there came a singular revelation from a former solicitor general. Eighteen years before, Erwin Griswold had stood before the Supreme Court representing the United States in the landmark Pentagon Papers case (*New York Times v. United States*), where the government, making national security claims, sought to prevent publication of leaked documents about the Vietnam War. Although Griswold, a former dean of Harvard Law School, had only skimmed a summary memo on what the Pentagon Papers contained, his legal brief warned the Court that publication of these papers would pose a "grave and immediate danger to the security of the United States." Now, on February 15, 1989, he stepped forward in a *Washington Post* op-ed piece to write: "I have never seen any trace of a threat to the national security from the publication [of the Pentagon Papers]. Indeed, I have never seen it even suggested that there was such an actual threat. . . . It quickly becomes apparent to any person who has considerable experience with classified material that there is massive overclassification and that the principal concern of the classifiers is not with national security but rather with governmental embarrassment of one sort or another."

By the time Griswold wrote this, not just unclassified but readily available public information, such as newspaper articles, had become subject to national security claims. Judges were requiring private *in camera* review of documents in less than a quarter of cases. Yet direct invocations of the state secrets privilege were by no means the broadest legacy of *Reynolds*. Merely by waving *Reynolds* in the background for "atmospheric effect," government lawyers had learned they could gain significant judicial deference.

This general judicial deference has been the greatest legacy of *Reynolds*. Faced with ominous claims about national security, judges in recent years have found it hard to deny governmental power. In fact, it's fair to say that over time, many judges embraced deference. They liked it: Deference let them off the hook. Understandably, no one wanted to be the judge whose ruling led to a disastrous cataclysmic apocalyptic event. Better to say, "We're not equipped . . . we can't tell whether it implicates national security . . . we need to leave this to those who know." The result: Justice Department lawyers now firmly possess—and use—what they sought more than sixty years ago.

Government assertions of the state secrets privilege particularly multiplied—and expanded in scope—with the Bush administration's post-9/11 war on terror. By the best available count, Bush over two terms made forty-eight claims, easily eclipsing all past administrations.[1] Hardly any were rejected by judges at a final legal stage.

The biggest difference from past practice: Without any back-and-forth litigating at all, government lawyers were now seeking instant, wholesale dismissal of every case challenging the constitutionality of the warrantless wiretapping and extraordinary rendition programs. They were saying the cases simply could not be adjudicated—even if they involved violations of the law by the government.[2]

In 2000, the CIA successfully moved to dismiss an employee's gender discrimination lawsuit by claiming the state secrets privilege; a U.S. district judge in Virginia found that the mere existence of a trial would jeopardize national security. In 2003, the Bush administration again blocked a lawsuit, this one brought by a senior engineer who charged that a military contractor had submitted false test results. That same month, the government, while seeking to block publication of a book by a former Los Alamos National Laboratory employee, refused to let the employee's own lawyer see the manuscript—and advised U.S. District Judge Emmet Sullivan that the matter was "not reviewable" in his court. When Judge Sullivan rejected this notion, ruling that the lawyer could read his client's manuscript—"this Court will not allow the government to cloak its violations of plaintiff's First Amendment rights in a blanket of national security"—he found himself reversed by an appellate panel.

Then came *The New York Times*'s revelation, in mid–December 2005, that President Bush, without judicial approval or knowledge, had secretly authorized the National Security Agency to eavesdrop on Americans and others in the country. During a Saturday radio talk on December 17 and a Monday press conference on December 19, Bush insisted he had the right to assert such sweeping executive powers in the war against terrorism. "The fact that we're discussing this program is helping the enemy," Bush said testily.

A cascade of lawsuits challenging the government's warrantless wiretapping began to fill courthouse dockets in May 2006. In all of them, the Bush administration invoked the state secrets privilege, seeking outright dismissal at the pleading stage because the very subject matter of the lawsuits involved state secrets. To support this assertion, government lawyers submitted no evidence for judges to examine, only affidavits signed by executive branch officials—officials who sometimes headed the very agencies being sued. For a time at least, the government lawyers finally appeared to have overplayed their hand. No longer could such claims of privilege be made with little notice or resistance. The NSA wiretapping cases drew wide attention and loud protest from commentators, lawyers, and citizen groups. There were complaints about the privilege being "judicially mishandled to the detriment of our constitutional system." There were proposals for change, including mandatory *in camera* judicial review of all claims. There were calls for judges to push back against the executive branch.

There were even a few occasions where federal district judges did just that. In the summer of 2006, U.S. District Judge Vaughn R. Walker in San Francisco (an unorthodox, independent-minded George H. W. Bush appointee, at the time Chief Judge of the Northern District of California) ventured to deny a state secrets claim in *Hepting v. AT&T,* a domestic eavesdropping case. Judge Walker wasn't overly impressed with the government's argument that the "very subject matter" of the action concerned privileged information. There's been a great deal of publicity about the wiretapping program, he pointed out, and public acknowledgments by President Bush, so "the very subject matter of this action is hardly a secret." What's more, "no case is dismissed because its 'very subject matter' was a state secret involved ongoing, widespread violations of individual constitutional rights." Walker thought it "premature" to decide whether the case should be dismissed on grounds that the plaintiffs, without privileged documents, couldn't make a prima facie case or AT&T couldn't defend itself. He would let discovery proceed, then assess that issue. This he would do despite the government's audacious argument that the court, "even if it were to find unlawfulness upon *in camera, ex parte* review," could not adjudicate the case because doing so would confirm the existence of the surveillance program and so jeopardize national security. "It is important to note that even the state secrets privilege has its limits," Judge Walker pointed out, his words echoing those of Albert Maris. "While the court recognizes and respects the executive's constitutional duty to protect the nation from threats, the court also takes seriously its constitutional duty to adjudicate the disputes that come before it. . . . To defer to a blanket assertion of secrecy here would be to abdicate that duty . . ."

In Detroit that summer of 2006, U.S. District Judge Anna Diggs Taylor also rejected the government's "very subject matter is secret" argument in another wiretapping case, *ACLU v. NSA*. Like Walker, she pointed out that the government's public admissions contradicted its claims of secrecy, and provided a basis for the plaintiffs to establish a prima facie case without using privileged documents. Yet she went further than Walker at this stage: Based on her findings, she granted the ACLU summary judgment and imposed a permanent injunction on the NSA wiretapping program, ruling it unconstitutional.

Then the appellate courts and Congress stepped in with responses that for the most part impeded or stopped the litigation. The U.S. Sixth Circuit Court of Appeals made it simple in *ACLU v. NSA*: It vacated Judge Taylor's decision, ruling that the plaintiffs (a group of journalists, academics, attorneys, and nonprofit organizations) lacked standing since they couldn't prove they, specifically, were subjects of surveillance—which, of course, they couldn't prove because the government considered the matter a state secret.

Other cases, such as the *Hepting* complaint before Judge Walker, stalled when Congress passed the FISA Amendments Act of 2008, which retroactively granted immunity to telecommunication companies that cooperated with NSA.

The surviving cases—those filed against NSA or the government, rather than a phone company—have bounced back and forth between trial and appellate courts. Judges fairly often have weighed whether plaintiffs can establish standing as victims without privileged information (sometimes yes, usually no). They have also considered, more than once, whether the wiretapping cases can be litigated under the procedures of the 1978 Foreign Intelligence Surveillance Act, which besides creating a FISA court to oversee surveillance warrants also provided a civil remedy for "aggrieved persons" subjected to unlawful surveillance. This suggested an intriguing possibility: If FISA could be applied to wiretapping cases, it would effectively preempt the state secrets privilege.

For a time, at least, that's what appeared to happen in *Al-Haramain v. Bush*, the most revealing, compelling, and all-embodying challenge to the warrantless surveillance program. This case merits close attention, for it proceeded further, and touched more issues, than any other challenge to the use of NSA wiretaps. Because the plaintiffs filed against the government rather than a company, the FISA Amendments Act didn't block it. And where other plaintiffs struggled to obtain standing, the government inadvertently provided the Al-Haramain Islamic Foundation, then a Muslim charity active in more than fifty countries, with a secret document (called the "Sealed Document" in litigation) proving that it had been subjected to warrantless NSA surveillance. The result of that surveillance: In February 2004, the Treasury Department temporarily froze Al-Haramain assets pending a proceeding that ultimately led to the foundation and one of its directors being declared "Specially Designated Global Terrorists." (The UN Security Council has also identified Al-Haramain as an entity belonging to or associated with al Qaeda.)

When Al-Haramain filed suit in Oregon in February 2006, attaching to its complaint a copy of the secret document, the government's first response was to try to seize that document from the court. This involved sending FBI agents to the federal courthouse in Portland and demanding, through a Department of Justice attorney, that U.S. District Judge Garr M. King hand over the document for storage in a top secret repository (the government calls it a "Sensitive Compartmented Information Facility"). The executive branch backed down only after Judge King, resisting the idea of the feds invading his files, asked the government attorney, "What if I say I will not deliver it to the FBI . . . ?"[3]

Next, as it did with all the wiretap cases, the government asserted the state secrets privilege, arguing the case must be dismissed because both the "Sealed Document" and the "very subject matter" of the proceeding were state secrets. Judge King rejected the "subject matter" claim (again because so much was already publicly known about the wiretapping program), but after *in camera* review of the Sealed Document, he accepted that it was a state secret. Still, Judge King didn't roll over. Reaching to find a way to keep the litigation going, he decided Al-Haramain lawyers could file an *in camera* affidavit attesting to the contents of the secret document they had seen.

On appeal, *Al-Haramain v. Bush* ended up before a three-judge Ninth Circuit panel—it was this case (combined with *Hepting*) that Judge Harry Pregerson had before him in the San Francisco federal courthouse on that day in August 2007 when he asked, "Who decides whether something is a state secret or not?" Pregerson, along with Judges Michael Hawkins and M. Margaret McKeown, listened on August 15 to government lawyers tell them they must give the executive branch "utmost deference," that otherwise they would be putting the country at "exceptionally grave harm." They also listened to both sides awkwardly dance around the matter of what the Sealed Document contained—something they couldn't discuss in the courtroom. The exchanges among lawyers and judges combined the best of Kafka and Lewis Carroll. "What's in the Document, I cannot mention it today," advised Jon Eisenberg, the lead lawyer for Al-Haramain. Nor could the DOJ attorney, Thomas Bondy, who nevertheless argued at length that what the plaintiffs *think* they know from the document isn't necessarily true—"it's entirely possible that everything they think they know . . . is completely false." At one point, Judge McKeown observed, "Boy, we are really splitting the 'knows.'" Added Judge Hawkins, "Sounds like Donald Rumsfeld."

The judges' eventual ruling reflected the difficulties that come into play whenever the government makes momentous claims about national security. In an opinion written by Judge McKeown and filed on November 16, 2007, the judges scoffed at the idea that the very subject matter of the TSP (terrorist surveillance program) was a secret. After *The New York Times* revelations in late 2005, McKeown pointed out, "government officials moved at lightning-speed to quell public concern and doled out a series of detailed disclosures." So "the government is hard-pressed to sustain its claim that the very subject matter of the litigation is a state secret. Unlike a truly secret or 'black box' program . . . the government has moved affirmatively to engage in public discourse about the TSP. . . . There has been a cascade of acknowledgments and information . . ." For that reason, the appellate judges "agree with the district court that the state secrets privilege does not bar the very subject matter of this action."

However, their *in camera* review of the Sealed Document had swayed them (as it did the district court) that this document was protected by the state secrets privilege. In explaining their finding, these judges seemed to convey a certain defensive discomfort: "We take very seriously our obligation to review the documents with a very careful, indeed a skeptical, eye, and not to accept at face value the government's claim or justification of privilege. Simply saying 'military secret,' 'national security,' or 'terrorist threat' or invoking an ethereal fear that disclosure will threaten our nation is insufficient to support the privilege . . ." Still, in the end "we acknowledge the need to defer to the Executive on matters of foreign policy and national security and surely cannot legitimately find ourselves second guessing the Executive in this arena."

That "need to defer" had an additional consequence: The appellate panel didn't agree with the district court that Al-Haramain could "reconstruct the essence of the document from memory." Such an approach "countenances a back door around the privilege and would eviscerate the state secret itself . . ." And without the secret document, Al-Haramain can't "prove it was a subject of surveillance," so "cannot establish standing." The result: Al-Haramain's claims "must be dismissed."

Unless, that is, FISA preempts the common law state secrets privilege—a claim Al-Haramain had made in its filings. In Oregon, Judge King had not addressed this question, and he'd made plain why: "I decline to reach this very difficult question at this time, which involves whether Congress preempted what the government asserts is a constitutionally based privilege." Though the judge didn't want to go there, the Ninth Circuit panel did. Does FISA preempt the state secrets privilege? The appellate judges thought a district court should first decide: "We remand for determination of this claim."

As a result of a transfer and consolidation of cases, *Al-Haramain v. Bush* ended up not back with the Oregon district judge, but before Judge Vaughan Walker in the Northern District of California, who (in *Hepting* and other cases) had already established a record of resisting Justice Department attempts to claim the state secrets privilege. He continued that pattern now. In July 2008, Walker held that FISA did indeed supersede the state secrets privilege. He rejected Bush's claim that the President's constitutional authority as commander in chief trumped the law, allowing him to order wiretaps without a warrant from a FISA court. "FISA preempts the state secrets privilege in connection with electronic surveillance for intelligence purposes," he wrote, "and would appear to displace the state secrets privilege for purposes of plaintiffs' claims." What's more, "FISA limits the power of the executive branch to conduct such activities and it limits the executive branch's authority to assert the state secrets privilege . . ."

However, that still didn't mean a victory for Al-Haramain: "FISA nonetheless does not appear to provide plaintiffs a viable remedy unless they can show that they are 'aggrieved persons' within the meaning of FISA." How to do that without the Sealed Document? How to do that, given the government's insistence that the entire wiretapping program was secret? Judge Walker thought the plaintiff should at least have the chance to try. So he dismissed Al-Haramain's FISA claim "with leave to amend." The plaintiffs "should have the opportunity to amend their claim to establish that they are 'aggrieved persons' . . ."

A half year later, in January 2009, Judge Walker found that the plaintiffs had met that burden by using public information, including a 2007 speech by an FBI official who acknowledged Al-Haramain had been placed under surveillance. Since the plaintiffs had proved they were "aggrieved" (wiretapped in a manner that required a warrant), they could proceed with discovery under FISA. To facilitate that, Walker ordered the government to grant security clearances to the Al-Haramain lawyers, but NSA officials and Justice Department attorneys (it was now, newly, the Obama administration's Justice Department) continued to defy orders to produce documents. In a February 27, 2009, filing, government lawyers (eerily echoing what they told Judge Kirkpatrick in 1950) advised Judge Walker that he lacked authority "to order the government to grant counsel access to classified information when the executive branch has denied them such access." Al-Haramain's lawyer, Jon Eisenberg, thought that pretty remarkable: "This is an executive branch threat to exercise control over a judicial branch function," he told a reporter at the time.

A year later, Judge Walker had finally heard enough. On March 31, 2010, he granted summary judgment to Al-Haramain on its FISA claim. More broadly, in an act of singular resistance by a federal judge, he ruled that the NSA warrantless wiretapping program was illegal, that the 1978 FISA was the law of the land, that when the government failed to get a warrant to wiretap, it broke the law. He also slammed the Obama administration's courtroom defense, which he called "argumentative acrobatics" that took a "flying leap" and missed "by a wide margin." It exasperated him no end that government officials argued they were not required to respond even to public evidence of illegal wiretapping because the entire issue was too secret to be discussed in a courtroom. "Under defendants' theory," he wrote, "executive branch officials may treat FISA as optional and freely employ the [state secrets privilege] to evade FISA, a statute enacted specifically to rein in and create a judicial check for executive branch abuses of surveillance authority."

Walker's ringing conclusion: "FISA takes precedence over the state secrets privilege in this case. . . . Plaintiffs have met their burden of establishing their 'aggrieved person' status using non classified evidence. Because defendants denied plaintiffs' counsel access to any classified filings in the litigation, even after top secret clearances were obtained for plaintiffs' counsel and protective orders . . . proposed, the court directed the parties to conduct this phase of the litigation without classified evidence. . . . The court now determines that plaintiffs have submitted . . . sufficient non classified evidence to establish standing on their FISA claim. . . . Plaintiffs are therefore entitled to summary judgment in their favor on those matters . . ."

Here was a rare—in fact unprecedented—breakthrough ruling, bucking the pattern of judicial deference that has informed the history of state secrets litigation. Applause came from commentators, advocacy groups, and major newspaper editorial pages. All eyes turned to the Obama administration's response: Would it appeal, or terminate a case that had been a political problem since the month after Obama took office? Would it honor its commitment, made in September 2009, to be more cautious in asserting the privilege, invoking it only when "absolutely necessary"?

In the end, the Obama administration did appeal—and prevailed. All through the litigation, even while asserting the state secrets privilege, the government also had been arguing that the doctrine of sovereign immunity prevented the executive branch from being sued over violations of FISA—you can't sue "the king" unless the relevant statute expressly waived immunity. In his opinion, Judge Walker had ruled that the government "implicitly" waived sovereign immunity under the FISA civil liability provision, which allows aggrieved persons to sue for damages. That word "implicitly" didn't quite go far enough.

The same three-judge panel that had been considering *Al-Haramain* since August 2007—Harry Pregerson, Michael Hawkins, M. Margaret McKeown—now, in August 2012, reversed Judge Walker's decision, finding that the FISA statute didn't waive sovereign immunity for this particular claim. Judge McKeown, writing for the unanimous panel: "It is well understood that any waiver of sovereign immunity must be unequivocally expressed." Since there was no *explicit* waiver, the judgment in favor of Al-Haramain had to be vacated.

What this meant: Despite a finding that the executive had violated FISA and broken the law, he could get away with it—he couldn't be sued and nothing more could be done. Even independent-minded judges like Michael Hawkins and Harry Pregerson hesitated to buck the government, particularly when the plaintiffs were designated terrorists rather than "good guy" citizens. The appellate panel at least recognized what they were doing: "This case effectively brings to an end the plaintiff's ongoing attempts to hold the Executive Branch responsible for intercepting telephone conversations without judicial authorization."

By early 2013, almost all of the NSA wiretapping cases had failed or stalled out. Just two long-running ones remained, the remnants of the dozens filed in 2006. *Jewel v. NSA* and *Shubert v. Obama* had been consolidated before U.S. District Judge Jeffrey S. White in the Northern District of California. Here was another federal judge willing to challenge the government's assertions. Like Vaughan Walker (who retired in February 2011), Judge White in July 2013 ruled that *Shubert* and *Jewel* could move forward despite state secrets claims because "Congress intended for FISA to displace the common law rules such as the state secrets privilege with regard to matters within FISA's purview."

Judge White went even further, though. In the month before his ruling, newspaper reports had started appearing based on Edward J. Snowden's much-publicized release of classified material regarding NSA intelligence activities. So now White ordered the government to evaluate how the disclosures and declassification decisions since Snowden's leaks had affected the government's earlier assertions of the state secrets privilege. He also ordered the government to review for declassification its prior declarations regarding the state secrets privilege. Did the government still maintain everything was a secret, despite the Snowden leaks and subsequent disclosures?

Yes, it did. Or rather, yes and no. In court filings late on Friday, December 20, 2013, James R. Clapper, the Director of National

Intelligence, declassified and publicly released eight previously classified declarations that the government had filed in support of state secrets claims. On May 5, 2014, he released ten more such declassified declarations. But in the proceedings before Judge White, Clapper continued to formally assert the state secrets privilege. Despite the impact of the disclosures by Snowden (which he called "extremely damaging to the national security of the United States"), Clapper argued that sensitive secrets remained at risk in any courtroom discussion. He was no longer asserting privilege, he explained, over "the existence of various presidentially authorized NSA intelligence activities, later transitioned to authority under FISA." But he was continuing to assert privilege over "still-classified information concerning the scope and operational details of these intelligence activities." This included information "that would tend to confirm or deny that particular persons were targets of or subject to NSA intelligence activities . . ."[4] Catch-22, in other words: The *Jewel* and *Shubert* plaintiffs still couldn't gain the evidence that might prove they were an "aggrieved party."

The NSA wiretapping cases at least featured some pushback from federal judges, however limited. Less of that has been apparent in the recent cases challenging the government's extraordinary rendition and targeted killing programs. Here judges, confronted with ominous affidavits full of references to terrorists' plots, apocalyptic threats, and secret foreign agreements—supported by materials provided in a sealed "cone of silence" environment—have largely accepted government arguments that the "very subject matter" of the lawsuits requires instant dismissal.

In doing so, they have been expanding the very notion of the state secrets privilege. Although *U.S. v. Reynolds* is widely viewed as the Supreme Court's first explicit recognition of the privilege, the Court considered a different form of it many years before, in

Totten v. United States (1875). *Totten* arose out of a contract between President Lincoln and a secret agent who was allegedly dispatched to spy on enemy troops. As the Court explained in a brief opinion: "It may be stated as a general principle, that public policy forbids the maintenance of any suit in a court of justice, the trial of which would inevitably lead to the disclosure of matters which the law itself regards as confidential. . . ." In other words, some cases just are not capable of being decided by a court of justice; they are what lawyers call "nonjusticiable." Much more recently, in 2005, the Court reconfirmed this in *Tenet v. Doe*, seemingly limiting such cases to those involving espionage agreements, which "are altogether forbidden." However, for a number of judges (prodded by government lawyers), this concept has now evolved into the more general principle that where the "very subject matter" of a lawsuit is a matter of state secret, the action must be dismissed without reaching the question of evidence. It has not escaped notice, by jurists and commentators, that these judges are essentially conflating *Reynolds* and *Totten* by approaching the state secrets doctrine as both a rule of nonjusticiability and as a privilege that may bar evidence needed to establish a prima facie case.[5]

There's no consensus, though. Federal judges' recent rulings have displayed considerable differences and confusion, particularly in the ways they interpret the connection between *Reynolds* and *Totten* and in their open desire for "non-judicial" routes to relief. Above all, they want Congress to act, they want Congress to provide solutions or guidance. In their opinions, they keep saying: Judges can't resolve these matters, this is up to the political branches.

El-Masri v. Tenet offers a particularly compelling example. The case began in December 2005, when Khaled El-Masri, a German citizen of Lebanese descent, filed a complaint against former CIA Director George Tenet and others (including CIA employees and private corporations). El-Masri's lawsuit asserted that he, in an apparent case of mistaken identity, had been kidnapped, tortured, and held in captivity for five months by the CIA. The details, as described in his complaint—which the court was obliged to take as true at this stage of the litigation—involved him being held repeatedly in isolation; being beaten, stripped, and sodomized with a foreign object; being blindfolded, shackled, and injected with sedatives; and being force-fed through tubes when he twice went on hunger strikes. Finally, according to El-Masri, his captors conceded to him that they'd detained him by mistake. On May 28, 2004, they flew him from Afghanistan to Albania, where they released him on the side of an abandoned road.

The United States, intervening, responded with a formal claim of state secrets privilege and motion for dismissal or summary judgment, on the grounds that continuing the suit would invariably lead to disclosure of state secrets. Pushing further—part of the new pattern—the government's dismissal motion also argued that the "*Totten* bar" renders this case nonjusticiable. In support of its claim, the government submitted to U.S. District Judge T. S. Ellis III (a Reagan appointee and former naval aviator) a classified *ex parte* declaration labeled JUDGE'S EYES ONLY. This declaration wasn't tangible evidence but rather a statement by the current CIA Director—a successor to George Tenet, the very person being sued—explaining that any admission or denial of El-Masri's allegations would reveal the "means and methods" employed in pursuing the clandestine rendition program. Such a revelation would present a "grave risk of injury" to national security.

By then the rendition program was hardly a secret: there'd been widespread publicity, an extensive Council of Europe report, and government officials' public affirmation of the program's existence. However, Judge Ellis found the government claims persuasive, seeing a difference between "a general admission that a rendition program exists" and "the admission or denial of the specific facts at issue in this case." So, however disturbing El-Masri's account,

Ellis did not believe the matter was "proper grist for the judicial mill." On May 12, 2006, the same day he heard oral argument in the case, he granted the government's motion for dismissal, based on its state secrets claim. He resisted only the government's assertion that the *Totten* bar also rendered this case nonjusticiable: "The *Totten* bar is quite distinct from the state secrets privilege; it is not a privilege or a rule of evidence. . . . Because the valid assertion of the state secrets privilege presents an adequate ground for dismissal . . . it is unnecessary to reach and decide the applicability of the *Totten* bar to the facts of this case."

Judge Ellis thought it "important to emphasize that the result reached here is required by settled, controlling law. It is in no way an adjudication of, or comment on, the merit or lack of merit of El-Masri's complaint." Nothing in his ruling "should be taken as a sign of judicial approval or disapproval of rendition programs." It just wasn't up to the judiciary: Courts must not "blindly accept" executive branch assertions, but courts must "bear in mind the Executive Branch's preeminent authority over military and diplomatic matters and its greater expertise relative to the justice branch . . ." If El-Masri's allegations are true, "all fair-minded people" must agree that El-Masri deserves a remedy. "Yet . . . the only sources of that remedy must be the Executive Branch or the Legislative Branch, not the Judicial Branch."

On March 2, 2007, the U.S. Fourth Circuit Court of Appeals not only affirmed Judge Ellis, but significantly expanded his view of the state secrets privilege. Citing both *Totten* and *Reynolds,* the appellate panel, in a decision written by Judge Robert King (a Clinton appointee and former U.S. Attorney in West Virginia), emphasized the notion that the state secrets privilege performs a "function of constitutional significance." Though the privilege usually was regarded as deriving from common law, the Fourth Circuit now asserted that it "has a firm foundation in the Constitution, in addition to its basis in the common law of evidence." Again citing

both *Totten* and *Reynolds*—openly conflating the two—Judge King
wrote that the "Supreme Court has recognized that some matters
are so pervaded by state secrets as to be incapable of judicial resolution. . . ." Though *Totten* traditionally had been seen as a narrow bar to lawsuits involving espionage contracts, the Fourth
Circuit now decided it more broadly established that a "cause cannot be maintained if its trial would inevitably lead to the disclosure of privileged information." Because "the central facts . . . that
form the subject matter of El-Masri's claim" remain state secrets,
the court said it had to dismiss his case.

Judge King appeared to anticipate the criticism this decision
would soon receive, even from brethren on the U.S. Ninth Circuit
Court of Appeals. Near the end of his opinion, he took heated exception to the notion that their ruling "would enable the Executive to unilaterally avoid judicial scrutiny merely by asserting that
state secrets are at stake." No, he wrote, "the state secrets doctrine
does not represent a surrender of judicial control. . . . As we have
explained, it is the court, not the Executive, that determines
whether the state secrets privilege has been properly invoked. . . .
We have reviewed the Classified Declaration, as did the district
court, and the extensive information it contains is crucial to our
decision . . ." It's worth repeating here that this pivotal "Classified
Declaration" was a statement signed by the current director of the
CIA—whose employees, past and present, were being sued.

In a petition urging the Supreme Court to review the Fourth
Circuit decision, El-Masri's ACLU lawyers cited the "substantial
confusion in lower courts" regarding when the privilege may be
invoked, what it covers, and whether it can ever properly be the
basis for dismissing cases at the pleading stage. Give judges guidance and help, the lawyers begged. The Supreme Court "has authority and obligation to amend *Reynolds* evidentiary burdens
if they interfere with the judiciary's constitutional role in reviewing
the legality of executive actions." Otherwise "the government may

engage in torture, declare it a state secret, and by virtue of that designation avoid any judicial accountability."

Responding on October 9, 2007, the Supreme Court declined to review the Fourth Circuit's *El-Masri* decision.

The judiciary's retreat continued in *Arar v. Ashcroft*. Maher Arar's claims sounded very much like El-Masri's: Returning from a vacation, this Syrian-born Canadian citizen, employed as a software engineer in Massachusetts, was retained while changing planes at JFK. He ended up confined, interrogated, and tortured in Syria for more than a year before being released without any charges being filed. His lawsuit against the attorney general, the Secretary of Homeland Security, and the FBI Director drew the same government response as El-Masri's: a motion, prior to discovery, for dismissal or summary judgment on state secrets grounds. Again the "secrets" didn't involve particular items of evidence but rather the "very subject matter" of the case.

And again a federal judge promptly granted the motion to dismiss, prior to any discovery. U.S. District Judge David Trager (a Clinton appointee, former U.S. Attorney and Brooklyn Law School dean) didn't directly address the state secrets claims, but explained he couldn't grant damages "given the national security and foreign policy considerations at stake." A U.S. Second Circuit Court of Appeals panel affirmed, saying the "claims under consideration involve significant national security decisions made in consultation with foreign powers" and so "counsel us to hesitate . . . in a domain so clearly inhospitable to the fact-finding procedures and methods of adjudication employed by the federal courts."

Acting on its own, the Second Circuit judges decided to hold a fuller *en banc* rehearing, which in December 2009 yielded an opinion that explicitly handed the ball to Congress. In affirming the district court, the *en banc* panel said, "Our ruling does not preclude judicial review and oversight. . . . But if a civil remedy in damages is to be created for harms suffered in the context of extraordinary rendition, it must be created by Congress, which alone has the institutional competence to set parameters, delineate safe harbors, and specify relief. If Congress chooses to legislate on this subject, then judicial review of such legislation would be available. . . . We decline to create, on our own, a new cause of action against officers and employees of the federal government. Rather we conclude that . . . it is for the Executive in the first instance to decide how to implement extraordinary rendition, and for the elected members of Congress—and not for us as judges—to decide whether an individual may seek compensation . . . for a constitutional violation."

Again the Supreme Court declined to review, this time after Obama's acting solicitor general, Neal Katyal, urged the justices not to take the case because it might affect national security and might raise questions about "the motives and sincerity of the United States officials who concluded that petitioner could be removed to Syria."

Then came what may very well be the most consequential state secrets case of them all, *Mohamed v. Jeppesen Dataplan, Inc. Jeppesen* offers a revealing comparison to *El-Masri,* both in the way the judges' decisions parallel and diverge from each other. *Jeppesen* by itself involves a fascinating mix of conflicting opinions: No case better illustrates the range of responses judges fashion when presented with a state secrets claim—responses that suggest more than a little perplexed agonizing.

The lawsuit, filed by ACLU lawyers in 2007 on behalf of five men who, in separate instances, had been detained, interrogated, tortured, and held in captivity by the CIA, sought damages not from the government, but from Jeppesen Dataplan, a Boeing subsidiary that had provided transportation services and logistical support for the extraordinary rendition program. The Bush administration instantly intervened before Jeppesen even answered the complaint, once again moving for dismissal on state secrets grounds. In February 2008, U.S. District Judge James Ware, after only limited review, granted the government's motion to dismiss because the allegations were "clearly . . . subject matter which is a state secret." This he decided even though the rendition program was public knowledge, recognized by the government, and even though Jeppesen Dataplan's role in the program had been the subject of a major *New Yorker* piece by Jane Mayer.

The ACLU appealed, and while the appeal was pending at the U.S. Ninth Circuit, Barack Obama was elected President. At oral argument in February 2009—two weeks into the Obama administration—a Justice Department attorney, Douglas Letter, seemed to startle a three-judge appellate panel when he declared that the Obama administration was taking "exactly" the same position as the Bush administration—even though Obama, during the campaign, had spoken against overuse of the state secrets privilege. Once again, a Ninth Circuit panel could be seen pushing back, wondering who decides what's secret. At one point, Judge Michael Hawkins, a Clinton appointee (and member of the appellate panel in *Al-Haramain*), asked the government lawyer, "So any time the executive branch of the government says the fact is classified, it means it cannot be examined?"

Letter, observing that national security was at stake, advised the court it should "not play with fire" by permitting the suit to go forward.

"Nor should the government in asserting [secrecy] privilege," Hawkins replied.[6]

This particular appellate panel (Hawkins, William C. Canby Jr., Mary M. Schroeder, all Democratic appointees) just was not going to defer or follow the Fourth Circuit's *El-Masri* holding. In an impassioned April 2009 opinion written by Hawkins, the panel reversed the district court's dismissal, saying that the state secrets privilege only excluded evidence from discovery or admission at trial, and didn't require dismissal at the pleadings stage. Dismissal at the very start, based on the "very subject matter" of the case, wasn't warranted except in the narrow case of spy contracts. This opinion, unlike the Fourth Circuit's, saw a clear difference between *Reynolds* and *Totten*: "Outside the extremely narrow *Totten* context, the state secrets privilege has never applied to prevent parties from litigating the truth or falsity of allegations . . . simply because the government regards the truth or falsity of the allegations to be secret. Indeed, to conclude that *Reynolds*, like *Totten*, applies to prevent the litigation of allegations, rather than simply discovery of evidence, would be to destroy the distinction between the two versions of the doctrine . . ."

Hawkins's incisive conclusion: "At base, the government argues here that state secrets form the subject matter of a lawsuit, and therefore require dismissal, any time a complaint contains allegations, the truth or falsity of which has been classified as secret by a government official. . . . This sweeping characterization of the 'very subject matter' bar has no logical limit. . . . According to the government's theory, the Judiciary should effectively cordon off all secret government actions from judicial scrutiny, immunizing the CIA and its partners from the demands and limits of the law."

These Ninth Circuit judges weren't so inclined. The structural elements of the Constitution, they believed, "including the principles of separation of powers and judicial review," strongly favor "a narrow construction of the blunt *Totten* doctrine and a broad construction of the more precise *Reynolds* privilege."

This decision seemed to promise a pruning of the ever-expanding reach of the state secrets privilege. Here was a chance for the Obama administration to reconsider its stance about use of the privilege, and live up to Obama's campaign promises. More than one editorialist called for the White House to not appeal.

However, that summer of 2009—even as the Justice Department prepared a memorandum establishing new, more restrained procedures for invocation of the state secrets privilege—the Obama administration did appeal the Ninth Circuit's decision. Rather than turn to the Supreme Court, the government sought a full bench (*en banc*) review before a larger panel of Ninth Circuit judges. In October, the appellate court agreed to hold such a hearing, later explaining it did so "to resolve questions of exceptional importance regarding the scope and application of the state secrets doctrine." As a result, on December 15, 2009, the lawyers gathered once again to argue about the state secrets privilege—this time before an eleven-judge panel.

What unfolded that day in the San Francisco federal courthouse made for compelling courthouse theater. There were many lively exchanges, with engaged judges challenging both sides, expressing a range of opinions and displaying an obvious sense of conflict. The sharply divided decision filed by these judges on September 8, 2010, clearly demonstrated that conflict. By a vote of 6–5 the *en banc* panel reversed the three-judge panel, affirmed the district court's ruling, and dismissed the plaintiff's action in *Mohamed v. Jeppesen Dataplan.*

While openly criticizing the Fourth Circuit's "erroneous conflation" of the *Totten* bar and the *Reynolds* privilege in *El-Masri*, the *en banc* panel's majority still concluded that dismissal at the pleading stage was required under *Reynolds* because there was "no feasible way to litigate Jeppesen's alleged liability without creating an unjustified risk of divulging state secrets." This reasoning, besides ignoring all the public information available about Jeppesen and the rendition program, required a tricky balancing act: Maintaining the distinction between the *Totten* bar and the *Reynolds* privilege "does not mean that the *Reynolds* privilege can never . . . result in a dismissal at the pleading stage . . ." In this way, the *Reynolds* privilege "converges with the *Totten* bar, because both require dismissal." Thus, the *Totten* bar and the *Reynolds* privilege form "a continuum of analysis."

From its very first words, the majority opinion, written by Judge Raymond C. Fisher (a Clinton appointee, former associate attorney general, and clerk to Supreme Court Justice William Brennan), conveyed the judges' struggle: "This case requires us to address the difficult balance the state secrets doctrine strikes between fundamental principles of our liberty, including justice, transparency, accountability and national security. Although as judges we strive to honor *all* of these principles, there are times when exceptional circumstances create an irreconcilable conflict between them. . . . After much deliberation, we reluctantly conclude this is such a case, and the plaintiffs' action must be dismissed . . ."

Near the end of his opinion, Judge Fisher again signaled a sense of conflict, offering comments that seemed to recognize the inability—or failure—of the judiciary to provide a satisfactory resolution to this case. Handing off responsibility, he proposed "other remedies" outside of the judicial system: "Our holding today is not intended to foreclose . . . possible *nonjudicial* relief. Denial of a judicial forum based on the state secrets doctrine poses concerns at both individual and structural levels. For the individual plaintiffs . . . our decision . . . deprives them of the opportunity to prove their alleged mistreatment and obtain damages. At a structural level, terminating the case eliminates further judicial review in this civil litigation, one important check on alleged abuse by government officials and putative contractors. Other remedies may partially mitigate these concerns . . ."

He looked to the executive branch: "That the judicial branch may have deferred to the executive branch's claim . . . does not preclude the government from honoring the fundamental principles of justice. . . . The government may be able to find ways to remedy alleged harms. . . . For instance, the government made reparations to Japanese Latin Americans abducted from Latin America for internment in the United States during World War II."

He looked to Congress: "Congress has the authority to investigate alleged wrongdoing and restrain excesses by the executive branch. . . . Congress also has the power to enact private bills. . . . When national security interests deny alleged victims of wrongful governmental action meaningful access to a judicial forum, private bills may be an appropriate alternative remedy."

Above all, he pointed out that Congress "has the authority to enact remedial legislation" regarding the state secrets privilege. He invited Congress to authorize "appropriate causes of action and procedures to address claims like those presented here."

In his conclusion, Judge Fisher once more made plain his unease: "For all the reasons the dissent articulates—including the impact on human rights, the importance of constitutional protections and the constraints of a judge-made doctrine—we do not reach our decision lightly or without close and skeptical scrutiny of the record and the government's case for secrecy and dismissal. . . . We acknowledge that this case presents a painful conflict between human rights and national security. As judges, we have tried our best to evaluate the competing claims of plaintiffs and the government and resolve that conflict according to the principles governing the state secrets doctrine . . ."

In yet another sign of discomfort, the court, in a highly unusual move, ordered the government to pay the plaintiffs' legal costs, even though they had lost the case and had not requested such a payment. The majority, in its opinion, also bowed several times to the five dissenters ("we accept and respect the principles that motivate the dissent") and allowed those judges to attach an 1,800-page appendix, submitted by the plaintiffs, that documented the voluminous public record about the rendition program.

Only by one vote had this majority decision prevailed. Writing for the *en banc* panel's five dissenting judges, Judge Michael Hawkins repeated many of the arguments he had offered in his earlier opinion. Then he turned to the majority's recommendation of alternative remedies, which he considered an ineffective abdication of the judiciary's role: "Suggesting, for example, that the Executive could 'honor the fundamental principles of justice' by determining 'whether plaintiffs' claims have merit' disregards the concept of checks and balances. Permitting the executive to police its own errors and determine the remedy dispensed would not only deprive the judiciary of its role, but also deprive Plaintiffs of a fair assessment of their claims by a neutral arbiter. . . . Similarly, a congressional investigation, private bill or enactment of 'remedial legislation,' leaves to the legislative branch claims which the federal courts are better equipped to handle."

Editorialists and commentators castigated the Ninth Circuit's *en banc* ruling, *The New York Times* reminding its readers that "torture is a crime, not a secret." The ACLU, as it did in *El-Masri*, appealed to the Supreme Court, again urging the justices to clarify conflicting case law and resolve widespread uncertainty as to whether the government can invoke the state secrets privilege at the pleading stage. In May 2011, the Supreme Court once more declined to review.

Just days after the *Jeppesen* decision, in a filing to the district court for the District of Columbia early on Saturday morning, September 25, 2010, the Obama administration again invoked the state secrets privilege—the first time it did so in defense of its own policies, rather than the Bush administration's. This came in response to an action filed August 30 by the father of Anwar al-Aulaqi, seeking to stop the government's plan for a targeted killing of his son, a dual U.S.-Yemeni citizen with alleged ties to the terrorist group al Qaeda in the Arabian Peninsula (AQAP). Anwar, hiding in Yemen, was in fact considered a central figure in AQAP, active in planning attacks, but he had not been charged with any crime.

In the legal arguments both sides offered (al-Aulaqi was represented by the ACLU and the Center for Constitutional Rights), it is easy to see the echoes and influences of all the previous NSA and rendition cases. Once again, the government sought an outright dismissal at the pleading stage—though this time, possibly sensitive to a mounting controversy, the government only proposed the state secrets privilege as a last choice "alternative" reason if all other defenses failed (among them: the plaintiff lacked standing, the court would have to decide nonjusticiable political questions). Once again, the plaintiffs pointed out that it made little sense for the government to claim secrecy for a targeted killing program that it had already acknowledged publicly through "an apparently co-ordinated media strategy." Once again, the government argued back that state secrets "would remain intertwined in every step of the case . . . and the inherent risk of disclosures that would harm national security should be apparent from the outset."

U.S. District Judge John D. Bates (a George W. Bush appointee, member of the FISA court, and former federal prosecutor) seemed genuinely troubled by what he, as a judge, was being asked to decide. "This is a unique and extraordinary case," he wrote at the start of the opinion he delivered on December 7, 2010. "Both the threshold and merits issues present fundamental questions of separation of powers involving the proper role of the courts in our constitutional structure . . ."

To Judge Bates, "stark, and perplexing, questions readily come to mind." Among them: "How it is that judicial approval is required when the United States decides to target a U.S. citizen overseas for electronic surveillance, but that, according to defendants, judicial scrutiny is prohibited when the United States decides to target a U.S. citizen overseas for death?"

Also: "Can a U.S. citizen . . . use the U.S. judicial system to vindicate his constitutional rights while simultaneously evading U.S. law enforcement authorities, calling for 'jihad against the West,' and engaging in operational planning for an organization that has already carried out numerous terrorist attacks against the United States?"

And: "Can the Executive order the assassination of a U.S. citizen without first affording him any form of judicial process whatsoever, based on the mere assertion that he is a dangerous member of a terrorist organization?"

Above all: "How can the courts, as plaintiff proposes, make real-time assessments of the nature and severity of alleged threats to national security, determine the imminence of those threats, weigh the benefits and costs of possible diplomatic and military responses, and ultimately decide whether, and under what circumstances, the use of military force against such threats is justified?"

Judge Bates didn't think the courts could do this. Though the "legal and policy questions posed by this case are controversial and of great public interest," he didn't believe he had jurisdiction, he didn't believe the plaintiff's stated claims fell "within the ambit of the Judiciary to resolve." In his legal reasoning, Bates cited and relied more than once on the Jeppesen *en banc* decision. He agreed that in some instances "the *Reynolds* privilege converges with the *Totten* bar," meaning "the assertion of the privilege will require dismissal because it will become apparent during the *Reynolds* analysis that the case cannot proceed without privileged evidence . . ."

In the end, though, Judge Bates decided he didn't have to reach the state secrets claim. Instead he found that al-Aulaqi's complaint raised political questions not answerable in a court of law. Once again, a judge looked elsewhere for a resolution. Because his finding required dismissal of the case at the outset, Bates wrote, "the serious issues regarding the merits of the alleged authorization of the targeted killing of a U.S. citizen overseas must await another day or another (non-judicial) forum."

Before that day came, the U.S. military acted: On September 30, 2011, an American drone strike in Yemen killed al-Aulaqi and several others.

Congress certainly is the "non-judicial forum" Bates and so many other judges have vainly been looking to in the past decade. Congress on its own, through hearings, investigations, legislation, and impeachment, could act as a check on the executive branch's war on terror programs. Or it could provide guidance and support for the judiciary. As various legal commentators have pointed out,[7] Congress has the power to define the federal courts' jurisdiction and affect the judicial response to claims of privilege. It can establish the parameters of the privilege and bolster the courts' authority. But it has never done so, it has never adopted legislation aimed at restricting use of the privilege.

Congress did consider codifying the state secrets privilege when it adopted the Federal Rules of Evidence in the 1970s, but decided not to. It also—at least according to a pair of federal court rulings—partly usurped the privilege in 1978 when it passed FISA, which provides judicial and congressional oversight of the government's covert surveillance activities. (FISA was introduced by Senator Ted Kennedy and cosponsored by a bipartisan group of nine senators, in response to congressional investigations into President Nixon's surveillance of political and activists groups). Congress again assigned judges responsibilities over national security matters in 1980, when it enacted the Classified Information Procedures Act (CIPA), which established procedures for how courts should respond to defense requests for classified documents in criminal cases.

The most direct effort to restrict use of the state secrets privilege came in 2008, when Senators Ted Kennedy, Arlen Specter, and Patrick Leahy introduced the State Secrets Protection Act, which among other things gave plaintiffs the "full opportunity" to complete nonprivileged discovery and required judges to examine (*ex parte, in camera*) actual evidence rather than trust the executive branch's affidavits. That same year Congressman Jerrold Nadler introduced a similar bill in the House. Hearings were held, press releases issued, speeches delivered, reports distributed—but the bills never made it to the floor of the Senate or House. The bills were reintroduced in 2009, with the same result. Nadler vainly tried again in 2012, then once more in October 2013. There just have not been enough votes to move the bills, and no consensus or common ground with either the Bush or Obama administration.

It likely didn't help when Bush's attorney general, Michael Mukasey, wrote a letter to the Senate Judiciary Committee in March 2008 threatening a Bush veto. He argued (pointing to the executive's constitutional role under Article II as commander in chief) that the privilege derived from the Constitution, so Congress couldn't modify it through statutory law—even though it apparently had done just that with FISA. "It is highly questionable," Mukasey wrote, "that Congress has the authority to alter the state secrets privilege, which is rooted in the Constitution and is not merely a common law privilege."

Then came the Obama administration's conciliatory words and September 2009 policy statement, outlining a modified, restricted use of the privilege. This apparently defused a lot of the momentum, leading some to assume the problem had been fixed. Others in Congress no doubt shied away from appearing "weak" on the war on terror. So rather than restrict use of the state secrets privilege, Congress, by passing the FISA Amendments Act, ended up broadening the government's power to eavesdrop, without individual warrants, on international phone calls and e-mails.

Congress's failure to check the executive, and failure to provide the courts with direction or reinforcement, has yielded consequences. At a 2008 oversight hearing, convened to support passage of Nadler's bill in the House, H. Thomas Wells Jr., American Bar Association president-elect, attributed executive abuse in part to "the absence of congressional guidance." Congressional silence, he added, has permitted courts to adopt "divergent" approaches to resolving cases and abdicating judicial oversight "without engaging in sufficient inquiry into the government's assertion of privilege."[8]

Congress, however, has not been entirely passive. In April 2014, the Senate Intelligence Committee, chaired by Senator Dianne Feinstein, voted to declassify hundreds of pages of a harshly critical report on the CIA's extraordinary rendition program—a report the committee had been working on since 2009, despite constant stonewalling and evasion by the CIA. This report promised to reveal the very type of operational information that courts have been treating as litigation-stopping state secrets. Those who read it in the summer of 2014 said the report would accuse the CIA of brutally torturing terror suspects and misleading Congress, the White House, and the public about the program's effectiveness. The declassification process was glacial, though, with CIA leaders past and present (including George Tenet) working behind the scenes to discredit and redact portions of the report—their goal clearly being to protect themselves, not national security. At the end of July, in a stunning revelation, an internal agency investigation confirmed that CIA officials had also hacked into a computer network used by the Senate Intelligence Committee in preparing its report, despite earlier denials by CIA Director John O. Brennan.

The agency's invasive, tenacious resistance—not unlike its response to lawsuits—had its effect: At the start of August, the executive branch, after review and declassification, returned to the committee a heavily censored version of its report. The CIA itself, along with the Office of the National Director of Intelligence, had done most of the censoring, in what the White House press secretary, Josh Earnest, called "a good faith effort . . . to make redactions that are consistent with the need to protect national security."

Feinstein bristled, saying there had been "significant redactions" which "eliminate or obscure key facts that support the report's findings and conclusions." She pushed back: "We need additional time to understand the basis for these redactions and determine their justification. Therefore the report will be held until further notice and released when that process is completed."[9]

The report's release finally came on December 9, 2014, despite vociferous objections from the CIA and Republican critics. It delivered an even more scathing indictment of the CIA's operation than expected. The report—a 524-page executive summary of a 6,000-page document—revealed that the CIA had regularly misled the White House and Congress about its methods in the war on terror—methods which were more brutal than the CIA had ever acknowledged either to Bush administration officials or to the public. In a speech in the Senate on the morning of the report's release, Senator Feinstein called the CIA program "a stain on our values and our history.[10]

Late July 2014 saw one other promising effort in the Senate to restrict the expansion of government surveillance power: Spurred by Edward Snowden's disclosures, Senator Patrick Leahy, with the backing of the White House, on July 29 introduced a version of the USA Freedom Act that improves on a gutted version the House passed in May. Although it doesn't go far enough, it would significantly restrict NSA's bulk collection of Americans' telephone records, requiring the agency to ask for the records of a specific person or address, rather than conduct a broad dragnet. It would also alter the workings of the secret FISA court: Where the court now hears only the government's case in a nonadversarial setting, and doesn't reveal decisions, it would have to listen also to a panel of advocates arguing in support of privacy rights and civil liberties, and it would have to issue public summaries of decisions.[11]

Whatever happens in Congress—past failures to act don't promise much—the courts retain a fundamental responsibility to serve as a check on executive excess and abuse. Judges should not keep looking to the "political branches" and "nonjudicial forums." As a number of jurists and commentators have pointed out, when judges dismiss cases challenging the legality of executive conduct, they abdicate their role in a system predicated on checks and balances.[12]

Judges should at the very least allow discovery of nonprivileged evidence before dismissing cases because the "very subject matter" is a state secret. To assure that an evidentiary privilege isn't used as an immunity shield, they should segregate evidence, structure discovery, and arrange security clearances for attorneys in a way that allows the courts a full *Reynolds* analysis. They should insist on *in camera* review of actual evidence, rather than just rely on government affidavits. They should recognize the substantive difference between a particular personal injury tort action (such as the B-29 crash in *Reynolds*), and the wholesale assertion of privilege to block judicial review of executive conduct in the war on terror.

Above all, they should think long and hard before trusting the government or accepting its claims—especially in the wake of the Senate Intelligence Committee report. They should understand it is in the self-interest of government operatives in the CIA and NSA to argue that the "very subject matter" is a secret. They should recognize that these cases are not truly about secrecy, but rather, immunity or impunity for people who have committed criminal acts. They should heed the words of the appellate judge who heard the *Reynolds* case in an era just as anxious and perilous as our post-9/11 world:

> To hold that the head of an executive department of the Government in a [law]suit to which the United States is a party may conclusively determine the Government's claim of privilege is to abdicate the judicial function.

In a system of three separate but equal powers of government, judges must do their job. Along with congressional action, what's needed are jurists with the nerve and wisdom of William Kirkpatrick and Albert Maris.

NOTES

* *An omnibus source, providing links to all major court decisions and related documents, can be found at the FAS Project on Government Secrecy Web site maintained by Steven Aftergood: "The State Secrets Privilege: Selected Case Files," www.fas.org/sgp/jud/statesec.*

1. Secrecy Report Card 2010. Indicators of Secrecy in the Federal Government, OpenTheGovernment.Org, as cited in Timothy Bazzle, "Shutting the Courthouse Doors: Invoking the State Secrets Privilege to Thwart Judicial Review in the Age of Terror," *Civil Rights Law Journal* 23, no. 1 (2012).
2. This pattern is discussed in various briefs and law journal articles, including:
   • Bazzle, "Shutting the Courthouse Doors."
   • Amanda Frost and Justin Florence, "Reforming the State Secrets Privilege," American Constitution Society for Law and Policy Issue Brief, 2008.
   • Amanda Frost, "The State Secrets Privilege and Separation of Powers," *Fordham Law Review* 75 (2007): 1931.
   • Todd Garvey and Edward C. Liu, "The State Secrets Privilege: Preventing the Disclosure of Sensitive National Security Information During Civil Litigation," Congressional Research Service Report for Congress, August 16, 2011.
3. Jon Eisenberg, "Suing George W. Bush: A Bizarre and Troubling Tale," *Salon,* July 9, 2008.
   Interview with Jon Eisenberg, July 30, 2014.

4. James R. Clapper, "Classified Declaration of James R. Clapper, Director of National Intelligence," May 5, 2014, http://icontherecord.tumblr.com.

Office of the Director of National Intelligence, "Declassified," May 6, 2014, icontherecord.tumblr.com/post/84748492788/.

5. Among commentators who discuss this:
   - Bazzle, "Shutting the Courthouse Doors."
   - Frost, "The State Secrets Privilege and Separation of Powers."
   - Garvey and Liu, "The State Secrets Privilege."

   U.S. Ninth Circuit Court of Appeals judges also discuss this in:
   - *Al-Haramain Islamic Foundation v. Bush.*
   - *Mohamed v. Jeppesen Dataplan* (both the three-judge and *en banc* panels).

6. Maura Dolan and Carol J. Williams, "Court Urged to Deny Rendition Trial," *Los Angeles Times,* February 10, 2009.

7. Most particularly, Amanda Frost in "The State Secrets Privilege and Separation of Powers," who persuasively suggests that "when the executive successfully argues that a federal court must dismiss whole categories of cases, it intrudes not just on the power of courts and the rights of individuals, but on the jurisdiction-conferring authority of the legislature as well . . . By seeking dismissal of these cases, the executive is stripping Congress of its ability to collaborate with the judiciary to curb executive power."

8. Bazzle, "Shutting the Courthouse Doors."

9. See the following:
   - Olivier Knox, "Feinstein puts Obama on the spot over CIA's 'torture report edits,'" Yahoo News, August 5, 2014.
   - Mark Mazzetti, "Redactions of Report on CIA Stoke Ire," *New York Times,* August 6, 2014.
   - Mark Mazzetti, "Ex-Chief of CIA Shapes Response to Detention Report," *New York Times,* July 25, 2014.
   - Mark Mazzetti, "Senators Clear Path for Release of Detention Report on CIA," *New York Times,* April 2, 2014.
   - Ken Dilanian and Eileen Sullivan, "State Dept: 'No American Is Proud' of CIA Tactics," Associated Press, July 31, 2014.
   - Josh Rogin and Eli Lake, "White House Must Decide Who Will Be Named in the CIA 'Torture Report,'" *Daily Beast,* August 7, 2014.

10. Mark, Mazzetti "Senate Torture Report Condemns C.I.A. Interrogration Program," *New York Times,* December 9, 2014.

11. Doina Chiacu and Joseph Menn, "US Senate bill proposes sweeping curbs on NSA surveillance," Reuters, July 30, 2014.
12. Among them:
    - Bazzle, "Shutting the Courthouse Doors."
    - Frost, "The State Secrets Privilege and Separation of Powers."

THE FUTURE OF PRIVACY IN THE SURVEILLANCE AGE

JON L. MILLS

JON L. MILLS is Dean Emeritus, Professor of Law, and Director of the Center for Governmental Responsibility at the University of Florida's Fredric G. Levin College of Law, where he served as Dean from 1999 to 2003. From 1978 to 1988 he served in the Florida Legislature and was Speaker of the House. As a lawyer, he has appeared in courts nationwide arguing on topics including voting rights and constitutional law. As a professor, he has directed major studies in Brazil, Poland, Haiti, and Central America. An expert on constitutional issues, Mills has been quoted by *The New York Times*, *The Wall Street Journal*, *The Los Angeles Times*, *The Chicago Tribune*, and *The Washington Post*. He has appeared on CNN, PBS, NPR, ABC, and the BBC, and produced an Emmy-winning report on the Florida Everglades. He has authored books, articles, and reports on environmental issues, voting rights, government ethics, and the Constitution, the most recent of which, *Privacy: The Lost Right*, was published by Oxford University Press in 2008.

I. THE HAYSTACK—PRIVACY VS. SECURITY

THE WORLD STOOD still on 9/11. Then it changed. President George W. Bush ordered security agencies to make certain the United States would never again wake up to crumbling towers and a burning Pentagon. Securing our homeland was the top priority. The primary tool we developed to achieve security became a strong surveillance system to find the new enemy.

The surveillance mission is to find and stop terrorists whose sole goal is to inflict pain on the United States. NSA Director General Keith B. Alexander's technique was said to be comprehensive: "Rather than look for a single needle in a haystack, his approach was, 'Let's collect the whole haystack.'"[1] Who comprises the haystack? Perhaps we all do.

The scope and breadth of the intelligence that Edward Snowden disclosed in 2012 suggest that government surveillance has overrun the boundaries of U.S. citizens' constitutional rights. By now, we all know that the NSA collected U.S. citizens' e-mails, family photos, and résumés. The data was gathered through PRISM, MUSCULAR, and other programs with memorable names.

Today, citizens are anxious not only about security but privacy as well. The concern about whether the U.S. government is becoming Big Brother has even led George Orwell's book *1984* to spike in sales.

The NSA intended for these programs to remain a secret. The intelligence overseers never expected them to become public— after all, they were compelled to spy on citizens in the interests of national security. Some argue that the public would be better off if the programs had remained secret. We cannot help but recall the words of Jack Nicholson's Colonel Jessup in *A Few Good Men*— "You can't handle the truth!" Regardless, the new wave of alarm that Snowden's intelligence leaks set into motion cannot reverse its course. We are presented with the inescapable conflict between security and personal privacy.

All human beings prioritize safety and security before any other earthly need. The idea of privacy as an intrinsic value cannot compete on this hierarchy. Recent trends in public opinion suggest that people regret the degradation of their privacy and its consequences. Perhaps this sentiment is a result of viewing the loss of privacy as a secondary security issue.

For example, we condemn authoritarian surveillance states like Nazi Germany where children informed on their parents and parents informed on their neighbors. In the Kafkaesque surveillance state, everyone is at risk. Being constantly observed or even the possibility of being observed has an effect on human conduct—it is intended to do so. Jeremy Bentham's panopticon prison was entirely based on controlling the inmates by merely presenting the *possibility* that an inmate might be observed at any time. Similarly, a Harris poll conducted after Snowden's disclosures revealed that 47 percent of 2,000 adult respondents reported changing their online behavior because of what they learned about government surveillance.[2] Twenty-four percent of respondents reported that they are less inclined to use e-mail and 26 percent of respondents reported that they engaged in less online shopping and banking. In other words, the possibility of observation affected behavior—just like in Bentham's panopticon.

Do today's citizens whose Internet use takes place in virtual glass houses really care if the government is watching them? The individuals in our contemporary culture post intimate details on Facebook and willingly trade off their location for discounts. Yet even in this sometimes exhibitionist society, being watched by government is different and more frightening. We care if Big Brother is eavesdropping without our permission. Americans do not want to live in a *1984* world. Our citizens still revere the values of privacy, dignity, solitude, free thought, and free speech. Increasingly, our actions demonstrate how the loss of privacy has real societal consequences. Chilling thought and speech has repercussions and is contrary to basic democratic principles.

Snowden's disclosures present the opportunity to take an inventory of the status of privacy and liberty. What is the toll of CCTV cameras, facial recognition software, DNA identification, comprehensive e-mail monitoring, cell phone collection, cataloging of Internet purchases, monitoring of Internet use and searches, location monitoring, drone surveillance, etcetera? And what is the danger of aggregating all of this information in one place? Has Big Data replaced Big Brother? If the NSA can successfully predict that a person will commit a terrorist act and detain him before he blows up the neighborhood mall, will we in turn tolerate more intrusions into personal life as a price for that security?

These are fundamental policy issues about what kind of society we want to live in. There are practical questions about what is essential for national security in an era when domestic safety has been compromised and foreign enemies will use all available resources to cause harm. There are also questions about the constitutional and legal boundaries of modern surveillance. The Constitution protects a citizen's reasonable expectation of privacy from governmental search and seizure. What is a reasonable expectation of privacy today?

Modern culture prioritizes privacy less than the one that existed even two decades ago when the Church Committee reviewed U.S. surveillance practices and warned of the real danger of increased intrusion. Today's consumer and surveillance capabilities go far beyond those in the Church Committee's pre-Internet era. In addition, the contemporary world has more domestic threats than ever before. The perfect storm of new technology, justifiable post-9/11 fears, and the vast voluntary disclosures of contemporary society provide the recipe for collecting unprecedented amounts of data on individuals. There are, however, still constitutional limits to government's data gathering in this new era.

II. PRIVACY, SECURITY, AND THE CONSTITUTION

Domestic surveillance creates an inevitable collision of two legal principles and basic human instincts—security and privacy. Security is arguably the very first ideal manifested in the U.S. Constitution. The preamble includes the phrases "insure domestic Tranquility," "provide for the common defense," and "secure the Blessings of Liberty to ourselves and our Posterity." On the other hand, the word "privacy" does not appear even once in the Constitution. However, the concept was included in the Fourth Amendment's codification of the right of the people to be free from unreasonable searches and seizures. That provision clearly allows individuals "to be secure in their persons, houses, papers and effects against unreasonable searches and seizures." This language specifically identifies "personal security" as a right that is held separate from and in addition to national security.

Personal security was deemed to be a natural right derived not from a government arbiter, but rather from God. Motivated by distaste for government and the invasion of personal space, recognition of this right was fueled by an era when the British government had vast authority to search people's homes and businesses. The British rulers were viewed as oppressors and the colonists had a healthy antagonism for what has come to be known as "Big Brother." The Founders did not anticipate drones, GPS surveillance, or the Internet. The possibility of a 9/11 terrorist attack was unthinkable. Technology and history have painted a vexing conflict between these principles of privacy and security that Americans have valued since the beginning of the republic.[3]

Technology has facilitated surveillance for national security purposes as well as law enforcement purposes. Constitutional protections from technology-assisted warrantless searches have changed dramatically. When telephone calls were made on shared lines, law enforcement officers frequently listened in, believing that existing wiretapping laws were not applicable. A landmark privacy case in 1928 involved precisely this circumstance. In *Olmstead v. United States,* a bootlegger appealed his conviction on the grounds that the admission of damning evidence obtained via the wiretapping of the home and office phones of the defendants violated the Fourth Amendment.[4] The relevant wiretapping lasted for many months. Chief Justice William Howard Taft, writing for the majority, determined that there was neither a "searching" nor a "seizure." He confined Fourth Amendment protections as pertaining only to a physical entry—"intervening wires are *not part of [a defendant's] house or office* [emphasis added], any more than are the highways along which they are stretched." Because the federal prohibition officers did not breach the homes, offices, or mail of the defendants, the actions were allowed. Justice Louis Brandeis was one of four dissenters. Thirty-eight years earlier, he coauthored "The Right to Privacy," a law review article that has since come to be known as the theoretical birthplace of American privacy.

Brandeis recognized that the single most important issue for privacy in the era of technology-based surveillance is that privacy protections should not be limited to a physical location. Affirming that the right to privacy was a basic principle, he advocated that every unjustified intrusion by government constituted a violation of the Fourth Amendment:

> *The makers of our Constitution undertook to secure conditions favorable to the pursuit of happiness. . . . They sought to protect Americans in their beliefs, their thoughts, their emotions and their sensations. They conferred, as against the government, the right to be let alone—the most comprehensive of rights and the right most valued by civilized men. To protect, that right, every unjustifiable intrusion by the government upon the privacy of the individual, whatever the means employed, must be deemed a violation of the Fourth Amendment.*

It was not until the 1967 decision of *Katz v. United States* that Justice Brandeis, then deceased, would be redeemed. Charles Katz was convicted on the basis of gambling information he transmitted via telephone from Los Angeles to Miami, which was captured by a recording device FBI agents had placed on the outside of a public phone booth.[5] He appealed his conviction on the grounds that the recording violated his Fourth Amendment rights. In a 7–1 ruling, the Supreme Court held that Fourth Amendment protections "do not vanish when the search in question is transferred from the setting of a home, an office, or a hotel room to that of a telephone booth." Justice John Marshall Harlan II's five-paragraph concurrence contains the reasoning supporting the expanded Fourth Amendment test for a search. In it he introduced the idea of a reasonable expectation of privacy:

> *[A]n enclosed telephone booth is an area where, like a home, . . . a person has a constitutionally protected reasonable expectation of privacy . . . and . . . the invasion of a constitutionally protected area*

by federal authorities is, as the Court has long held, presumptively
unreasonable in the absence of a search warrant.

This opinion was a major change from the *Olmstead* decision.
Whereas the Fourth Amendment had previously only guaranteed
a right to privacy in one's physical home, *Katz* now permitted a
more expansive application that protected privacy beyond the home.

The Court took another landmark step in 2014. In a 9–0 decision, the Court held that citizens can legitimately assert a reasonable expectation of privacy in their personal information.[6] In fact,
Justice John Roberts concluded, "a cell phone search would typically expose to the government far *more* than the most exhaustive
search of a house." The *Riley v. California* case epitomizes the realization that obtaining a technological accumulation of data
intrudes on personal privacy. Observation of the phone's accumulation of e-mails, location information, Internet browsing, personal communications, and personal schedule creates a mosaic of
a person's entire life. The Court decided that the warrantless governmental search of this information is illegal. Is the warrantless
accumulation of similar data through Internet surveillance acceptable for national security purposes, or are the current practices of
the NSA also a violation?

III. HISTORY AND PERSPECTIVE OF PRIVACY AND SURVEILLANCE

Today, privacy is eroding because of a flood of security threats.
History teaches that governments can use surveillance to control
people rather than protect them. The examples are legion. Rulers
and kings prefer to avoid, outsmart, or behead opponents. Knowing
who they are and what they are doing is a wonderful advantage.
While there are instances in U.S. history where surveillance was

used to create enemies lists—such as those employed by President Richard Nixon—that type of oppression is not the U.S. norm. There are historic and contemporary precedents for surveillance societies in which the government's motive is to identify its disruptive or outspoken critics in order to limit dissent. China and North Korea are obvious examples.

Fear motivates a government or its leaders to find out as much about its enemies as possible. Historically, little restraint was applied to spy technology. If you had it, you used it. That certainly seems justified when fighting against a foreign military enemy—especially when the enemy uses a similarly unbridled approach. While Nazis were trying to break our codes and deceive us any way they could, we were doing the same thing to them.

Post-9/11, the motivation to protect the homeland was very high and the technology had advanced to a stage where it was possible to watch, listen to, and monitor individuals in unprecedented ways. This technology gave birth to Stellar Wind (aka The Program), PRISM, and so many other spy surveillance operations. However, before looking at the specifics of contemporary privacy invasions, it is worth exploring the rich history of spying.

When Hamlet feared that the "walls have ears," he was right. In the Middle Ages, some castles were constructed with built-in coves covered in curtains where observers or spies could listen to conversations. Intelligence on the thoughts and actions of enemies and friends alike has always been incredibly important to governments during both war and peace. In fact, it could arguably be considered negligent not to surveil your enemies, and sometimes even your friends. Perhaps it should not have been surprising when it was revealed that British and U.S. intelligence agencies had hacked the phone of German Chancellor Angela Merkel.[7]

After the advent of the telegram, eavesdroppers had the ability to tap into communications from a remote location and without the knowledge of those directly involved. In the same mold as the Internet, the technology of the telegraph improved communication and at the same time made spying easier.

During the Civil War, both the Union and Confederacy intercepted each other's telegrams. Abraham Lincoln would personally review some of these Confederate communications during his presidency.[8] Confederate General Jeb Stuart even traveled with his own wiretap specialist.[9] In fact, when President Bush was under pressure following the disclosure of the government's warrantless wiretapping program, Attorney General Alberto Gonzales referenced the long-standing tradition of wartime enemy surveillance within the United States, including during the Civil War.[10] It was the attorney general's contention that a legislative grant to use "'all necessary and appropriate force'" to combat the enemy included the warrantless surveillance of even *potential* enemies.

During both World War I and World War II, domestic surveillance was widespread. In World War I, prior to substantial telephone use, the government employed postal workers to examine 30 million letters sent to approximately 10 million German-Americans.[11] This spying later expanded to a force of agents who conducted surveillance on not only immigrants, but also union members and socialists. During World War II, the FBI continued to surveil domestically, but with a greater focus on tapping telephones. Keep in mind that the U.S. Supreme Court had not yet decided that wiretapping was an illegal search and seizure. Therefore, it was a plausible argument that the FBI's domestic wiretaps did not violate existing law.

President Franklin Roosevelt entrusted FBI Director J. Edgar Hoover with domestic espionage operations. However, Hoover did not limit his surveillance to wartime. In 1945, Project SHAMROCK was launched to read all telegraphs entering and exiting the United States.[12] Continuing into the 1950s and 1960s, this counterintelligence program (COINTELPRO) investigated "dissidents" ranging from Vietnam War protesters to Dr. Martin Luther King Jr.[13]

In the early 1970s, a new set of intrusions on American citizens was brought to the front pages by a Senate investigation that was in some ways a response to Watergate-era revelations of surveillance used to monitor perceived enemies of the FBI, the CIA, and the President. Senator Frank Church of Idaho chaired the select committee chosen to investigate intelligence activities relating to American citizens. The Church Committee exposed mail-opening programs, domestic wiretapping, COINTELPRO, and a multitude of other constitutionally questionable activities. The types of intrusions described in the report sound eerily familiar—the collection of too much information for too long, the use of illegal or improper means, general ignorance of the law, deficiencies in accountability, and the adverse impact of improper intelligence activity.[14]

Three intelligence activities caused particular alarm: physical data collection, subsequent dissemination, and the purposeful targeting of individuals who were "far beyond persons who could properly be characterized as enemies of freedom." The essential finding was that "[t]oo many people have been spied upon by too many Government agencies and *to* [*sic*] *much information has been collected.*" The most significant result of the Church Committee was passage of the Foreign Intelligence Surveillance Act of 1978, which established the court and secret processes that are a central issue in today's debate. Although the act was intended to provide needed oversight of the intelligence gathering process, the reform of 1978 was arguably a flawed secret process that allowed or facilitated some of the excesses disclosed by Edward Snowden.

IV. THE TURNING POINT—9/11

The tragedies of 9/11 produced a focused effort to preserve and protect the security of the U.S. homeland. The War on Terror was launched against the specific enemy, al Qaeda, and the amorphous specter of foreign and domestic terrorists threatening our safety.

That strong motivation to protect the homeland combined with new technical capabilities created a perfect storm for vastly expanding surveillance.

Attorney General John Ashcroft recounted his experiences in the days following the 9/11 attacks, relaying how President Bush admonished, "Never let this happen again."[15] The Department of Justice and others now had the broad task of prevention in addition to the focused task of prosecuting wrongdoing. Preventing a crime from happening is a far different task than punishing it. Under the broad banner of preventing terrorism, collecting information about innocent Americans was simply collateral damage.

To prevent another tragedy, information had to be gathered about potential acts of terrorism and about potential terrorists. There was, however, a legal barrier to unfettered surveillance of U.S. citizens on U.S. soil. Under the Foreign Intelligence Surveillance Act, intelligence wiretaps inside the United States are impermissible without a FISA court warrant. In general, surveillance must be targeted in order to obtain such a warrant. But the FBI and National Security Agency wanted to engage in the newer practice of data mining, the antithesis of a targeted effort. They intended to search a broad range of data in a continuing effort to find the needle in the data haystack.

To enable this collection, a legal theory was necessary. David Addington, legal counsel to Vice President Dick Cheney, engineered a legal basis to engage in the collection of metadata without the authority of the FISA court.[16] His justification was the national security power of the President. Three separate NSA lawyers approved the authorization order for the collection of domestic information without a warrant pursuant to the President's Article II authority. Article II, Section 2 of the U.S. Constitution reposes military authority with the commander in chief. The scope of authority granted to the President by these NSA attorneys' interpretations has yet to be disclosed. However, former Deputy

Assistant U.S. Attorney General John Yoo has posited two inter-pretations.[17] First, he has argued that the wording of the Fourth Amendment leaves open the possibility of reasonable warrantless searches. Secondly, he has claimed that the restriction on unreason-able search and seizure does not govern wartime operations. The administration of this new program, known only to a handful of people under the code name Stellar Wind, was left to the NSA.

Stellar Wind gathered phone and Internet traffic from U.S. citi-zens and searched it for any suspicious activity. The technology was based upon an earlier prototype code-named ThinThread.[18] But whereas ThinThread had built-in privacy protections that ano-nymized the source of captured communications, those protections were stripped out in Stellar Wind. In other words, communications derived from U.S. persons were no longer encrypted, and a court order was no longer required to disclose the identity behind any communications. Whereas prior surveillance programs included only communications where either the sender or recipient was out-side the United States, Stellar Wind tracked communications that both originated and terminated within the United States. It is deba-table exactly how clearly or how fully this program was described to members of Congress. We now know that under Stellar Wind, the government was conducting warrantless and personally identifiable domestic searches of personal communications of American citizens.

In response to questions about overreaching surveillance, there was always the possibility that a limitation on surveillance could result in the loss of American lives in another 9/11. Nonetheless, there was internal dissension over the constitutionality of Stellar Wind and other domestic surveillance programs. In October 2001, shortly after 9/11, three NSA employees retired after refusing to use ThinThread technology domestically. One of those employ-ees later joined forces with a Republican congressional staffer on the House Intelligence Committee. Another NSA employee sepa-rately took his concerns to the NSA's general counsel and director.

After what he believed constituted retaliation for his questioning, he turned over unclassified domestic surveillance documents to a *Baltimore Sun* reporter.

Jack Goldsmith, the former head of the DOJ's Office of Legal Counsel and a true conservative, brought his objection to the e-mail collection directly to David Addington. James Comey, who was acting attorney general during General Ashcroft's illness, refused to sign a reauthorization of the domestic surveillance program until warrantless e-mail data collection came to a stop. Alberto Gonzales, who was White House Counsel at the time, signed the reauthorization order in the attorney general's stead. This constitutionally vague action was made moot when the NSA Director later obtained a FISA order permitting the wholesale reinstitution of e-mail metadata collection.

Standing up for privacy is not a partisan or unpatriotic act. DOJ Attorney Thomas Tamm was heir to an FBI legacy; his uncle and father worked with J. Edgar Hoover. While preparing warrants, Tamm became concerned that the NSA conducted electronic surveillance on American citizens without warrants and then bootstrapped the information gathered to obtain FISA warrants. He was unable to persuade the NSA that these actions were illegal. He took his outrage to *The New York Times*.[19]

On December 16, 2005, James Risen and Eric Lichtblau of *The New York Times* wrote an article disclosing the phone and e-mail monitoring.[20] They had previously attempted to do so, but *Times* editors had acquiesced Bush administration requests to scuttle the story. Amid the public outrage subsequent to the disclosure of Stellar Wind, Congress passed the FISA Amendments Act of 2008 in an attempt to rein in warrantless activity. However, the act was largely criticized for its excessive loopholes. Just as the post–Church Committee reforms did not foresee the problems of the FISA courts, in the ongoing attempt to balance privacy and security, privacy lost again in 2008.

Even when the FISA Amendments Act was reauthorized in 2012, the Congressional Research Service noted, "[i]n at least two important ways, the standard that must be met . . . before the [Foreign Intelligence Surveillance Court] will issue an order authorizing an acquisition is less stringent than the standard that has been traditionally required under FISA."[21] The 2012 reauthorization did away with two significant requirements. First, FISA applications were no longer required to identify the facilities that would be subject to surveillance. Secondly, U.S. citizens could now be targeted even if they were not linked to international terrorism or clandestine activities. The roller-coaster evolution of surveillance and privacy policies in the United States has been crisis driven. As of 2012, it is fair to say that privacy protections in the surveillance area had not been significantly expanded in the last fifty years.

V. SECURITY AND PRIVACY THROUGH THE PRISM OF 2012

Enter Edward Snowden. In December 2012, Snowden reached out to journalist Glenn Greenwald via e-mail. Approximately six months later, Greenwald, documentary film director Laura Poitras, and *Guardian* correspondent Ewen MacAskill flew to Hong Kong to meet with Snowden in person. Snowden showed the journalists documents that directly contradicted earlier Senate testimony of Director of National Intelligence James Clapper. On June 5, 2013, *The Guardian* published a story by Greenwald, which detailed a secret court order requiring Verizon to disclose to the NSA all telephone calls in its systems, including phone numbers of both parties to a call, location data, call duration, and other unique identifiers.[22]

Just two days later, *The Washington Post* published an article by Barton Gellman and Laura Poitras outlining the PRISM program.[23] PRISM allowed the NSA and FBI to extract "audio and video chats, photographs, e-mails, documents, and connection logs" directly from the servers of nine U.S. Internet service providers. PRISMS's Internet providers were Microsoft, Yahoo, Google, Facebook, Paltalk, YouTube, Skype, AOL, and Apple. In Snowden's first video interview with Greenwald and Poitras, he expressed his concern that the storage of communications content gives the government the ability to go back in time to "derive suspicion from an innocent life and paint anyone in the context of a wrongdoer."[24] Later it was discovered that PRISM went even further than the mere collection of metadata. It also collected the actual content of e-mails and other online communications and storage.[25]

On October 30, 2013, Gellman and Ashkan Soltani authored another *Washington Post* article, which claimed that the NSA and its British counterpart had been secretly capturing data from overseas fiber optic cables.[26] The program was code-named MUSCULAR. Whereas PRISM represented a disclosure of data pursuant to a court order, MUSCULAR was an outright hacking of Google and Yahoo's networks abroad. In one of the NSA presentations outlining MUSCULAR, a sketch of how the government overcomes Google's security systems is notated with a smiley face. Although Google and Yahoo officials expressed dismay at these revelations, by and large, telecommunications and Internet corporations have submitted themselves to FBI National Security Letters without challenge, even though such

> *I think it's important to recognize that you can't have 100 per cent security and also then have 100 per cent privacy and zero inconvenience.... In the abstract you can complain about Big Brother and how this is a potential program run amok, but when you actually look at the details then I think we've struck the right balance.*
>
> —President Barack Obama
> June 7, 2013

NSLs are not issued under the signature of an Article III judge. NSLs are comparable to administrative subpoenas in criminal investigations. The Patriot Act, which was signed in the wake of 9/11, greatly expanded the use of NSLs.[27] Previously, the threshold for NSL use required specific facts that showed that the target of the NSL was an agent of a foreign power. After the Patriot Act revision, the records sought needed only to be "'relevant' to an authorized investigation."

Another critical revelation is that NSLs were used to obtain intelligence from corporations. There was little resistance to NSLs, and ISPs became significant sources of information. Internet providers are an excellent source of information. Big providers such as Google and Facebook work hard to develop the best analytics about customers. That information is tremendously valuable to advertisers. The NSA utilized these advanced analytics to improve surveillance.

All of these revelations paint a frightening picture. Discussing these disclosures, President Obama described what we see in the privacy security conflict. His view was that it is impossible to have perfect security and absolute privacy. That statement is obviously true. The real issue is how to reach a reasonable balance.

The table below represents an effort to provide an overview of most of the known surveillance programs. This overview includes a description of the technological process employed by the NSA and its subsidiaries to retrieve the data, the manner in which the technological process intrudes upon one's privacy, and the legal authority that is cited to justify the actions.

The technological processes discussed feature not only the programs that target specific individuals, but also the broader data collections and efforts to weaken encryption platforms. The totality of these programs demonstrates the extensive amount of information available to the government and the substantial efforts exerted to collect it. This breadth and sum of the parts represent an unprecedented gathering of data on citizens by the U.S. government.

The programs described below rely primarily on the guidelines established by three sources: Executive Order 12333, the Patriot Act, and the Foreign Intelligence Surveillance Act.

EXECUTIVE ORDER 12333

Issued by Ronald Reagan in 1981, EO 12333 governs the collection of foreign intelligence by American intelligence agencies.[28] Under EO 12333, these agencies can only collect intelligence on American citizens with the approval of the attorney general. This approval is further contingent on the collection meeting one of the following categories: information that is publicly given or given with consent; information obtained during the course of a lawful foreign intelligence, counterintelligence, international counternarcotics, or international counterterrorism investigation; information necessary to preserve the safety of persons or organizations; information obtained from persons reasonably believed to be potential sources or contacts in order to determine credibility; information necessary to protect intelligence sources and methods; and information incidentally collected that may indicate involvement in activities that violate federal law.

PATRIOT ACT

Passed by Congress in 2001 in response to the 9/11 terrorist attacks, Title II of the Patriot Act increased government agencies' powers of surveillance.[29] Section 215 expands agency access to telephony (and potentially Internet) metadata under the FISA business records provision to include "tangible things" relevant to an investigation of a foreign target. This section authorizes the collection of phone records. Section 505 permits the issuance of NSLs in order to obtain information deemed relevant to national security investigations.

FOREIGN INTELLIGENCE SURVEILLANCE ACT

Signed into law in 1978, FISA establishes the guidelines for foreign collection intelligence.[30] Congress has since amended FISA to include Title VII, 702, 703, and 704. Section 702 specifies the guidelines for collecting data of non-U.S. citizens. Specifically, Section 702 allows the targeting of any individual reasonably believed to be located outside of the United States. The section also specifies that these organizations cannot *intentionally* target any American citizen. Sections 703 and 704 discuss the targeting of Americans overseas. These sections authorize the warrantless surveillance of Americans located abroad.[31] The Foreign Intelligence Surveillance Court, which is not subject to public view, then oversees these FISA collections. The overwhelming majority of the government's requests for warrants are granted, leading one to question whether it really provides adequate oversight as opposed to the mere appearance of legitimacy.[32]

SUMMARY OF SURVEILLANCE PROGRAMS			
PROGRAM NAME	TECHNOLOGICAL PROCESS	IMPACT ON PRIVACY	LEGAL JUSTIFICATION
Stellar Wind (also known as The Program)	Bulk metadata collection of American phone calls and Internet traffic.[33]	Until 2011, the NSA could collect information about Americans' phone calls and e-mail messages without receiving individual warrants. This information includes whom you called and e-mailed.	FISA court The Constitution does not apply because there is no reasonable expectation of privacy for Americans.

SUMMARY OF SURVEILLANCE PROGRAMS			
PROGRAM NAME	TECHNOLOGICAL PROCESS	IMPACT ON PRIVACY	LEGAL JUSTIFICATION
PRISM	Direct content extraction by the NSA from the servers of data providers. Program was initiated with apparent consent of Microsoft, Yahoo, Google, Facebook, Paltalk, YouTube, Skype, AOL, and Facebook.[34]	NSA can collect shared content (e.g., e-mails, chats, videos, photos, stored data, voice-over Internet protocol, file transfers, videoconferencing, log-ins, and social networking details) of any individual— American or foreign—sharing content with anyone reasonably believed to be outside the United States. This collection can occur without individual court orders or authorization from the service providers.	"Legally compelled collection" and "cooperation"[35] Sec. 702 FISA[36] The Constitution does not apply because there is no reasonable expectation of privacy for Americans.
Upstream Undersea Cable Tapping (OAKSTAR, STORM-BREW, BLARNEY, and Fairview);	A joint NSA and British Government Communications Headquarters Program (GCHQ) that the NSA may	Cable communications collected include phone call recordings, e-mail messages, Internet history, and Facebook content. The NSA makes	Sec. 702 FISA[39] The Constitution does not apply because the actions take

Continued

SUMMARY OF SURVEILLANCE PROGRAMS			
PROGRAM NAME	TECHNOLOGICAL PROCESS	IMPACT ON PRIVACY	LEGAL JUSTIFICATION
(Tempora [in the UK])	access. Using intercept probes and physical taps, the organizations access undersea fiber optic cables throughout the world with occasional permission of the nearest country and intercept cable communications. Data is preserved for three days and metadata is stored for thirty days. Mass Volume Reduction is used to filter the data with the help of thousands of selectors.[37]	a copy of everything collected, searches through this data using selectors and target information, and then stores the data that matches. There also appears to be no distinction between innocent individuals and targeted suspects.[38]	place outside the United States.
Cell Phone Records (RAGTIME and MARINA)	Court order requiring the provision of electronic copies of "telephony metadata" in bulk to the NSA by Verizon.[40] This data is then stored in an NSA database.[41]	Verizon provides the NSA with information in bulk about phone calls (e.g., location, length, and session identifying information) placed by U.S. citizens. The	Sec. 215 Patriot Act: a FISA court order falls under FISA "business records" provision 50 USC § 1861. The Constitution does not

SUMMARY OF SURVEILLANCE PROGRAMS			
PROGRAM NAME	TECHNOLOGICAL PROCESS	IMPACT ON PRIVACY	LEGAL JUSTIFICATION
		order allows this collection to occur without any evidence of wrongdoing by the caller or the person being called. The NSA can then search through these results within three hops of a preapproved seed number connected to a foreign terrorist organization. Individual warrants are not required to collect the information.[42] However, the NSA supposedly would need an additional warrant to access the data.[43]	apply because (i) there is no reasonable expectation of privacy for Americans; and (ii) foreign targets do not receive constitutional protections.
CO-TRAVELER	To perform "target development," the NSA taps into global cable network connections (i.e., telephony links) and intercepts	Allows the NSA to track locations of mobile users—including those suspected of no wrongdoing who are inadvertently included in	EO 12333[45] The Constitution does not apply because (i) there is no reasonable expectation of

Continued

SUMMARY OF SURVEILLANCE PROGRAMS			
PROGRAM NAME	TECHNOLOGICAL PROCESS	IMPACT ON PRIVACY	LEGAL JUSTIFICATION
	data pertaining to the location of cell phones through cellular networks, GPS, Wi-Fi, and triangulation.[44]	the data sweep— in order to locate unknown associates of targeted suspects.	privacy for Americans; and (ii) foreign targets do not receive constitutional protections.
MUSCULAR	Extraction of unencrypted data in bulk from Google and Yahoo's overseas fiber optic cables by hacking into their internal networks, supposedly without the authorization of the Internet service providers. After being copied, the data is then filtered and stored.[46]	Despite the existence of PRISM, the NSA extended its collection of Internet metadata from over a million users of the two providers. This allows the NSA to copy data and content in real time without the knowledge or permission of the providers.[47]	Attorney general approved processes[48] The Constitution does not apply because (i) there is no reasonable expectation of privacy for Americans; and (ii) foreign targets do not receive constitutional protections.
XKEYSCORE	Using over 700 servers, this program indexes unfiltered metadata from other data extractions into tables and provides the	Allows the NSA to retrospectively search through their bulk data collection for any type of information (e.g., a telephone number, name, or an	Unknown

SUMMARY OF SURVEILLANCE PROGRAMS			
PROGRAM NAME	TECHNOLOGICAL PROCESS	IMPACT ON PRIVACY	LEGAL JUSTIFICATION
	ability to perform strong-selector searches.[49]	individual's Google searches) without a warrant. This program also provides the NSA with the ability to conduct a much more effective and specific search within its massive storage of data. These searches are conducted by NSA analysts who select a "foreign factor" to bypass a FISA court warrant.[50]	
Boundless Informant	Tracks, categorizes, and maps NSA collections of metadata by geographical location.[51]	Those with access to the program can select a country on the map and view the amount and type of information collected by the NSA within the country.	The Constitution does not apply because foreign targets do not receive constitutional protections.
MYSTIC and SOMALGET	Interception, recording, and archiving of the telecommunications of select countries.[52]	While MYSTIC only provides the NSA with the power to collect metadata from the selected	EO 12333 The Constitution does not apply because foreign targets

Continued

SUMMARY OF SURVEILLANCE PROGRAMS			
PROGRAM NAME	TECHNOLOGICAL PROCESS	IMPACT ON PRIVACY	LEGAL JUSTIFICATION
		countries, SOMALGET provides access to the actual content of every phone conversation in the Bahamas and one additional unnamed country (speculated to be Afghanistan). The NSA is also seeking to expand SOMALGET to include more countries.	do not receive constitutional protections.
SIGINT Enabling Project and Egotistical-Giraffe	Digital insertion of vulnerabilities into encryption systems, IT networks, and Tor.[53]	Weakens encryption systems utilized by network providers and Internet users to protect private data.[54]	Unknown
Follow the Money	Collection of financial data.[55]	Monitoring of international payments and banking and credit card transactions.	Unknown

The Constitution does not apply because foreign targets do not receive constitutional protections. |

SUMMARY OF SURVEILLANCE PROGRAMS			
PROGRAM NAME	TECHNOLOGICAL PROCESS	IMPACT ON PRIVACY	LEGAL JUSTIFICATION
National Security Letters	After an ISP or phone company receives an NSL, they are required to submit user profile information to the FBI.[56]	While the law supposedly limits the FBI from content such as e-mail or text messages, the companies are usually under a gag order and cannot alert their users that this information has been shared.	18 USC § 2709— expanded by Sec. 505 Patriot Act[57] USCA Second Circuit held § 2709(c) and § 3511(b) unconstitutional based on their lack of judicial oversight for the nondisclosure requirements.[58]

Together, these programs have the capability to form a comprehensive electronic profile on any American citizen. This profile includes different types of data:

1. Public information on an individual in public records, the press, and open Web sites
2. Personal communications (e-mail, text, Twitter, cell phone)
3. Internet usage including site visits (Google)
4. Commercial internet use including purchases and contractual disclosures (Amazon)
5. Social media sites (Facebook)
6. Location information (cell phone locator, GPS)
7. Nonpublic stored information (medical records, financial records)

Each program relates to this data in a distinct way. There are also varying levels of intrusion and legality. For example, PRISM, upstream cable tapping, and XKEYSCORE all extract or analyze data from social networks like Facebook. This data is obtained in one of three ways: NSL/FISA warrant, private agreement between the government and the Internet company, or hacking into the system. We know that Facebook can be legally compelled to hand over user metadata and content if they are served with an NSL or a FISA warrant. Facebook can also enter into a private agreement with the government and allow them direct access to their servers. The government could even hack into its internal networks and extract data without its knowledge or consent as is presumably done in MUSCULAR with Google and Yahoo. How much access Facebook gives to the government remains unknown. The PRISM slides that Snowden leaked indicate that the NSA has direct access to Facebook servers. They also indicate that this extraction is done with the cooperation of Facebook and is not necessarily the product of a FISA warrant or NSL. Facebook has ardently denied that the NSA has direct access to their servers, but admits that they comply with individual warrants.[59]

Can the government really do that? This is the question that crossed every American's mind when he or she heard of the Snowden leaks. Even if the motivations were noble, at some point warrantless and random collection of personal information steps over the line. Of course not all surveillance is illegal, and intelligence gathering is a necessity. The following legal principles support surveillance activities:

- The surveillance is conducted on foreign soil.
- The information gathered does not contain information subject to a reasonable expectation of privacy.
- The information gathered is necessary to protect national security.

As a baseline, our historic conception of surveillance involved spying on the "enemy." The enemy was a foreign power. Of course the United States wanted to find out the war secrets of Nazi Germany. The public perception of spies included images of James Bond and Mata Hari. Conducting surveillance of foreign enemies on foreign soil was expected. Today the dominant profile of a spy is different. The new master spies are faceless computer geeks like Edward Snowden. They use PRISM and MUSCULAR to sweep up information about foreigners and Americans alike in searching for a terrorist needle in the haystack. Remember, the Constitution protects Americans from warrantless searches—it does not prohibit surveillance on foreign soil. What happens when otherwise constitutional surveillance conducted on "foreign soil" contains data on American citizens? Obviously, global Internet surveillance changes the impact of foreign surveillance.

The government is not spying if it simply collects publicly available information. When a citizen voluntarily discloses information, he or she generally abandons a reasonable expectation of privacy in that information. There are some fundamental flaws in the current legal definition of voluntarily abandoning information. For example, the current state of the law dictates that there is no reasonable expectation of privacy in certain bank records and phone logs that have been "voluntarily" disclosed to third parties. Is it rational to hold that all disclosures to third parties represent a conscious acquiescence to make that information available to the NSA?

Another legal justification to allow collection of information for surveillance is the straightforward assertion of the "special needs" of government to protect national security. After 9/11, at least one court recognized potential terrorist activity as one of these "special needs."[60] The justification of national security may have the broadest implications. Since 9/11, our concept of national security includes protecting domestic locations within the United States. The motivation of national security and the availability of new technology have enabled the surveillance environment in which we find ourselves today, but there has always been a motivation for national security and a thirst to use the new technology of the time.

Is the situation today more extreme and difficult than ever before? Yes, based on global terrorism issues and unprecedented technology.

There are multiple contradictions among statements by the NSA, ISPs, and stories based on Snowden's leaks. As of this writing, there is no final definitive determination about the methods, techniques, and extent of surveillance. The analysis here is based primarily on the Snowden leaks and official statements by government agents.

> I'm glad that the NSA is trying to find out what the terrorists are up to overseas and in our country. I'm glad that activity is going on, but it is limited to tracking people who are suspected to be terrorists and who they may be talking to. . . . Yes, I am sure that that's what they're doing.
>
> —Senator Lindsey Graham
> June 6, 2013

How do these programs actually affect the average American citizen or company? The NSA stresses that the only Americans that should be worried are either terrorists or those who contact terrorists. Recent reports indicate that the majority of data being collected concerns nonsuspects whose information is swept up indiscriminately. And nearly half of this bulk of information is from American citizens.[61] Geoffrey R. Stone, a legal scholar and member of the President's Review Group, emphasized that no American's data is being accessed unless there are connections between him or her and a suspected terrorist target.[62] However, this statement paints an incomplete, if not dishonest, picture. The actual operation of these programs is better demonstrated by hypothetical stories that describe the interrelationships of programs and how they could affect real people.

THREE HOP JANE DOE: SEARCH

Wake up with your Verizon phone fully charged. Text message a friend who is reasonably believed to be outside the United States and who happens to be under surveillance as part of a contact chain. Your contact is the second hop from the original suspected terrorist target. You are the third hop. This information alone targets you as a suspect. The data sweep begins. CO-TRAVELER tracks your location through your phone throughout the day. PRISM collects your Gmail messages and tagged Facebook photos. Verizon has provided your call records to the NSA for years and the NSA can now potentially access the data because of your text message. After realizing the breadth of metadata collected on you over time, an NSA programmer uses XKEYSCORE to search through this collected data retroactively and review all of your Google searches for the past five years. Innocent searches about TSA regulations, meth labs, or breathing techniques that were made to allay your curiosity or solve an argument suddenly become incriminating. Your prior efforts and use of Tor to encrypt your data are rendered useless because of EgotisticalGiraffe and other NSA efforts to weaken encryption programs. This analysis continues until you are cleared—if you are ever cleared.

INCIDENTAL SWEEP JOHN DOE: COLLECTION

Throughout the day, John Doe constantly shares information that is incidentally swept into one of the NSA's servers. The NSA collects his Verizon phone records daily and saves this information for five years. If John calls a relative in the Bahamas or a patriotic friend serving in Afghanistan, the entire content of his phone conversation is recorded and archived. Any additional Internet communication he conducts with a foreign person or server is collected in real time by the undersea fiber optic cables. This content is then copied, searched, and potentially stored for up to thirty days.

PROFILE OF ISP DOE, INC.: COMPLIANCE

Doe, Inc., is a small Internet service provider that offers its users an encrypted platform to send e-mails, chat with friends, and store photos and videos. Using its Section 702 FISA powers, the NSA compelled Doe, Inc., to cooperate with the investigation of a specific terrorist target. While Doe, Inc., prioritizes the privacy of their users, the national security concern appeared too vast to disregard. The information that the NSA needed only infringed upon one user's information. Doe, Inc., begrudgingly complied. A couple of months later, Doe, Inc., received a National Security Letter that required the ISP to submit the content of 150 Doe, Inc., users. Doe, Inc., viewed this request as illegal, but the NSL directs them to contact no one and not seek legal advice. Knowing no other option, Doe, Inc., obeyed and then shut down its service forever in fear of future requests made by the NSA.

VI. PREDICTING AND PREVENTING CRIMES—IS MINORITY REPORT THE NEXT STEP?

In the wake of some of the tragedies documented by social media in recent years, officials discovered confession videos and Facebook entries that either predicted or threatened the tragedy to come: students promised to hurt others or themselves, or worse, cried out for help when none was forthcoming. Sometimes the documentation simply suggests the pending tragedy by showing pieces of it coming together: a search for how to build a bomb coupled with a Google map result for street views of a city park. If the government has enough information to indicate that an individual is going to bomb the Boston Marathon, should the authorities stop him before he does it?

Predicting future human behavior is increasingly valued, particularly as understanding consumer behavior becomes the holy grail of Internet search engines and marketers. The defense contractor Raytheon has also developed a program that uses social networking data to track people's movements and predict future behavior. The Rapid Information Overlay Technology (RIOT) uses GPS from photographs posted on Facebook and Foursquare check-ins to determine where individuals have been and where they will likely go in the future. Raytheon has not sold RIOT to any clients, but has shared its technology with the U.S. government.[63] Amazon recently gained a patent for anticipatory shipping. The company is so sure about what we are going to buy that it plans to ship it to us before we order it.[64] Why not use the same tools to predict and thereby prevent criminal behavior?

> We have a system of pervasive, pre-criminal surveillance where the government wants to watch what you're doing just to see what you're up to, to see what you're thinking, even behind closed doors.
>
> —Edward Snowden
> May 29, 2014

Of course trying to punish individuals *before* they actually commit a crime is tricky business. Thankfully we are not living in the sci-fi dystopia of Steven Spielberg's film *Minority Report*. The 2002 film portrayed a United States in 2054 where "precrime police" in D.C. worked with preventive government to protect citizens. They stopped murders before they happened with the help of "precogs" and computers. As long as the "precrime" system was 100 percent correct, the public supported it and there seemed to be no more murders. When the fictional system in *Minority Report* was found to be flawed, it collapsed. There may be a logical appeal or longing for a perfect system that prevents all crime and terrorism. Using the name "Minority Report" is simply a reminder that perfection is elusive.

In order to prevent terrorist acts amid rapidly advancing technology, there is a need for rational assessment of future surveillance actions. If predictive technology is deemed accurate, then most people would likely support employing it to prevent crime. The issue then becomes the degree of accuracy of the prediction.

The government currently has technology that provides predictions on criminal behavior. The Department of Homeland Security developed Future Attribute Screening Technology (FAST) and tested it publicly in 2011. FAST uses sensors and video and audio recordings to assess the probability that an individual—not yet suspected of any crime—will commit a crime in the future. These sensors and recordings evaluate an individual's psychophysiological signals to determine malintent. This behavioral biometric data includes cardiovascular signals, pheromones, skin conductivity, eyeblink rate, and respiratory patterns. The public field test occurred in an undisclosed location in the Northeast. The details of the field test have not been disclosed, but a 2011 Privacy Impact Assessment discussed limited operational tests planned to occur in large public places—temporarily closed to the public—where volunteers would undergo screenings (image alone, questions alone, or images and questions combined).[65] While the DHS did not reveal the results of the public test, it has reported a success rate of 70 percent in its lab tests.[66] The evolution of this program from lab tests and volunteer participation to public tests signifies the continued development of the predictive incident avoidance agenda.

Although the Snowden disclosures did not focus on any specific predictive preventive programs, another NSA employee revealed the NSA program AQUAINT (Advanced Question

Answering for Intelligence) in 2009. This artificial intelligence system uses the massive amount of data shared on the Internet (and likely already collected by the NSA) to answer predictive questions about future events. The unnamed researcher, who quit for moral reasons related to AQUAINT, explained that the system is incredibly similar to the robot HAL 9000 from *2001: A Space Odyssey*. In addition, and similar to AQUAINT, the Center for Advanced Study of Language (CASL) has initiated a program that seeks to determine whether a person is lying by studying his behavior and listening to him speak.[67] CASL is a national security research lab accessible to the NSA.[68] Snowden worked at CASL as a security specialist in 2005 before he worked as a private contractor for the NSA.[69]

> *Think of 2001: A Space Odyssey and the most memorable character, HAL 9000, having a conversation with David. We are essentially building this system. We are building HAL.*
>
> —former NSA employee

The use of predictive programs to avert future crimes is rationally appealing in many ways. Obviously there are major risks relating to accuracy or abuse. We are now aware that bulk data collection was used to construct search warrants. The existence of so much data coupled with enhanced predictive coding could move a search warrant up to an arrest warrant. Luckily, no identified "precrime" program has yet been disclosed.

The motivation to stop crime and terrorist events is strong, and technology is certainly able to make better predictions than ever. The ability to predict is well established and well honored. Based on evidence about the behavior of different celestial bodies, astrophysicists mathematically predicted the existence of Neptune before it was observed.

In a precrime analysis, if surveillance of a suspected terrorist operative indicated that he had trained for bomb making, acquired bomb materials, was diagnosed as psychotic, had threatened to bomb a stadium, and had two tickets to a football game for the next day, he would likely be detained. As a matter of perspective, even crimes that have already occurred are often hard to solve. Crimes are also difficult to stop even with today's best technology.

By the time of the Boston Marathon bombing, Boston had a comprehensive CCTV network, with some 500 cameras mounted throughout the city. Omnipresent surveillance did not deter the Boston bombers from detonating their homemade bombs near the finish line. In the hours following the bombing, local, state, and national intelligence and security officials combed through hundreds of hours of footage captured by CCTV cameras near the bombing site. This terrorist attack was the first committed in a place with comprehensive surveillance and with the tools to search suspects' Facebook pages, Twitter feeds, geolocation posts, and blog posts. Technology provided real advantages to the investigation. In addition, thousands of Bostonians and others across the world viewed images and contributed resources through crowdsourcing. Yet the first suspects identified were the wrong people.

A combination of media, technology, and the crowdsourcing element contributed to the wrongful identification of these individuals as the perpetrators; then it published their pictures. Ultimately technology played a major role in indentifying Dzhokhar and Tamerlan Tsarnaev as the principal suspects. Even comprehensive surveillance will not deter a determined or suicidal terrorist. Second, technology does not always provide an instant or accurate answer. Third, technology and surveillance can nonetheless be useful in uncovering and proving a crime.

The Snowden disclosures have opened the programs described above to serious scrutiny. Some of the programs are apparent intrusions and give us motivation to analyze rational approaches to reforms that protect privacy and national security. They also challenge us to consider the overzealous extension of modern technology, and whether it might deeply harm our personal freedoms.

VII. SHORT-TERM REACTIONS TO THE DISCLOSURES OF 2012

The disclosures beginning in 2012 generated a series of responses to the actions of the NSA as well as efforts to remedy perceived privacy intrusions. In May 2014, the House passed a gutted version of the USA Freedom Act. That proposal lost support from the Electronic Frontier Foundation and major Internet companies because it does little to prevent bulk data collection. In December 2013, the U.S. District Court for the District of Columbia held that the *Smith v. Maryland* case that allows the collection of certain targeted data entrusted to a third party without a warrant does not apply to bulk data collection.[70] *Smith*, which was decided in 1979, has been used as the primary legal basis to review data "voluntarily" disclosed to a third party. There, the Supreme Court reasoned that there was not a reasonable expectation of privacy in a warrantless search of pen registers.[71] Pen registers are records of phone calls from landlines. Although it has been treated as precedent, in many ways this case symbolizes the law's failure to catch up with reality and new technology. In 1979, there was no Internet, and there were no cell phones, and no programs that could easily collect, aggregate, and analyze masses of information.

In *Klayman*, Judge Richard Leon reasoned that this long-term collection and analysis likely violates the Fourth Amendment and our reasonable expectation of privacy. Other cases dealing with the modern aggregation of data such as warrantless GPS tracking and warrantless review of smartphones show that the law is changing to catch up with the times. It is time to view the *Smith* holding as obsolete.

Perhaps the most important case regarding the data privacy of citizens was the previously mentioned Supreme Court ruling in *Riley* that the search and seizure of a cell phone's digital data is unconstitutional. The fact that the aggregation of sensitive personal data on a cell phone cannot be obtained without a warrant sends a message to the legal system. Even though the case applied to a criminal search and not the more compelling purpose of national security, the logic is the same as applied to protect surveillance of bulk data. Both types of aggregated personal data create an intrusive personal mosaic.

The information affected corporations as well. The Snowden disclosures—particularly the tech industry's involvement with NSA—have led several Internet companies to invest in better encryption services. In June 2014, Google even announced a new Chrome extension, End-To-End, that encrypts sent messages with an easier process than the other PGP and GnuPG encryption software. They also released the code before the official extension was available on the Chrome Web store and offered financial awards to anyone who finds a security defect in the code.[72]

Following the PRISM disclosures, Mark Zuckerberg wrote on his Facebook page that "it's up to us—all of us—to build the internet we want. Together, we can build a space that is greater and a more important part of the world than anything we have today, but is also safe and secure."[73] However, the competition to feed the information race is fierce, and it continues to drive innovations that feed on consumer privacy. For instance, more recently, Facebook faced scrutiny after releasing a new feature for their app that uses your phone's microphone to listen to the background noise to determine what television show you are watching or song you are listening to.[74]

All these reactions show that policy makers, courts, citizens, and corporations are struggling with the new realities without a clear outcome.

VIII. THE FUTURE: PROTECTING THE HOMELAND AND THE HAYSTACK

Spying, surveillance, and privacy are different in the twenty-first century. They are different because the "enemy" is different, technology is different, and society is different. First, there are domestic and foreign terrorists in the United States who play by their own rules. Second, new technology gives the terrorists more options and also provides us with more options for surveillance. Third, today's global society is dominated by technology and gathers more information than at any time in history.

The intense focus brought by the Snowden disclosures provides a moment in time to reflect on two predominant themes of modern life—national security and individual privacy in the technology age. The 9/11 tragedies raised the stakes for security and the Snowden disclosures have raised the visibility of privacy. No doubt there will be "reform." There is sufficient outcry that something will happen. Congress will pass a bill with a well-designed acronym (Uniting and Strengthening America by Fulfilling Rights and Ending Eavesdropping, Dragnet Collection, and Online Monitoring Act, for example). Agencies will provide new processes to guard against abuses and future Snowdens. Reforms, even when well intended, sometimes turn out well and sometimes do not. Some argue the well-intended FISA courts that were part of the Church Committee's reforms in 1978 have ended up allowing abuses under the appearance of court review.

The reforms under way will ultimately be judged by their ability to protect the public from danger and restore the public's faith. There are a variety of stakeholders that want faith restored, including the Internet companies that rely on public acceptance and use. From my point of view reform should focus in four areas:

1. Establish transparency in domestic surveillance.
2. Provide for effective, independent, and trustworthy oversight of surveillance.
3. Design a whistleblower system that will encourage the disclosure of abuse, but still protect national security.
4. Define rational limits of search and seizure law that protects citizens in the new technical world.

Rational, effective, and pragmatic remedies are hard. As previously mentioned, there is no option for absolute security and total privacy. Real solutions must recognize that reality. However, there must be a balance restored to protect the privacy and dignity of U.S. citizens and restore faith in the systems that protect us. We must accept that rational solutions should not abandon surveillance or disclose every surveillance program used by the United States. Legitimate foreign surveillance of foreign enemies can still exist. We should not have to ask permission from the Taliban to tap their communications or surveil their operations with drones.

The Snowden disclosures renewed focus and interest on overreaching government surveillance and privacy intrusions. However, the interest in security has not disappeared. Citizens want protection from the Boston and Oklahoma City bombers just as well as the foreign-based 9/11 terrorists, but the process of sifting through the haystack of communications and data to thwart domestic and foreign terrorists should be able to still honor the U.S. Constitution and its principles. Our legal system and criminal justice system should be agile enough to perform needed searches of citizens in a constitutional way.

There are four major categories of reform that can better protect privacy and still recognize the importance of national security. Overall, these reforms seek to increase transparency of domestic surveillance, provide trustworthy oversight of intelligence and surveillance programs, improve whistleblower processes to disclose abuses, but protect national security, and finally, seek a constitutional standard that actually protects U.S. citizens from surveillance intrusions.

Congress has the authority to respond to many of the claims of privacy intrusions. They can amend or further define the authority to gather domestic intelligence and address the policy changes discussed below. In fact, at the time of this writing there are proposed legislative solutions that deal with some of these issues. One version of the USA Freedom Act would ban the bulk collection of Americans' personal data. The details and definitions are important. For example, a "specific selection term" is an important definition because that term defines the scope of a surveillance warrant. Can a "selection term" allow the surveillance of a whole geographic region, like a city? While the House's version defined "specific selection term" broadly,[75] the draft Senate version at the time of this writing narrows the definition and specifically prohibits the collection of entire geographic regions or particular service providers.[76]

The basic principles relating to reform of our intelligence system are fairly straightforward. Be transparent, avoid intruding on U.S. persons, and review the legal process that authorizes surveillance.[77] Those issues are being considered by Congress. If legislative reforms fail or fall short, legal challenges to surveillance policies may well define the constitutional boundaries of surveillance. Ultimately, the Constitution itself defines the limits of government surveillance, and the courts are perfectly capable of enforcing those boundaries. This option is further discussed below in the analysis of the rational constitutional limits on government surveillance.

1. Establish Transparency in Domestic Surveillance

Snowden's leaks identified secret government intrusions on American citizens. A central need for restoring public faith is for the U.S.

government to tell its citizens why it is conducting domestic surveillance and how. Of course there cannot be public disclosures about secrets dealing with foreign and enemy intelligence. No rational British citizen was upset that his or her government failed to disclose that it possessed technology to crack German "Enigma" communications during World War II.[78] Americans can hardly complain about their government's methods of surveilling international actors when those actions identify and locate potential and known terrorist threats. However, there are true constitutional limits when it comes to surveillance of American citizens. That constitutional limit is discussed more extensively below. This issue of transparency is about telling the truth about how our government is conducting itself. As it stands now, after the Snowden disclosures and before major reforms are in place, the American public does not know or trust the surveillance system.

In 2013, the Office of the Director of National Intelligence and the Department of Justice explicitly recognized the need for transparency. They said there was a need for the public to have an "understanding of how the Intelligence Community uses the legal authorities provided by Congress to conduct surveillance and gather foreign intelligence."[79] They also articulated the "need not to disclose information that our adversaries could exploit to evade surveillance and harm our national security."

There is some public disclosure based on a post-Snowden presidential directive. The Office of the Director of National Intelligence's Civil Liberties and Privacy Office now publishes guidelines for protecting privacy when gathering intelligence[80] and releases an annual report, describing the nature of intelligence agencies' surveillance programs.[81] This information includes data on the number of targets and the definition of an intelligence target. This information is declassified and published online. The ultimate issue is what is future policy for the disclosure of domestic surveillance.

The goal of transparency is to disclose the truth and to promote public understanding and trust. Therefore, disclosures must indeed be accurate. By disclosing the rules of the game to the public, Congress, an oversight agency, or a whistleblower can point to acts that exceed and violate rational policies to protect privacy. Compare that with the current situation, where citizens were not told of surveillance policies and then discovered that the secret and intrusive policies were being legally justified or legally approved by the FISA court. If the future policies are transparent, we can evaluate those justifications for ourselves rather than having blanket domestic surveillance determined in secret.

2. Provide for Effective Independent Oversight of Intelligence Activities

An important element of having a clear policy for domestic surveillance is to have reasonable and independent oversight of surveillance actions to assure compliance. Two groups currently oversee surveillance activities that are otherwise secret: members of the Privacy and Civil Liberties Oversight Board (PCLOB) and the federal judges who sit on the FISA court. Additionally, leaders of the intelligence community brief congressional intelligence and judiciary committees on their surveillance activities. Congress is also required to authorize mass data collection activities under Section 215 of the Patriot Act. Despite congressional approval and oversight, the discovery of the current ongoing domestic surveillance activities has been a shock to the American people. Perhaps as big a shock to Congress was that the CIA surveilled the computers of staffers on the Senate Intelligence Committee, the congressional committee charged with direct oversight of the intelligence community.[82] Therefore, the restoration of public trust is going to require more or different oversight.

The PCLOB has released reports on NSA and other agency compliance with Section 702 of the Foreign Intelligence Surveillance Act. It is generally tasked with balancing civil liberties and surveillance. Reviews have been mixed. Its reports indicate that many surveillance activities of Internet communications were in compliance.[83] However, the report also indicated that outside of Section 702's "fundamental core," certain practices "push the program close to the line of constitutional reasonableness." The fundamental core is collection of foreign intelligence, but other practices go beyond that. The analysis of the constitutional issue is greatly limited by the fact that the board was unable to evaluate "the unknown and potentially large scope" of Section 702's incidental collection of U.S. persons' data. In other words, the board was not informed of the full impact of the government's "incidental collection." The oversight impact of the PCLOB is defined by two indisputable shortcomings. First, they have no authority to implement or control policy. Second, they apparently do not or cannot consider the full scope of government surveillance. The reports are, however, important and useful in understanding intelligence activities.

The FISA court, which the Church Committee created in 1978, consists of eleven federal judges appointed by the Chief Justice of the United States. It has been the principal authority to approve surveillance activities. Statistics show the court approved the overwhelming majority of surveillance proposals that have been part of the disclosures that offended many Americans.[84] Further, detractors criticize the makeup of the court and suggest a change in the appointments process. For instance, one critic of the current FISA court system, Connecticut Senator Richard Blumenthal, has proposed increasing the number of judges on the court from eleven to thirteen, and shifting the appointment power from the Chief Justice of the United States to the chief judges of the eleven circuit courts of appeals.[85]

Equally important to some structural reform in the FISA court is the scope of jurisdiction of that court in approving surveillance activities. In other words, legislation may prohibit or limit the FISA court's jurisdiction to grant bulk domestic warrants. Another proposal, suggested by President Obama, would add an adversary requirement to the FISA court.[86] This option provides a counterbalance in situations where a zealous advocate for a broad surveillance request would need to respond to an advocate who might question the breadth and constitutionality of a domestic request.

Oversight is critical in the post-Snowden era. But oversight in the form of a nonadversarial court review system, such as the present FISA court system, has proven to be inadequate to protect privacy interests. Reform is needed, perhaps in the guise of the proposal advanced by Senator Blumenthal. The independent PCLOB is a promise of greater oversight, but the board's small budget and staff hamper its promise. Furthermore, since the President appoints all of its members, some might view the board as less than completely independent.

For an oversight function to help restore public faith, the policy to be overseen must be rational and supportable. The fact that the oversight board recently suggested that many NSA surveillance techniques were legal suggests to the general public that either the oversight or the laws are flawed. At this point, it may well be the latter.

3. Design a Whistleblower System That Will Encourage Disclosure of Abuse, But Still Protect National Security Secrets

Critics of Edward Snowden say he knew about internal whistleblower avenues at the NSA but chose to approach *The Guardian* for the greater possibility of international acclaim and notoriety. Supporters accept Snowden's argument that the NSA's internal whistleblower options were not effective. Irrespective of your view of Snowden, the existing whistleblower system is flawed. It did not attract Snowden nor did it work for Thomas Tamm. We should explore a better system that appeals to both the computer nerds and the patriotic Justice Department lawyers who might uncover unconstitutional or illegal violations. Many of the new spies and contractors are different. Spy agencies recruit from hacker conventions as much as or more than from the Ivy League. Some question the maturity of a few of these young genius hackers and spies. There are even credible stories of hiring cyber criminals and using their techniques to help law enforcement and spy agencies.[87] Remedies must recognize the nature of the people involved in the new intelligence game.

A new framework must acknowledge the dramatic failures of the current system over the last decade. Chief among them is access to the courts. Right now there is no external avenue for whistleblowers in the intelligence community. The first time a whistleblower has the opportunity to see a judge is after he or she is charged with a crime.[88] Post-Snowden reforms have included unguaranteed appellate opportunities to inspectors general of other intelligence communities, but they still fall well short of a workable framework. Two former NSA employees believe that Snowden's actions in terms of misappropriating vast amounts of confidential data was in part a reaction to their own previous failed attempts at whistleblowing within the system. William Binney and Thomas Drake experienced investigations and intimidation by armed FBI agents. The government ended up prosecuting Drake for violating the Espionage Act, although he settled for a misdemeanor plea bargain after the government withdrew the bulk of evidence it had planned to present.[89] Snowden recognized that he would need to physically possess the data in order for individuals to believe him.

Binney and Drake had several specific thoughts about what kind of system would work better. They wanted a lawyer and a court. While there should still be an internal inspectors general system for whistleblowers, there is an advantage to devising a process that allows a whistleblower to have private counsel and access to the courts. There is a well-established legal process that could be adapted to whistleblowers in the intelligence community.

The *qui tam* proceeding was devised to identify misconduct that cost the government money. Latin for "who as well," *qui tam* lawsuits originated in medieval England as a legal action against parties undermining the king. The action was brought on behalf of the king. We have no king. We have a government by the people. So, *qui tam* actions in the United States are brought to vindicate and protect the people rather than the crown. Since the passage of the 1863 federal False Claims Act in America, *qui tam* lawsuits have been a tool for citizens to "assist in the detection and prosecution of fraud against the government."[90] In a very real sense illegal acts of surveillance are a fraud against the government and its citizens.

The False Claims Act works. *Qui tam* actions recovered billions of dollars in wasteful spending over 150 years. The private party, or relator, is rewarded for identifying the fraud on government. He may recover 30 percent of the amount the government lost. The process allows the government to prosecute the fraud if it chooses. If it does, and thereby reduces the burden on the private citizen, that individual shares in the recovery because he or she alerted the government to the potential fraud. An important part of the *qui tam* remedy is the fact that attorneys' fees are paid if the fraud is proven and the government recovers. This facilitates the process of a whistleblower obtaining counsel. Another critical quality of the *qui tam* process is confidentiality.

An adaptation for security violations could be patterned after these confidentiality qualities. A *qui tam* claim is initially filed under seal, where the accusations and evidence supporting them are only made known to the court. The potential national security *qui tam* would allow the whistleblower to remain confidential, and provide an incentive to not disclose national secrets to the public, but to disclose the allegations to a court. This alternative would place review in the hands of a federal judge without compelling a whistleblower to go to his boss or his agency. He could go to his lawyer with the allegations of unlawful conduct. Even if the court ultimately found that no violations occurred, the federal Whistleblower Protection Act of 1989 could be amended to offer protection from current or future employment retaliation to whistleblowers who exercised their rights under the privacy *qui tam* system.[91]

Rather than proving the government has been injured or defrauded, a privacy *qui tam* suit would require proving a violation of American citizens' civil liberties. A whistleblower would file a *qui tam* claim under seal in federal court, alleging the nature of the civil liberty violation. Filing under seal minimizes the danger of disclosing harmful secrets and is surely better than a whistleblower making his or her own determination of whether to leak to the media. The court conducts a closed proceeding to allow the government to decide how it wishes to proceed. If the government decides the allegations are worthy of proceeding, they may then notify the government agency accused of wrongdoing. The judge conducts a confidential review of the evidence presented. If the judge determines the surveillance activities were unlawful, the agency is ordered to cease the surveillance activity and the relator is compensated. The compensation would be based on a fine levied against the government for violating Americans' civil liberties, and as an award to the whistleblower for uncovering the violation.

If the government decides not to proceed, the relator may then proceed to attempt to prove the case against the agency in question. In this case, the fines paid to the whistleblower would be doubled because he or she was compelled to prosecute the case. The same logic is used in the existing *qui tam* proceedings.

In either case, if the surveillance were determined to be unlawful, the nature of the violation would be made public to the extent that disclosure does not harm national security.

The privacy *qui tam* system advanced here encourages whistle-blowers to report government violations of civil liberties while providing a regime that protects sensitive intelligence.

4. Define Rational Limits of Search and Seizure Law That Protects Citizens in the New Technical World

Defining a basic constitutional concept like "reasonable expectation of privacy" is all the more difficult when technology changes overnight and law evolves over decades. Constitutional protection for privacy can and has evolved in the past. As noted previously, at one time wiretapping was legal; then it was deemed illegal as constitutional interpretation caught up with reality. The Snowden disclosures and search and seizure cases in the past several years have set the stage for another step forward.

Justice Sonia Sotomayor's concurring opinion in *United States v. Jones* asked if the law could redefine a reasonable expectation of privacy to fit twenty-first-century realities rather than legal theories better suited to the time when the U.S. mail was the dominant means of communication.[92] She stated that the older approaches are "ill suited to the digital age, in which people reveal a great deal of information about themselves to third parties in the course of carrying out mundane tasks." In the *Jones* opinion from a lower court, one judge called the information from a 24/7 GPS tracking involved in that case, by itself, an intrusive mosaic that could be definitive of a person's life.

The *Riley* case is another example of new recognition of the impact of technology on the legal concept of constitutional privacy. As previously discussed, a unanimous Court, with Chief Justice Roberts writing, concluded a warrantless search of the aggregated data in a modern cell phone was more intrusive than the search of a home.

The reasoning of these Courts can be applied to the domestic surveillance issues raised by the Snowden disclosures. According to various reports, NSA surveillance may have included e-mails, texts, Internet searches, online purchases, cell phone records, location records, and social network records. If they occurred, did these searches violate the existing law or the Constitution? To answer that question we must know if the information was collected pursuant to the issuance of an individual warrant, a FISA warrant for bulk collection, or an NSL directing private companies to grant access, or whether it was done with some other authorization. The PCLOB recently found that some of the NSA activities were lawful.[93] It may be that certain surveillance was authorized by the FISA court or collected through NSLs that may have been legally justifiable at the time under existing interpretations and statutes. Maybe. The determination that they were legally justified in some way is an entirely different question than whether those programs should be legal in the future.

To be specific, the central issue is defining the limits of bulk data collection from U.S. citizens. If a warrant based upon probable cause is issued for an individual for cause determined by a judge, that search is, at least facially, within the Fourth Amendment. The salient issue is to what extent can the government sift through the "haystack" without a warrant. Also, how broad is the authority of the FISA court to authorize bulk collection of data through a warrant?

To analyze these issues effectively, it is important to understand the types of data that can be collected with modern technology. The programs listed in the section describing surveillance programs, including PRISM, MUSCULAR, and XKEYSCORE, are programs that collect or analyze information. The following is the list of the classes of information that might be collected by these programs.

1. Public information on an individual in public records, the press, and open Web sites
2. Personal communications

3. Internet usage, including site visits
4. Commercial Internet use, including purchases and contractual disclosures
5. Social media sites
6. Location information
7. Nonpublic stored information

This list includes all the potential sources needed to create a thorough profile of an average American today. As this list is analyzed, realize that some of this information is freely and readily publicly available. Consequently, the collection of that kind of information is not an invasion of personal privacy. In the modern society that lives in figurative glass houses, much of people's lives are transparent to anyone, including the government. There are some gray areas where information is available on a limited basis. And there are some situations where that data is clearly personal, private, and not generally available. All of this information can be characterized as electronic information. Importantly, modern technology can allow the assembly and aggregation of all of this data to create an electronic profile.

Other technical issues affect the level or nature of the collection. For example, is it surveillance or a search if only a computer scans information and no human ever observes the information? For example, what if a computer algorithm is programmed to review all e-mails during a certain date but only retain and identify those e-mails that are sent to a known terrorist? Has the scan violated any rights of a person whose e-mails are scanned but not identified? Yet another issue to be aware of is the distinction between collecting metadata and content. Collection of metadata, or data about data, is sometimes considered less intrusive. For example, is a warrant necessary to collect a person's e-mail metadata (i.e., the "To" and "From" lines with the destination address) as long as the computer does not collect the content of the e-mail?

If anyone thinks metadata is unimportant, consider former NSA head Michael Hayden's statement on ABC News in May 2014: "We kill people based on metadata." Of course he was referring to non-U.S. persons.

PUBLIC INFORMATION

One does not have a reasonable expectation of privacy in public data accessible to any individual with an Internet connection. This is true for both metadata and content. Public data can include public blog entries and YouTube videos, as well as information publicly provided by government, such as arrest records, tax records, personal licenses, and ownership history. Many of these records are freely available on the Internet and are routinely aggregated by commercial data brokerage firms. Data brokers bank on the fact that there is a vast amount of information available from public files. In addition, media publications, broadcasts, and blogs are certainly public information and collectible by government. Without a warrant, government can often capture a great deal of information about individuals from this category of publicly available information.

PERSONAL COMMUNICATIONS

The Fourth Amendment should protect the content of personal communications, such as e-mail messages and conversations via phone. In fact, phone wiretapping cases are significant benchmarks in search and seizure law. Personal communications such as the content of a written letter are also protected. However, the addressed destination on a letter is different than content and has always been considered unprotected because the addressee is voluntarily disclosed to multiple postal workers. The commonly used analogy is that the written address on a letter is the same as an e-mail address on an e-mail communication. Under this reasoning, e-mail metadata (i.e., the addressee of the e-mail) is fair game for surveillance without a warrant. New technology should require a reexamination of this analogy. With new technology, it is easy to collect and classify thousands of e-mails and analyze their destination. The collection and classification of months of personal communications is qualitatively different than knowing the destination of one or two letters. Surveillance of communication metadata needs to be reexamined.

The government should clearly be required to obtain a warrant to collect the content of any personal electronic communication. However, if the communication is a Facebook public posting to 300 friends or a mass e-mail to 500 business associates, the privacy of that communication diminishes. These communications are more akin to public statements. Certainly a Twitter posting from an unrestricted account is not private.

The Fourth Amendment may also protect the metadata of personal communications. The Supreme Court has yet to explicitly overturn the holding in *Smith* that treats information disclosed to third parties as available without a warrant, but the *Klayman* decision that found bulk collection telephony metadata unconstitutional, and some other legislative proposals in the USA Freedom Act of 2014, indicate that warrantless bulk collection of telephony metadata may soon come to an end. This same reasoning should be applied to the metadata of all electronic communications, including e-mail. Communication data, particularly personal communications, often disclose very sensitive data that should require a warrant to allow government surveillance.

INTERNET USE

The Fourth Amendment protection of Internet use is an intricate concept. The metadata of Internet use is presumably the URL of a Web site or how many times an individual visits a Web site. The content would be determining the actual substance of the Web site that an individual observed. The Fourth Amendment does not prevent an investigator from observing the content placed on public Web sites by an individual if the Web site is generally available to the public. Therefore, if an investigator knows a suspect is posting his views or blogging on a public Web site, the investigator can look at those postings. The URLs of public Web sites are tantamount to public information data. However, the Fourth Amendment may protect the content of more interactive Web sites that are password protected. The government would need to issue an NSL, obtain a warrant to access this information, or reach an agreement with the Web site.

COMMERCIAL WEB SITE

One likely does not have a reasonable expectation of privacy for the metadata and content hosted on commercial Web sites like Amazon or eBay. These commercial Web sites depend on the collection of personal information to cross-market and provide future recommendations. Many of these sites have terms and conditions allowing data collection to which the user agrees. While the government may not need a warrant to access this information, the Fourth Amendment should prevent the government from a warrantless hacking into Amazon or Google to obtain the metadata or content without the consent of the company as was done through MUSCULAR. It seems the government could obtain information with a targeted individual warrant, but should they be able to obtain bulk data with a bulk warrant like an NSL that could allow the collection of data on a broad number of Internet users? This invasive type of intrusion could constitute a Fourth Amendment violation. The area of bulk data collection from Internet providers is one of the central and most controversial issues that came out of the Snowden disclosures. If NSLs are to be allowed to continue, they should not be allowed for an indiscriminate vacuuming of information about the entire haystack. The government should be compelled to state a cause for obtaining domestic information and conduct a rationally targeted search.

PERSONALLY SENSITIVE (STORED INFORMATION)

Individuals have a reasonable expectation of privacy for certain personally sensitive information like health records. This expectation is true for both metadata and content. For example, the fact that a person had an operation and the fact that it was a heart transplant are both facts that are nonpublic. For certain kinds of information like medical information, there are explicit standards for confidentiality. Of course, the government already collects health data for health regulation purposes. The 2003 Health Insurance Portability and Accountability Act Privacy Rule included a national security exception that authorizes the collection of medical records by federal agents if part of a national security investigation.[94] Therefore, collection of health data is specifically authorized by HIPAA, and the NSA may therefore use a FISA warrant or other legal justifications to obtain health information on a target.

Beyond health records, the Fourth Amendment should also protect bank records. Currently, warrantless review of certain bank records is justified under a 1976 Supreme Court decision. This type of transaction surveillance is one of the most unregulated forms of government surveillance. Record holders such as banks have vast access to our personal data only because "we cannot otherwise realistically function in the modern world."[95] If an individual wants to keep money in a bank, he or she must consent to the bank's issuance and knowledge of his or her account number. This ordinary participation in the modern world is not a voluntary submission to general observation of financial information by government. The only way to avoid this "voluntary disclosure" is to put your cash in a mattress. In this instance, transaction surveillance is an illogical justification for warrantless surveillance that is completely inconsistent with reality. Courts have extended a person's reasonable expectations of privacy to zones outside the home and to private information. Bank records should be considered sensitive information, and the limited disclosure to a bank should not equate to voluntary disclosure. The government should be obligated to obtain a warrant before procuring this kind of sensitive information for both metadata and content.

Cloud-based services have become one of the easier methods to store and access data. Is the cloud data fair game for the government to obtain without a subpoena? Probably not. Both the metadata and content of stored data are comparable to that which a person saves on her computer's hard drive. There is no intent to broadly share this information, which is stored in a hypothetically secure place. The Stored Communications Act (SCA) should provide a basis for protection.[96] As with the other types of data, a person's conduct can limit her expectation of privacy. If a person shares a Dropbox folder with a hundred people, then it would be easier for the court to grant the government a warrant.

SOCIAL MEDIA

Oversharing is the norm on social media sites like Twitter and Facebook. Yet many users are surprised to learn that the government may gain access to the same information they share with their Facebook friends through programs like PRISM. Where posts are made broadly available, without any limitations, then the individual may have abandoned a reasonable expectation of privacy. Government viewing of such unrestricted information is not likely to require a warrant. In addition, Facebook might be compelled through an NSL or FISA warrant to disclose additional information. In contrast, the Fourth Amendment may protect individual messages sent through Facebook from one user to another. In addition, if a person places specific limits on distribution and viewing, then those communications may be more protected and more similar to the content of e-mail.

While some disclosure of information is necessary to participate in the modern technological world, such as the disclosure of the destination address of an e-mail to an ISP, the disclosure of one's birthday, home address, vacation plans, book preferences, or best friends on a Facebook page may be different. Courts have evaluated Facebook pages for claims of confidentiality by parties to criminal and civil lawsuits. Basically, the courts will grant a subpoena for Facebook posts when a party identifies the relevancy of the underlying information.[97] They will not usually grant blanket access to an individual's Facebook account.[98]

There are numerous social networks with different markets and purposes. They have in common the purpose of a broad disclosure of information—not confidentiality. People have a lower expectation of privacy in the social networking arena than in some of the other classifications discussed here, such as personal communications. However, certain social network posts that more closely resemble personal communications than public disclosures may be entitled to a higher expectation of privacy.

LOCATION DATA

GPS tracking of an individual's location through a smartphone or any other device can be very intrusive. The Supreme Court has held that the government cannot place a GPS tracker on a suspect's car 24/7 for a criminal investigation without a warrant. The majority's opinion focused on the property or trespassing nature of the placement on the defendant's car. Justice Sotomayor went further in her concurrence. She reasoned that the GPS placement was an unconstitutional search and seizure. While this opinion provides helpful reasoning for Fourth Amendment protections in the future, there are many other instances of voluntary disclosure of a person's location that may be legally obtained by the government. A person who posts his or her location on Foursquare or checks in on Facebook may be deemed to have voluntarily disclosed the information to the public. However, the Fourth Amendment may prevent the government from obtaining an individual's Google Maps searches or Find My iPhone data without a warrant because the individual did not intentionally share that information with any particular person by consenting to use the application. Nevertheless, Google possesses and retains that information and the government may attempt to obtain it directly from such a third party.

Ultimately, a person's conduct and choices regarding how much he or she chooses to share with the world can determine his or her privacy rights. Furthermore, distinguishing the relative intrusiveness of content collection versus metadata collection is challenging. Most collections of metadata are intrusive because of the aggregation effect. It is arguable that the GPS coordinates or address constitutes the metadata while what occurs in the location is the content.

THE SURVIVAL OF PRIVACY

There are clearly many issues to be resolved as technology evolves. Currently, two of the biggest concerns are aggregation and bulk collection. The sensitive nature of aggregated information from phone records, browser history, stored data, personal communications, etcetera, has influenced recent Supreme Court decisions.

The *Jones* case dealing with continuous GPS monitoring and the majority opinion in *Riley* concerning a warrantless search of a smartphone indicate the recognition that the aggregation of data is a major threat to privacy. While the extraction of personal communication metadata from a phone may not yet constitute a Fourth Amendment violation, the aggregation of multiple types of data—including personal communication metadata—does. The technological aggregation of data changes the qualitative nature from nonintrusive information to an intrusive comprehensive data profile. For example, GPS tracking showing "location information" that someone was at a bar one day does not provide much insight. However, when a thirty-day record indicates that the individual spends three hours every afternoon for thirty days at that bar, that location information *aggregation* paints a picture.

Bulk collection is intrusive for a different reason. By its nature, bulk collection is a randomized sweep of information from mostly unaware and innocent people. Keep in mind that the technical capabilities described in the previous section may enable the collection of large amounts of information about those random individuals subject to bulk collections. If bulk surveillance is allowed to sweep communications (e.g., cell phone contacts or e-mails) and Internet use through upstream collection as well as easily collected public records, a quite specific profile may be stored even if it is not observed. It is at this point that the haystack argument is central to the discussion. Bulk collection allows the "incidental" collection of nonsuspect American data that can be stored and searched through in the future utilization of programs like XKEYSCORE. This collection is a serious intrusion and may well be found to be a Fourth Amendment violation. As mentioned above, Congress may statutorily limit bulk collection of information.

Further, other bulk collection programs like the undersea cable tapping that indiscriminately collects domestic information must be reexamined. In that case, a technical solution exists that preserves the ability to conduct foreign surveillance and preserve Americans' privacy.

When the NSA developed ThinThread, programmers created a code that immediately extracted or blocked American information from the data collected. This code prevented any domestic data from being seen or stored by the NSA. Unfortunately, the NSA decided to forgo the use of this code under post-9/11 pressures.[99] To rectify privacy concerns, the NSA should reinstate this code and coding similar to it to filter out domestic data. Beyond coding modifications, FISA warrants should require more targeted bulk collection practices. For example, if there is a suspected terrorist with known connections to a New York mosque, should the NSA be allowed to perform a bulk collection of all the data from any individual who attends that same mosque? That seems to be an overreach without more explicit reasons. The collection should instead be limited to those individuals with whom the suspect directly communicates or who are suspects for other specific reasons. Without some more specific limitations, bulk collection of otherwise confidential domestic information is a major focus for reform.

Other programs like MUSCULAR and XKEYSCORE raise other issues of legality. Purportedly, MUSCULAR allows NSA programmers to hack into the internal networks of ISPs. XKEYSCORE functions with the use of a dropdown menu that allows an NSA worker to determine the justification of his or her own search. The NSA worker—or contractor, like Snowden—may justify his own search of all the data collected under this program. Each of these programs appears to allow the hacking of private information without a specific statutory justification or judicial oversight. Instead, the NSA worker chooses from dropdown options including "the person has stated that he is located out-side of the US," "human intelligence source indicates person is located outside the US," and "open source information indicates that person is located outside the US."[100]

The legality of overseas surveillance programs like SOMAL-GET presents more complicated legal issues. Recall that SOMAL-GET is recording entire cell phone conversations. With millions of Americans visiting the Bahamas yearly, the NSA is clearly intercepting the phone conversations of American citizens. This action would be illegal in the United States, and a person's mere presence in the Bahamas is, by itself, a highly suspect justification to wiretap an American citizen. However, the fact that a U.S. person is in a foreign country may be cited as legal justification for the surveillance. Beyond domestic legal issues, there are also real concerns that SOMALGET violates international laws.[101]

Reforms require a complex balancing of national security and personal privacy. The motivation to protect the homeland is strong and justified. The new concern about individual privacy is substantial and a comprehensive response is imperative. Programs spurred by 9/11 and enhanced by new technology have created a toxic environment of public distrust. Put in the best light, NSA officials were not candid in describing surveillance programs in response to the Snowden disclosures. It seems clear that these programs gathered massive amounts of information about innocent Americans without the NSA ever intending to tell the American public. No wonder there is a trust gap.

The public can handle the truth and there is likely a general willingness to support a strong surveillance program. However, transparency and real change are just the beginning. The above-suggested changes are a start at a critical moment when our nation has a chance to restore the core element of an effective democracy—faith of the people in the government.

NOTES

The author would like to thank Matthew Christ, Kelsey Harclerode, Emily Snider, and Andrew Starling for their excellent research work.

1. Ellen Nakashim and Joby Warrick, "For NSA chief, terrorist threat drives passion to 'collect it all,'" *Washington Post,* July 14, 2013, www .washingtonpost.com/world/national-security/for-nsa-chief-terrorist -threat-drives-passion-to-collect-it-all/2013/07/14/3d26ef80-ea49 -11e2-a301-ea5a8116d211_story.html.

2. Stephen Cobb, "New Harris poll shows NSA revelations impact on-line shopping, banking, and more," *We Live Security,* April 2, 2014, http://www.welivesecurity.com/2014/04/02/harris-poll-nsa-revelati ons-impact-online-shopping-banking/.

3. Chuck McCutcheon, "Government Surveillance," *CQ Researcher* 726, vol. 23, no. 30 (August 2013).

4. *Olmstead v. United States,* 277 U.S. 438, 456–57 (1928).

5. *Katz v. United States,* 389 U.S. 347, 347 (1967).

6. *Riley v. California,* 134 S. Ct. 2473, 2495 (2014).

7. Laura Poitras, Marcel Rosenbach, and Holger Stark, "'A' for Angela: GCHQ and NSA Targeted Private German Companies and Merkel," *Spiegel Online,* March 29, 2014, http://www.spiegel.de/international /germany/gchq-and-nsa-targeted-private-german-companies-a -961444.html.

8. Christopher Woolf, "The history of electronic surveillance, from Abraham Lincoln's wiretaps to Operation Shamrock," *Public Radio International,* November 7, 2013, http://www.pri.org/stories/2013 -11-07/history-electronic-surveillance-abraham-lincolns-wiretaps -operation-shamrock.

9. Whitfield Diffie and Susan Landau, *Privacy on the Line: The Politics of Wiretapping and Encryption* (Cambridge, MA: MIT Press, 1998), 177.

10. Edward Epstein, "Wiretap defense invokes Lincoln, Roosevelt/At-torney general says they didn't get warrants, either," *San Francisco Chronicle,* January 25, 2006, http://www.sfgate.com/politics/article /Wiretap-defense-invokes-Lincoln-Roosevelt-2505999.php.

11. Alfred W. McCoy, "How NSA Surveillance Fits Into a Long History of American Global Political Strategy," *Mother Jones,* January 24, 2014,

http://www.motherjones.com/politics/2014/01/nsa-surveillance-history-global-political-strategy-domestic-spying.

12. "Factbox: History of mass surveillance in the United States," Reuters, June 7, 2013, http://www.reuters.com/article/2013/06/07/us-usa-security-records-factbox-idUSBRE95617O20130607.

13. McCutcheon, "Government Surveillance."

14. U.S. Senate Select Committee to Study Governmental Operations with Respect to Intelligence Activities, *Final Report: Book II,* Report No. 94–755 (Washington, D.C.: United States Government Printing Office, 1976), xi–xii.

15. Rick Young, "Spying on the Home Front," PBS *Frontline* (2007), http://www.pbs.org/wgbh/pages/frontline/video/flv/generic.html?s=fro102p6d&continuous=1.

16. Michael Kirk, "United States of Secrets (Part One): The Program," PBS *Frontline* (2014), http://www.pbs.org/wgbh/pages/frontline/united-states-of-secrets-(part-one)-the-program.

17. Young, "Spying on the Home Front."

18. Kirk, "United States of Secrets (Part One): The Program."

19. Michael Isikoff, "The Whistleblower Who Exposed Warrantless Wiretaps," *Newsweek,* March 13, 2010, http://www.newsweek.com/whistleblower-who-exposed-warrantless-wiretaps-82805.

20. James Risen and Eric Lichtblau, "Bush Lets U.S. Spy on Callers Without Courts," *New York Times,* December 16, 2005, http://www.nytimes.com/2005/12/16/politics/16program.html?_r=3&sq=James%20Risen%20nsa%20surveillance&st=cse&scp=1&pagewanted=all&.

21. Edward C. Liu, "Reauthorization of the FISA Amendments Act," Congressional Research Service, April 8, 2013, http://fas.org/sgp/crs/intel/R42725.pdf.

22. Glenn Greenwald, "NSA Collecting Phone Records of Millions of Verizon Customers Daily," *Guardian,* June 5, 2013, http://www.theguardian.com/world/2013/jun/06/nsa-phone-records-verizon-court-order.

23. Barton Gellman and Laura Poitras, "U.S., British intelligence mining data from nine U.S. Internet companies in broad secret program," *Washington Post,* June 7, 2013, http://www.washingtonpost.com/investigations/us-intelligence-mining-data-from-nine-us-internet-companies-in-broad-secret-program/2013/06/06/3a0c0da8-cebf-11e2-8845-d970ccb04497_story.html.

24. Edward Snowden, "NSA whistleblower Edward Snowden: 'I don't want to live in a society that does these sort of things'—Video," *Guardian*, June 9, 2013, http://www.theguardian.com/world/video/2013/jun/09 /nsa-whistleblower-edward-snowden-interview-video.

25. Martin Smith, "United States of Secrets (Part Two): Privacy Lost." www.pbs.org/wqbh/pages/frontline/ united-states-of-secrets-(part-two).

26. Barton Gellman and Ashkan Soltani, "NSA Infiltrates Links to Yahoo, Google Data Centers Worldwide, Snowden Documents Say," *Washington Post*, http://www.washingtonpost.com/world/national-security /nsa-infiltrates-links-to-yahoo-google-data-centers-worldwide-snowden -documents-say/2013/10/30/e51d661e-4166-11e3-8b74-d89d714ca4 dd_story.html.

27. Peter P. Swire, "The System of Foreign Intelligence Surveillance Law," *George Washington Law Review* 72 (2004): 1332–33.

28. Executive Order 12333, 46 Fed. Reg. 59941 (December 4, 1981), http:// www.archives.gov/federal-register/codification/executive-order /12333.html.

29. H.R. 3162, 107th Congress (2001).

30. S. 1566, 95th Congress (1978).

31. H.R. 6304, 110th Congress (2008).

32. Evan Perez, "Secret Court's Oversight Gets Scrutiny," *Wall Street Journal,* June 9, 2013, http://online.wsj.com/news/articles/SB100014 24127887324904004578535670310514616.

33. Glenn Greenwald and Spencer Ackerman, "NSA Collected US Email Records in Bulk for More Than Two Years Under Obama," *Guardian,* June 27, 2013, http://www.theguardian.com/world/2013 /jun/27/nsa-data-mining-authorised-obama.

34. Glenn Greenwald and Ewen MacAskill, "NSA Prism Program Taps in to User Data of Apple, Google and Others," *Guardian,* June 6, 2013, http://www.theguardian.com/world/2013/jun/06/us-tech-giants -nsa-data.

35. Dominic Rushe and James Ball, "PRISM Scandal: Tech Giants Flatly Deny Allowing NSA Direct Access to Servers," *Guardian,* June 6, 2013, http://www.theguardian.com/world/2013/jun/07/prism-tech -giants-shock-nsa-data-mining.

36. Glenn Greenwald and James Ball, "The Top Secret Rules that Allow NSA to Use US Data Without a Warrant," *Guardian,* June 20, 2013, http://www.theguardian.com/world/2013/jun/20/fisa-court-nsa -without-warrant.

37. Ibid; Olga Khazan, "The Creepy, Long-Standing Practice of Undersea Cable Tapping," *Atlantic,* July 16, 2013, http://www.theatlantic.com/international/archive/2013/07/the-creepy-long-standing-practice-of-undersea-cable-tapping/277855/.

38. Greenwald and Ball, "The Top Secret Rules that Allow NSA to Use US Data Without a Warrant."

39. Craig Timberg, "NSA Slide Shows Surveillance of Undersea Cables," *Washington Post,* July 10, 2013, http://www.washingtonpost.com/business/economy/the-nsa-slide-you-havent-seen/2013/07/10/32801426-e8e6-11e2-aa9f-c03a72e2d342_story.html.

40. Verizon Forced to Hand Over Telephone Data—Full Court Ruling," *Guardian,* June 5, 2013, http://www.theguardian.com/world/interactive/2013/jun/06/verizon-telephone-data-court-order.

41. Marc Ambinder, "How the NSA Uses Your Telephone Records," *Week,* June 6, 2013, http://theweek.com/article/index/245285/how-the-nsa-uses-your-telephone-records.

42. Greenwald, "NSA Collecting Phone Records of Millions of Verizon Customers Daily."

43. Ambinder, "How the NSA Uses Your Telephone Records."

44. "How the NSA Is Tracking People Right Now," *Washington Post,* December 4, 2013, http://apps.washingtonpost.com/g/page/national/how-the-nsa-is-tracking-people-right-now/634/.

45. Kimberly Dozier, "NSA Defends Global Cellphone Tracking as Legal," NBC News, December 6, 2013, http://www.nbcnews.com/tech/security/nsa-defends-global-cellphone-tracking-legal-f2D11708514.

46. "How the NSA's MUSCULAR Program Collects Too Much Data from Yahoo and Google," *Washington Post,* October 30, 2013, http://apps.washingtonpost.com/g/page/world/how-the-nsas-muscular-program-collects-too-much-data-from-yahoo-and-google/543/.

47. Gellman and Soltani, "NSA Infiltrates Links to Yahoo, Google Data Centers Worldwide, Snowden Documents Say."

48. "NSA Statement on Washington Post Report on Infiltration of Google, Yahoo Data Center Links," *Washington Post,* October 30, 2013, http://www.washingtonpost.com/world/national-security/nsa-statement-on-washington-post-report-on-infiltration-of-google-yahoo-data-center-links/2013/10/30/5c135254-41b4-11e3-a624-41d661b0bb78_story.html.

49. Glenn Greenwald, "XKeyscore: NSA Tool Collects 'Nearly Everything a User Does on the Internet," *Guardian,* July 31, 2013, http://

www.theguardian.com/world/2013/jul/31/nsa-top-secret-program-online-data.

50. Ryan Gallagher, "NSA Even Spied on Google Maps Searches, Documents Suggest," *Slate*, July 11, 2013, http://www.slate.com/blogs/future_tense/2013/07/11/xkeyscore_program_may_have_allowed_nsa_to_spy_on_google_maps_searches.html.

51. Glenn Greenwald and Ewen MacAskill, "Boundless Informant: The NSA's Secret Tool to Track Global Surveillance Data," *Guardian*, June 11, 2013, http://www.theguardian.com/world/2013/jun/08/nsa-boundless-informant-global-datamining.

52. Ryan Devereaux, Glenn Greenwald, and Laura Poitras, "Data Pirates of the Caribbean: The NSA Is Recording Every Cell Phone Call in the Bahamas," *Intercept*, May 19, 2014, https://firstlook.org/theintercept/article/2014/05/19/data-pirates-caribbean-nsa-recording-every-cell-phone-call-bahamas/.

53. Secret Documents Reveal N.S.A. Campaign Against Encryption," *New York Times*, September 5, 2013, http://www.nytimes.com/interactive/2013/09/05/us/documents-reveal-nsa-campaign-against-encryption.html?ref=us; James Ball, Bruce Schneier, and Glenn Greenwald, "NSA and GCHQ Target Tor Network that Protects Anonymity of Web Users," *Guardian*, October 4, 2013, http://www.theguardian.com/world/2013/oct/04/nsa-gchq-attack-tor-network-encryption.

54. Nicole Perlroth, Jeff Larson, and Scott Shane, "N.S.A. Able to Foil Basic Safeguards of Privacy on Web," *New York Times*, September 5, 2013, http://www.nytimes.com/2013/09/06/us/nsa-foils-much-internet-encryption.html?_r=0; Ball, Schneier, and Greenwald, "NSA and GCHQ Target Tor Network that Protects Anonymity of Web Users."

55. "'Follow the Money': NSA Spies on International Payments," *Spiegel Online*, September 15, 2013, http://www.spiegel.de/international/world/spiegel-exclusive-nsa-spies-on-international-bank-transactions-a-922276.html.

56. Declan McCullagh, "Justice Department Tries to Force Google to Hand Over User Data," CNET, May 31, 2013, http://www.cnet.com/news/justice-department-tries-to-force-google-to-hand-over-user-data/.

57. "National Security Letters," Electronic Frontier Foundation, https://www.eff.org/issues/national-security-letters.

58. *John Doe, Inc. v. Mukasey,* 549 F.3d 861 (2d Cir. 2008).
59. Mark Zuckerberg's Facebook page, accessed August 4, 2014, https://www.facebook.com/zuck/posts/10100828955847631.
60. *Cassidy v. Chertoff,* 471 F.3d 67, 82 (2d Cir. 2006).
61. Jennifer Jenkins and Carol D. Leonnig, "In NSA-Intercepted Data, Those Not Targeted Far Outnumber the Foreigners Who Are," *Washington Post,* http://www.washingtonpost.com/world/national-security/in-nsa-intercepted-data-those-not-targeted-far-outnumber-the-foreigners-who-are/2014/07/05/8139adf8-045a-11e4-8572-4b1b969b6322_story.html.
62. Geoffrey R. Stone, "The NSA's Telephone Metadata Program Is Unconstitutional," *Huffington Post,* http://www.huffingtonpost.com/geoffrey-r-stone/the-nsas-telephone-meta-d_b_4571523.html.
63. Ryan Gallagher, "Software that Tracks People on Social Media Created by Defense Firm," *Guardian,* February 10, 2013, http://www.theguardian.com/world/2013/feb/10/software-tracks-social-media-defence.
64. Joel R. Spiegel, Michael T. McKènna, Girish S. Lakshman, and Paul G. Nordstrom. Method and System for anticipatory package shipping. U.S. Patent 8,615,473, filed August 24, 2012, and issued December 24, 2013.
65. "Privacy Impact Assessment Update for the Future Attribute Screening Technology (FAST)/Passive Methods for Precision Behavioral Screening," Department of Homeland Security, December 21, 2011, http://www.dhs.gov/xlibrary/assets/privacy/privacy_pia_st_fast-a.pdf.
66. Sharon Weinberger, "Terrorist 'Pre-Crime' Detector Filed Tested in United States," *Nature,* May 27, 2011, http://www.nature.com/news/2011/110527/full/news.2011.323.html.
67. James Bamford, "The New Thought Police," PBS, January 1, 2009, http://www.pbs.org/wgbh/nova/military/nsa-police.html.
68. "Assisting the Language Analyst: Multi-disciplinary Research at CSL," *The Next Wave: The National Security Agency's Review of Emerging Technologies* 18 (2009): 1, http://www.nsa.gov/research/tnw/tnw181/articles/pdfs/TNW_18_1_Web.pdf.
69. Peter Finn, Greg Miller, and Ellen Nakashima, "Investigators Looking at How Snowden Gained Access at NSA," *Washington Post,* June 10, 2013, http://www.washingtonpost.com/world/national-security/investigators-looking-at-how-snowden-gained-access-at-nsa/2013/06/10/83b4841a-d209-11e2-8cbe-1bcbee06f8f8_story_1.html.

70. *Klayman v. Obama,* 957 F. Supp. 2d 1, 37 (D.D.C. 2013). In the case of *ACLU v. Clapper,* 959 F. Supp. 2d 724 (S.D.N.Y. 2013) the judge reached a different conclusion on similar facts.

71. *Smith v. Maryland,* 442 U.S. 735, 743 (1979).

72. Stephen Somogyi, "Making End-to-End Encryption Easier to Use," Google Online Security Blog, June 3, 2014, http://googleonlinesecu rity.blogspot.com/2014/06/making-end-to-end-encryption-easier -to.html.

73. Mark Zuckerberg's Facebook page, accessed August 4, 2014.

74. Aryeh Selekman, "A New, Optional Way to Share and Discover Music, TV and Movies," Facebook, May 21, 2014, http://newsroom .fb.com/news/2014/05/a-new-optional-way-to-share-and-discover -music-tv-and-movies/.

75. H.R. 3361, 113th Congress (2014).

76. USA Freedom Act of 2014, S. 2685, 113th Congress (2014).

77. The proposed policy changes of the PCLOB 2014 report provide a reasonable background for reform ideas (e.g., define NSA targeting more completely, avoid U.S. person surveillance, review the FISA court's role, evaluate upstream collection on purely domestic subjects, promote transparency and accountability, and evaluate the efficacy of the surveillance programs).

78. Andrew Lycett, "Breaking Germany's Enigma Code," BBC, February 17, 2011, http://www.bbc.co.uk/history/worldwars/wwtwo /enigma_01.shtml.

79. U.S. Senate, *Joint Testimony of the Office of the Director of National Intelligence and the Department of Justice Before the Committee on the Judiciary,* 113th Congress, November 13, 2013, http://fas.org/irp/congress/ 2013_hr/111313litt.pdf.

80. Civil Liberties and Privacy Office of the Office of the Director of National Intelligence, *Civil Liberties and Privacy Guidance for Intelligence Community Professionals: Properly Obtaining and Using Publicly Available Information,* July 2011, http://www.dni.gov/index.php/newsroom/repo rts-and-publications/204-reports-publications-2014/1093-civil-libe rties-and-privacy-guidance-for-intelligence-community-profes sionals.

81. Office of the Director of National Intelligence, *IC on the Record: 2013 Transparency Report,* http://icontherecord.tumblr.com/transparency /odni_transparencyreport_cy2013.

82. Mark Mazzetti and Carl Hulse, "C.I.A. Inquiry Affirms It Spied on Senate Panel," *New York Times*, July 31, 2014, http://www.nytimes .com/2014/08/01/world/senate-intelligence-commitee-cia-inter rogation-report.html?_r=1.

83. Privacy and Civil Liberties Oversight Board, *Report on the Surveillance Program Operated Pursuant to Section 702 of the Foreign Intelligence Surveillance Act*, accessed July 3, 2014, http://www.pclob.gov/All%20Docu ments/Report%20on%20the%20Section%20702%20Program /PCLOB-Section-702-Report.pdf.

84. Perez, "Secret Court's Oversight Gets Scrutiny."

85. Office of Senator Richard Blumenthal. "Blumenthal Unveils Major Legislation To Reform FISA Courts," 2013, http://www.blumenthal .senate.gov/newsroom/press/release/blumenthal-unveils-major-legi slation-to-reform-fisa-courts.

86. Peter Wallsten, "Lawmakers say obstacles limited oversight of NSA's telephone surveillance program," *Washington Post*, August 10, 2013, http://www.washingtonpost.com/politics/lawmakers-say-obstacles -limited-oversight-of-nsas-telephone-surveillance-program/2013 /08/10/bee87394-004d-11e3-9a3e-916de805f65d_story.html.

87. Mike Lennon, "Researchers Out Spy Tools That Let Governments Hack Your Smartphone," *Security Week*, June 24, 2014, http://www .securityweek.com/researchers-out-spy-tools-let-governments-hack -your-smartphone.

88. David Welna, "Before Snowden: The Whistleblowers Who Tried to Lift The Veil," National Public Radio, July 22, 2014, http://www .npr.org/2014/07/22/333741495/before-snowden-the-whistle blowers-who-tried-to-lift-the-veil.

89. Marcy Wheeler, "Government Case Against Whistleblower Thomas Drake Collapses," *Nation*, June 13, 2011, http://www.thenation.com /article/161376/government-case-against-whistleblower-thomas -drake-collapses.

90. Beverly Cohen, "Kaboom! The Explosion of Qui Tam False Claims Under the Health Reform Law," *Penn State Law Review* 116 (2011): 77–78.

91. Whistleblower Protection Act of 1989, Pub. L. No. 101–12, 103 Stat. 16 (1989). The act is intended to protect federal employees from re-taliation if they report unlawful practices occurring at their place of work.

92. *United States v. Jones*, 132 S. Ct. 945, 957 (2012).

93. David E. Sanger, "U.S. Privacy Panel Backs NSA's Internet Tapping," *New York Times*, July 2, 2014, http://www.nytimes.com/2014/07/03 /world/privacy-board-backs-nsa-program-that-taps-internet-in-us .html?_r=0.

94. Health Insurance Portability and Accountability Act of 1996, Establishing the 2003 Privacy Rule, *Code of Federal Regulations*, title 45 (2003): 160, 162, 164, http://www.hhs.gov/ocr/privacy/hipaa/ad ministrative/combined/hipaa-simplification-201303.pdf.

95. Christopher Slobogin, "Transaction Surveillance by the Government," *Mississippi Law Journal* 139, no. 75 (2005).

96. Passed in 1986, the SCA provides Fourth Amendment–like protection to digital communications stored on third-party servers and remote computing servers.

97. Agnieszka A. Mcpeak, "The Facebook Digital Footprint: Paving Fair and Consistent Pathways to Civil Discovery of Social Media Data," *Wake Forest Law Review* 48 (2013): 892–93. Courts have generally required a showing of relevancy when considering motions to compel access to the entirety of a Facebook account.

98. *EEOC v. The Original Honeybaked Ham Co. of Georgia*, No. 11-CV -02560-MSK-MEH, (D. Co. November 7, 2012). A federal magistrate judge reasoned in one recent employment discrimination case that production of social media account passwords was warranted when the requested information was specific and relevant to the matter in dispute.

99. Kirk, "United States of Secrets (Part One): The Program."

100. Greenwald, "XKeyscore."

101. Devereaux, Greenwald, and Poitras, "Data Pirates of the Caribbean."

SECRECY, SURVEILLANCE, AND THE SNOWDEN EFFECT

Thomas Blanton

THOMAS BLANTON is Director of the National Security Archive at George Washington University in Washington, D.C. In April 2000, the Archive won U.S. journalism's George Polk Award for "piercing self-serving veils of government secrecy, guiding journalists in search for the truth, and informing us all." A graduate of Harvard University, he filed his first Freedom of Information Act request in 1976 as a weekly newspaper reporter in Minnesota. His articles have since appeared in *The International Herald Tribune, The New York Times, The Washington Post, The Los Angeles Times, The Wall Street Journal, The Boston Globe, Slate, The Wilson Quarterly,* and many other publications. He is the author of numerous books, most recently *Masterpieces of History: The Peaceful End of the Cold War in Europe, 1989,* coauthored with Svetlana Savranskaya and Vladislav Zubok, which won the Arthur S. Link-Warren F. Kuehl Prize for Documentary Editing.

THE EDWARD SNOWDEN leaks starting in June 2013 not only challenged the U.S. government's surveillance policies but also forced major change in the national security classification system. In fact, only a year after the Snowden documents began hitting the headlines, and directly in response to those disclosures, the U.S. government and particularly its intelligence agencies had actually declassified and published more pages of previously secret surveillance documents (over 3,000 pages) than had the combined media partners holding Snowden materials (2,227 pages as of August 2014).[1] At one point in the summer of 2013, the former National Security Agency Director General Michael Hayden—giving yet another interview defending the surveillance programs—complained he could hardly keep up with the official disclosures, so he did not really know what was still a secret and what was not.

Of course, before Snowden, every single page of those new official releases was withheld from the public. The government even claimed—before Snowden—that wiretap court orders and pleadings had to be withheld in full; even the sections of the documents that simply cited and repeated the text of the Fourth Amendment (the Constitution)—were now "top secret."[2] Even after Snowden, the newly declassified pages contained so many redactions, blackouts, and whiteouts—ostensibly on continued national security grounds—that a single Snowden page arguably amounted on substantive grounds to two or even three of the official pages.

The U.S. secrecy system had long privileged at the highest level the communications intercept activities of the National Security Agency, so much so that the standing joke among NSA watchers held that the initials stood for "No Such Agency." Intelligence products that contained COMINT almost automatically qualified for top secret controls (the definition of "top secret" holds that release of this information would cause "exceptionally grave" damage to national security). From 1950 to 1982 (when the statute protecting CIA agent identities was passed), only one category of "national defense information" was precisely defined in statutes like the Espionage Act, and that was the COMINT Act, Section 798 of Title 18—covering "communications intelligence activities" and "any code, cipher, or cryptographic system" and any classified information obtained from communications intelligence.[3] That history of privileged secrecy—presumptive secrecy—is worth a closer look, particularly the lessons it holds for today about the abuses of surveillance power enabled by secrecy, and the potential balance we might strike with public demands for transparency.

This chapter attempts to situate the current debates over secrecy and transparency of surveillance activities in the policy argument as old as this republic, dating back to the revolutionary and necessarily secret activities of the Continental Congress. The narrative here reviews the various and diverse analyses of the national security secrecy system and its incentive structures, and sketches the rise of the NSA itself, as secrecy masked its origins in the Cold War and its vast expansion parallel to the Internet in the 1980s and 1990s. The chapter will describe the renewed secrecy shrouds after the terrorist attacks of 9/11, how this fed the agency's culture of reflexive secrecy and enabled the aggressive surveillance activities now being partially rolled back—after Snowden. Finally, the chapter will offer the comparisons from more than a dozen examples of the sea change in secrecy from before and after Snowden, and how these belated acknowledgments by the government actually illuminate the credibility gap between what officials claimed and what we now know.

The analysis here, though, cannot offer encouragement that the post-Snowden transformation in the secrecy system amounts to sustainable, much less permanent, change. The credibility of the NSA and its supervisors is shot right now, as the result of demonstrably false statements made to the Congress, the courts, to the public, and to each other—all revealed by the Snowden documents. The new intelligence community transparency is transparently an attempt at public relations rather than systemic reform, although a few institutional arrangements such as the Privacy and Civil Liberties Oversight Board offer some real promise. Right now the trends are in the openness direction, but the same was true of the CIA in the mid-1970s in the midst of congressional investigations and front-page stories, many of them provided by the CIA coming clean itself. Yet within only a few years, the cowboys were back in charge at Langley, and such abuses and fiascos as the Iran-Contra scandal resulted.

Justice Potter Stewart in the famous concurring opinion in the Pentagon Papers case (1971) provided a lasting, useful guide to national security secrecy: "For when everything is classified, then nothing is classified, and the system becomes one to be disregarded by the cynical or the careless, and to be manipulated by those intent on self-protection or self-promotion. . . . The hallmark of a truly effective internal security system would be the maximum possible disclosure, recognizing that secrecy can best be preserved only when credibility is truly maintained."

Arguably, the national security classification system is trending right now, thanks to Snowden, toward Justice Stewart's definition of a truly effective system. But to date, the new disclosures pertain mostly to the surveillance activities that Snowden had access to, with only a few transparency impacts on the rest of the U.S. national security colossus (the most important involve the intelligence budget and drone targeting). The new openness may turn out to be a temporary condition rather than the "zero-based budgeting" that would rebuild the classification system from the ground up. Even with the Snowden revelations—in fact, as proven by Snowden's ability to leak—we still have a secrecy system that places low fences around vast prairies of classified information, when we actually need very high fences around the tiny graveyards that hold the real secrets that would get someone killed.[4]

President Obama wrongly defined the surveillance and secrecy challenge in his January 17, 2014, speech as that of "maintain[ing] the trust of the American people, and people around the world." He was more correct, in the same speech, to say, "Given the unique power of the state, it is not enough for leaders to say: Trust us, we won't abuse the data we collect. For history has too many examples when that trust has been breached. . . . [O]ur liberty cannot depend on the good intentions of those in power; it depends on the law to constrain those in power."[5] Building a credible national security secrecy system will require much less secrecy, many more checks and balances built into law, and, yes, much to the discomfort of those in power, more Snowdens.

THE SECRECY DEBATE

U.S. government today ranks among the most open in the world, even in matters of national security. Foreigners look in awe at the public and often contentious confirmation process for American spymasters; the frequent debates over specifics on cost overruns in weapons systems; the regular military and foreign policy reporting to Congress, much of which takes place in televised hearings; the wide variety of internal and external audit mechanisms, such as inspectors general; and the often routine openness in other areas of government, which reformers in the rest of the world are trying to emulate. At the same time, however, the U.S. government creates and keeps more secrets than any other state in the world—in fact, if the size of the U.S. national security establishment is any guide, U.S. agencies have more secrets than the next ten largest countries put together. Most open and most secret—such is the paradox of U.S. national security secrecy.

The scholar Daniel Hoffman's analysis of the Founders of the American republic shows they deliberately meant to overturn monarchical notions of secrets of state, the absolutism found in King Louis's famous exhortation, *"L'état, c'est moi."*[6] Publicity for congressional proceedings would be the norm, for example—the U.S. Constitution only specifically mentions secrecy a single time, in Article I, Section 5: "Each House shall keep a Journal of its Proceedings, and from time to time publish the same, excepting such Parts as may in their judgment require secrecy; and the Yeas and Nays of the Members of either House on any question shall, at the Desire of one fifth of those Present, be entered on the Journal."

Conceptually, the Founders' formulation offers some real guidance for today. An echo may be found in statutes 200 years later, like the Freedom of Information Act, and even in President Obama's "Day One" commitments to open government—that we need a presumption of openness for government information, with "exceptions" for real secrets as established by some democratic and legal process. Of course, this concept is turned on its head by the almost absolute secrecy around modern communications intelligence matters, before Snowden, where the presumption was secrecy, leaving exceptions to be staked out by leakers or guessed at by the public. This issue—whether a presumption of openness or of secrecy—lies at the heart of the current debate over surveillance transparency.

As on slavery, the Founders' intent failed to settle the issue. Even at the time, the debate over secrecy raged, and both reformers and securocrats can today find support for their views in what the Founders said and did. Reformers like to cite James Madison's admonition that "a people that mean to be their own Governors, must arm themselves with the power which Knowledge gives." However, Madison also defended, against Thomas Jefferson's criticism, the closed doors of the Constitutional Convention, so that delegates could be protected from outside pressures, change their minds, avoid posturing, and build consensus (the 1787 proceedings were not published in full until 1819, thirty-two years later).[7] The Continental Congress, of course, ran the revolution through various secret committees, which had permission to hide even from the rest of Congress the identities of their correspondents; and the first legislative appropriation of the newly independent country gave President George Washington a secret fund to use for ransoming American hostages abroad, or bribing foreign officials—the historic precursor to intelligence budget secrecy today.[8]

Secrecy figured centrally in the constitutional debates over the leading role of the executive. Alexander Hamilton insisted, in his Federalist Paper number 70, that "[d]ecision, activity, secrecy, and dispatch" were the main qualities required of the executive (he was arguing against those trying to weaken the President's powers). Yet John Dickinson of Delaware, also arguing for a strong but checked and balanced presidency, pushed back: "Secrecy, vigor & dispatch are not the principle properties reqd. in the Executive. Important as these are, that of responsibility is more so. . . ."[9]

These examples illustrate a tension as old as the republic. Perhaps most eloquent of the Founders was Patrick Henry, who wrote, "to cover with the veil of secrecy the common routine of business is an abomination. . . ." Yet Henry also explained, "Such transactions as relate to military operations or affairs of great consequence, the immediate promulgation of which might defeat the interests of the community, I would not wish to be published, till the end which required their secrecy should have been effected." However, in the context of an endless war against terror, when would that be? And who would judge?

These questions become most difficult in the context of the modern administrative state. By the 1930s, an alphabet soup of new federal programs joined the regulatory agencies invented by the Progressives, and as government expanded, so did pushback by interest groups and reformers, creating transparency mechanisms like the *Federal Register* (1936) and rules that would become the notice-and-comment requirement in the Administrative Procedure Act of 1946. During World War II, the U.S. government dramatically grew into what analyst Harold Relyea (of the Congressional Research Service) has described as the "national security state," with secrecy as "one of its primary characteristics."[10] Writing just before World War I, as corporate and governmental bureaucracies began to proliferate, the German sociologist Max Weber situated the secrecy problem in core bureaucratic practice: "Every bureaucracy seeks to increase the superiority of the professional informed by keeping their knowledge and intentions secret. Bureaucratic administration always tends to be an administration of 'secret sessions'; in so far as it can, it hides its knowledge and actions from criticism. . . . The concept of the 'official secret' is the specific invention of bureaucracy, and nothing is so fanatically defended by the bureaucracy as this attitude. . . . In facing a parliament, the bureaucracy, out of a sure power instinct, fights every attempt of the parliament to gain knowledge by means of its own experts or from interest groups."[11]

There were of course real reasons for the national security secrecy, to keep enemies in the dark, but mixed motivations characterized the American secrecy system from the start. Take the Manhattan Project, which built the atomic bomb and also gave birth to most of the features of the modern classification system, such as security clearance investigations, compartments, "need to know" restrictions, and document markings. When the Manhattan Project's commander, the legendary General Leslie Groves, later worked on his memoir with his son, Groves produced a fascinating list of eight justifications for the shroud of secrecy he had placed over all atomic matters, according to his biographer, Robert S. Norris. The Germans and the Japanese provided the top two motivations for secrecy, of course, and the then-allies-future-enemies of the Soviet Union were number three. But "all other nations" including the other allies, like Great Britain, were target number four. Most revealing was number five, "those who would interfere directly with the progress of the work, such as Congress and various executive branch agencies"! Number six limited discussion to a small group of officials; number seven aimed for military "surprise"; and number eight mentioned "need to know" as a management tool, perhaps to control those unruly scientists.[12] Max Weber would find much to work with in the Groves list.

Those scientists had been the inventors of nuclear secrecy, not the military, not the security officers. Enrico Fermi credits the Hungarian refuge Leó Szilárd as the one who came up with the idea of self-censorship, of removing physics research related to fission from the scholarly literature after 1939. What Groves and the security officers did in the Manhattan Project was to take the scientists' peer-review censorship committees and turn them into a pervasive bureaucratic system. Afterward, Szilárd himself complained that in fact the controls on information imposed on the scientists contradicted everything he knew about how scientific progress occurs, and specifically that the compartmented approach—separating scientists into small groups based on "need to know," as if Groves possessed enough omniscience to decide the need—prolonged the war in the Pacific for more than a year by holding up recognition of how quantities of U-235 could be produced in mass.[13] However, the securocrats, not the scientists, were in charge.

Communications intelligence joined nuclear weapons as the main drivers of the new information security system during World War II and after. Breaking the Japanese and German codes ranked among the most sensitive secrets in the U.S. government. When the *Chicago Tribune*'s front-page coverage of the U.S. victory at the Battle of Midway in 1942 revealed—without explicitly saying so—that the United States was reading Japanese naval messages, security officials wanted to prosecute the newspaper and the Justice Department convened a grand jury to do so. Ultimately the Navy Secretary called off the proceedings because apparently Japan had missed the *Tribune* story as well as the subsequent controversy (including a Member of Congress actually confirming the fact of the intercepts)—thus the U.S. government feared that any further legal action might bring the matter to Japan's attention.[14] Here, the judgment call in effect concluded that the maximal pursuit of secrecy in the name of security would actually damage that security.

Broken codes also figured prominently in the widely read critiques of secrecy after the Cold War by U.S. Senator Daniel P. Moynihan, especially in the 1997 report of the commission he chaired. The commission's very title—"On Protecting and Reducing Government Secrecy"—reflected some cognitive dissonance among its congressional sponsors and cochairs (Moynihan the Democrat from New York and Larry Combest, conservative Republican from Texas), although reformers would argue that one better protects the real secrets by reducing the rest. For Moynihan, most striking were the ways in which institutional secrecy enabled the security establishment to get the main problems wrong, and to forestall public knowledge and debate of major Cold War issues, from the true dimensions of Soviet spying in the 1940s to the coming collapse of the Soviet Union in the 1980s. Moynihan focused his argument on "Venona"—the U.S. intelligence community's decrypted intercepts of 1940s Soviet diplomatic and military cable traffic that proved the existence of multiple Soviet spy rings in the United States. While the U.S. government brought high-profile (and highly controversial) prosecutions against many of these accused spies in the late 1940s, the government refused to declassify even the existence of the intercepts or their use in driving the prosecutions—which Moynihan subsequently believed would have settled the public debate.

Moynihan argued that the excessive secrecy about the "Venona" COMINT left free rein for both McCarthyism and denial, both hysterical overreach and a false conclusion of persecution. All this because of a secrecy system that ironically enabled both understating the real Soviet spy threat of the 1940s and misunderstanding how the United States had largely eliminated that threat by the early 1950s, when the Red Scare mounted into paranoia. For Moynihan, the real cost of national security secrecy included the McCarthyism divisions in society, and the subsequent inflation and overinvestment in military power from overstating the strength of the Communist system by the 1970s and 1980s.[15]

Moynihan's subsequent 1998 book, Secrecy, joined the volumes that have been written on the history of Cold War secrecy, and on the periodic scandals that threw back the national security shrouds for significant periods of time. Suffice it here to say that this history is notable for the patterns of enormous growth in classified information since World War II, interrupted in almost every decade by scandal-driven openness, soon followed by retrenchment and more secrecy. The 1970s forced the greatest openness on the U.S. intelligence community, from the Pentagon

Papers revelations to the Watergate abuses to the Church and Pike committee investigations of spy agency lawbreaking. For the National Security Agency, that period represents perhaps the only analog to the current post-Snowden period of investigation and exposure (about which much more below).

But during the 1980s, the Iran-Contra scandal showed how limited the 1970s reforms really were, and exposed the return of some of the worst practices of Cold War secrecy and covert operations on and off the books. Investigators later complained that the National Security Agency was the only intelligence agency that stuck to its secrecy claims—forcing unwarranted redactions in the official Iran-Contra reports. Those same reports actually gave NSA some credit for refusing to edit its briefing flow to top officials (intercepts of the arms-for-hostages negotiations, for example) despite White House attempts at cover-up, and those officials' attempts to seem "out of the loop."[16]

The end of the Cold War of course brought large reductions in the military and intelligence budgets, and a parallel decline in national security secrecy during the 1990s. Perhaps most notably, then–Vice President Al Gore's interest in longitudinal environmental data drove the declassification of decades of spy satellite photos, when less than ten years earlier, a Navy analyst had gone to prison for leaking one of them to *Jane's Defence Weekly*. The Clinton administration wrote a new executive order on secrecy, prompting the declassification of hundreds of millions of pages of historic secrets. Also during the 1990s, Congress drove major declassification programs, responding to the hit conspiracy film *JFK* by establishing a blue-ribbon commission responsible for releasing the classified records around the 1963 Kennedy assassination— including the CIA's covert operations files on Cuba. Similarly, responding to news reports of Nazi war criminals living in the United States under protection from agencies like the CIA, Congress set up another panel to drive the release of both Nazi and Japanese war crimes records, including the unprecedented release of CIA "name files" on key Nazis like Adolf Eichmann.[17]

The Moynihan report of 1997 paradoxically represented the high point of the 1990s secrecy reform movement. By 1998 Congress had lost its interest in JFK- and Nazi-style declassification projects, as Chinese spying hysteria swept Capitol Hill (ultimately to collapse with a governmental apology to the poster child, nuclear scientist Wen Ho Lee). The simultaneous Clinton impeachment process devoured the available oxygen in the public policy sphere and undermined the previous progress on open government. The CIA reneged on its declassification program promises on the day the House of Representatives impeached Clinton; and Congress even passed an official secrets act, criminalizing leaks to the media, only to have Clinton veto the bill at the last minute in 2000.

Intelligence officials had persuaded Congress to pass that vetoed official secrets act by presenting classified briefings about cases of leaks that allegedly did severe damage to national security, but some years later, when the FOIA opened those case studies to public view, the stories fell apart.[18] Two in particular centered on communications intelligence leaks with relevance to Snowden today. The classified briefings to Congress in 2000 had claimed that a leak to the columnist Jack Anderson in 1971 had cut off U.S. access to the car phones of Soviet Politburo members driving around Moscow, thus depriving the United States of an extraordinary intelligence source. However, Anderson's biographer Mark Feldstein found Anderson's notes of phone calls checking with government officials in which Anderson agreed to hold the story. After the CIA Director and the Justice Department confirmed that the Soviets knew about the intercepts, Anderson then wrote about the intelligence coup, but not about the specifics of the car phones: "For obvious security reasons, we can't give a clue as to how it's done."[19] The CIA's James Bruce, the "Vice Chairman of the Director of Central Intelligence Foreign Denial and Deception Committee," responsible for the classified case studies briefed to Congress, committed his own denial and deception, either advertently or inadvertently missing the entire sequence of events.

The CIA and James Bruce compounded the error by focusing Congress's attention—in secret sessions—on the purported loss from leaks of U.S. intelligence's ability to listen to Osama bin Laden's satellite phone. The Bruce briefing artfully used a quote from White House Press Secretary Ari Fleischer on June 20, 2002 (repeated by President George W. Bush in 2005), blaming a leak and a press report in *The Washington Times* for Bin Laden's ceasing to use his satellite phone in 1998, thus thwarting the National Security Agency's intercepts. The claim also appeared in a best-selling book on terrorism written by former Clinton administration aides, and even in the 9/11 Commission's final report after Bruce and his team gave classified briefings to the Commission. However, once the Bruce/Bush/Fleischer claim could actually be fact-checked in public, it fell apart, as the 9/11 Commission cochair Lee Hamilton subsequently acknowledged. The purported 1998 leak had been preceded by Bin Laden's own discussion in a 1997 CNN interview of his satellite phone use, by the 1996 assassination of the Chechen leader Dzhokhar Dudayev by a Russian cruise missile targeted on his satellite phone, and by the August 1998 U.S. cruise missile attack on Bin Laden's own training camp in Afghanistan, from which he had departed only hours earlier. Like so many alleged secrets, this one turned out to be public information; and *The Washington Post* concluded the leak story actually ranked as an "urban myth."[20]

The backstory of the official secrets act that Congress passed and Clinton vetoed in 2000 shows that secrecy was on the rise even before the terrorist attacks of 9/11. After 9/11, with a heightened sense of threat and even paranoia, government at every level moved its operations under wraps. The massive increases in new security classification decisions might well have happened anyway with the surge in military and intelligence activities, the doubling of those budgets, and the two wars in Afghanistan and Iraq ordered by President George W. Bush, but in addition to the perhaps understandable secrecy related to current war fighting, the securocrats took the opportunity to go back and reverse decisions about historic records, about the documents released in the 1990s, and about whole categories of records having nothing to do with the war on terror that now were pulled back to the vaults. Securocrats at the Department of Energy, the CIA, and the Air Force even began formal but secret reclassification programs (actually full employment programs for their retirees, now working as contract reviewers) to take back the millions of pages released in the 1990s.[21]

And the new secrecy generated its equal and opposite reaction in the form of leaks. Or more precisely, the overreaching claims of government authority that drove both the new secrecy and even more controversial programs of detention, interrogation, surveillance, and assassination also sparked a pluralistic system's internal antibodies against authority in the form of whistleblowers. Cases like those of Thomas Drake at the National Security Agency and Thomas Tamm at the Justice Department are discussed elsewhere in this book, as are the advances in electronic surveillance that empowered government prosecutors who started under George W. Bush and then continued under Barack Obama, to bring more leak prosecutions in the last five years than all previous administrations put together.

Thus, even before Snowden, the policy debate over secrecy had reached a new level of ferocity, with members of Congress and conservative analysts calling for prosecution of *The New York Times*, for example, over various stories based on leaks.[22] The media vigorously defended itself with two arguments, first the one about journalistic ethical responsibility for getting comment from any affected parties, especially on national security issues in which reporters must have a dialogue with knowledgeable government officials before publishing classified information. Such a responsibility extended even to the point of censoring themselves (as did *The Washington Post* on the location of the CIA's secret prisons in countries like Poland, as did even WikiLeaks on the names of people who talked to U.S. embassies in the Wiki cables). Famously, *The New York Times* held the first version of its story on warrantless wiretapping under President George W. Bush for over a year, until reporting by its Justice Department correspondent (Eric Lichtblau) both confirmed its intelligence correspondent (James Risen) and established that senior officials at Justice believed parts of the program to be illegal.[23]

The other media argument of course has the virtue of historical consistency. At the core of this argument is the analysis in the famous affidavit in the Pentagon Papers case by *New York Times* editor Max Frankel:

> *Presidents make "secret" decisions only to reveal them for the purposes of frightening an adversary nation, wooing a friendly electorate, protecting their reputations. The military services conduct "secret" research in weaponry only to reveal it for the purpose of enhancing their budgets, appearing superior or inferior to a foreign army, gaining the vote of a congressman or the favor of a contractor. The Navy uses secret information to run down the weaponry of the Air Force. The Army passes on secret information to prove its superiority to the Marine Corps. High officials of the Government reveal secrets in the search for support of their policies, or to help sabotage the plans and policies of rival department. Middle-rank officials of government reveal secrets so as to attract the attention of their superiors or to lobby against the orders of those superiors.*

Or to quote President John F. Kennedy, the ship of state is the only vessel that leaks from the top.[24] In such a context, the media must report and parse the leaks, and does so under the protection of the First Amendment.

Yet the Constitution is not "a suicide pact," as we are reminded by the securocrats.[25] An absolutist First Amendment position remains untenable, according to the federal courts. So in between the securocrats and the First Amenders come the hairsplitters. The most thoughtful of the fencewalkers, Princeton professor Rahul Sagar, situates the problem—the lack of balance between secrecy and openness—in a series of constitutional silences. Sagar argued—before Snowden—that while leaks of national security information like the *Times*'s 2005 story on warrantless wiretapping are necessary to accountability, they should be maximally discouraged, involving as they do the breaking of oaths, the undercutting of representational democratic channels for decision-making about what information should be public, and mixed motivations by the leakers and the reporters.[26]

Rebutting Sagar are some interesting apostates. Foremost would be Harvard Law professor Jack Goldsmith, himself no slouch in defending executive privilege as a former head of George W. Bush's Office of Legal Counsel. Goldsmith wrote some of the still-secret legal opinions justifying warrantless snooping. After Snowden, he became more forthright in his conclusions. Before Snowden, Goldsmith only argued that Bush had made a mistake in seizing executive power unilaterally and secretly, when Congress and the public would have granted almost but not quite all of that power had Bush asked.[27] After Snowden, Goldsmith argued against Sagar's notions by maintaining that secrecy in a democracy has a presumption of illegitimacy. Not because there are no real secrets—of course there are—but because "in a constitutional democracy where the People ultimately rule, secrecy from the People is aberrant (for they cannot govern what they do not know), and it demands special justification (thus the presumption against its legitimacy)."[28] Similarly, Suffolk University law professor

Alasdair Roberts has argued that the technologies and specifics of intelligence gathering can and likely should be classified, but the policies surrounding their applications cannot be secret and still have legitimacy or accountability. The Snowden revelations have now given even more force to the Goldsmith and Roberts formulations.

NO SUCH AGENCY

The National Security Agency before Snowden enjoyed a presumption of secrecy—an idyllic form of self-protection that came in handy in surviving all kinds of scandal. There was some real basis to the secrecy—cryptological codes and methods and technologies were appropriately classified—but the absolute secrecy covered matters ranging from the pizza boxes produced from the NSA's shredded papers all to the way up to the policy decisions that allowed, as Snowden's leaks showed, the collection of the "to-from-date-time-duration" metadata on every single phone call made in the United States on the Verizon phone network, to name just one such company. The contradiction was present at the creation of the NSA—presidential orders pursuant to the National Security Act of 1947 established the NSA in 1952, but not until 1957 was the agency publicly acknowledged in the Government Manual. As mentioned, the initials quickly became a quip, "No Such Agency," yet the "secret" of its existence actually showed the limits of the secrecy system: Washington-area newspapers had revealed the NSA's existence in stories as early as 1954 about the building of its sprawling Ford Meade, Maryland, campus.[29]

That campus would ultimately become what writer James Bamford called "Crypto City"—an enormous collection of thousands of employees and even more thousands of contractors housed in dozens of buildings and spending tens of billions of taxpayer dollars each year. Bamford's trilogy of books on the NSA argues that the technological opportunities drove much of the expansion of NSA from 1952 onward. In 1929, at the time of Herbert Yardley's "Black Chamber," the entire code-breaking apparatus of the U.S. government could fit into a single 25-foot-square room. By the time of the 9/11 attacks, the NSA occupied a whole campus at Ford Meade, with 32 miles of roads, parking lots amounting to 325 acres, and more than 7 million square feet of office space. All covered by a presumption of secrecy.[30]

For the purposes of a post-Snowden analysis, what is most striking about the NSA's secret history has been the dramatic ebbs and flows of secrecy around the agency's operations. The NSA's secret creation in 1952 took five more years before public acknowledgment in 1957, but actual operational exposure like Snowden's would come two decades later, in the 1970s. From its earliest days, the NSA picked up a preexisting program, called Project SHAMROCK, that intercepted every single overseas telegram starting in 1945, millions each year, with the secret cooperation of all three cable companies (RCA, Western Union, and ITT). This ultimately produced (as of the early 1970s) some 150,000 messages each month that were selected for NSA's analysts to review.[31] Then, starting in 1962 with some Mafia figures whose names were provided by the FBI and the Justice Department, the NSA cooperated with the CIA on a watch list program, code name MINARET, that ultimately included some 300,000 people in the index, mostly antiwar dissidents and political activists and public figures.[32] Here is the precedent for the post-9/11 warrantless wiretapping, but the earlier program at least had specific targets rather than mass collection of data. The targets included the Reverend Martin Luther King Jr., Tom Wicker of *The New York Times*, even *Washington Post* humor columnist Art Buchwald! The list also featured two U.S. senators, the Democrat Frank Church from Idaho and Republican Howard Baker of Tennessee.

Senator Church went on to lead the congressional investigations (1975–1976) that exposed the SHAMROCK and MINARET programs—with much help from insider leaks and investigative reporters. Church concluded: "The United States government has perfected a technological capability that enables us to monitor the messages that go through the air. . . . That capability at any time could be turned around on the American people, and no American would have any privacy left, such is the capability to monitor everything—telephone conversations, telegrams, it doesn't matter. There would be no place to hide."[33] Those conclusions, along with considerations of immunity for the corporations that had cooperated with wiretapping, and considerations of admissibility of evidence in court, led to the Ford and Carter administrations' support for what ultimately became the FISA Act of 1978.[34]

For the NSA, the mid-1970s exposure of their darkest secrets meant a sea change in both operations and self-perception. One senior NSA officer wrote up their new realization in a secret internal newsletter: "We might as well get used to it, used to feeling exposed and unprotected at moments when our accustomed and familiar anonymity seems to be snatched away." She hoped that their "time of indecent exposure" was coming to an end, but concluded: "Packs of hungry animals of various breeds, having caught the scent, are out there gnawing at the foundations of the storehouses, sniffing and rooting for more beans."[35]

Indeed, more "beans" about the SHAMROCK and MINARET programs have emerged in the years since the Church Committee. Through Freedom of Information and Mandatory Review requests, the nongovernmental National Security Archive pried loose the NSA history with the actual names from the watch lists, and a remarkable observation by the agency's own historian: "The project, which became known officially as Minaret in 1969, employed unusual procedures. NSA distributed reports without the usual serialization. They were designed to look like HUMINT reports rather than SIGINT, and readers could find no originating agency. Years later the NSA lawyer who first looked at the procedural aspects stated that the people involved seemed to understand that the operation was disreputable if not outright illegal."[36]

The pendulum swings of NSA secrecy have been perhaps most visible in the agency's treatment of its outside biographer, journalist James Bamford. Through diligent interviewing of NSA retirees and spelunking in their private archives in the late 1970s, Bamford amassed such documentary gems as a complete series of the NSA employee newsletter and the Justice Department's internal discussion (as of 1978) of possible prosecution of the NSA over MINARET and SHAMROCK. Before his 1981 book could be published, Bamford faced prosecution threats himself from the government, and the NSA's security agents repossessed various archival collections used by him from the open shelves of libraries. However, when undertaking his sequel in the 1990s, Bamford enjoyed direct interview time with the NSA Director, a tour of the facilities at Fort Meade, and ultimately even an NSA-hosted book party—so, perhaps not surprisingly, when the book, *Body of Secrets,* came out in 2001 (before 9/11), there was a noticeably more favorable tone in his depiction of the NSA.[37] Likewise, in the 1990s, the NSA actually declassified key directives like the 1993 USSID and the minimization procedures used, for example, to protect First Lady Hillary Clinton's privacy during foreign travel, along with the NSA's own 1998 organizational chart. After 9/11, the next version of the organizational chart came out almost completely blacked out, redacted.[38]

Between 9/11 and the warrantless wiretapping controversy that began with *The New York Times* story on December 16, 2005, the main secrecy battle at the NSA concerned ancient history—the Vietnam War. An enterprising NSA historian had gone back to the original raw signals intercepts from the controversial Gulf of

Tonkin episode in August 1964, in which the Johnson administration claimed two unprovoked attacks by North Vietnamese ships on the U.S. Navy as the basis for bombing the North and escalating the war in the South. The historian's classified article uncovered the way in which intercepted North Vietnamese naval messages had been mistakenly prioritized, conflated, even merged (and later covered up) in such a way as to reinforce what policy makers wanted to hear, confirming a second attack that never happened but that would justify military response and a ramping up of the Vietnam War. It took years of Freedom of Information pressure, news media coverage, a leak of part of the history, and embarrassment for the NSA before the underlying historical article would be declassified in 2005.[39]

These ebbs and flows of NSA secrecy illustrate some of secrecy's costs. Because of the reflexive secrecy, the government fails to understand its own history. The secrecy reinforces that eternal temptation for policy makers to cherry-pick information that suits their preferred policies; suppress dissent and alternative views; and cover for incompetence, inaccuracy, and illegality. In fact, the record shows the 9/11 attacks themselves were enabled by excessive secrecy. Likewise, the dirty little secret of the vastly expanded national security secrecy after 9/11 is that the new shrouds were actually counterproductive. This may seem a controversial finding, but it is one shared by both of the major official investigations of the 9/11 attacks.

For example, the joint congressional investigation of 9/11 found "the U.S. Intelligence Community was involved in fighting a 'war' against Bin Ladin largely without the benefit of what some would call its most potent weapon in that effort: an alert and committed American public." The 9/11 Commission found the problem was not a lack of dots to connect, a lack of haystacks to search, or a lack of intercepts to read, but the active withholding of information inside the government by the CIA from the FBI that might have caught the two future hijackers living in San Diego. According to the 9/11 Commission, the CIA's interrogations of 9/11 planner Ramzi bin al-Shibh revealed the hijackers would have called off the attacks if there had been any publicity about the arrest of Zacarias Moussaoui, the Minnesota flight school student who only wanted to learn to steer, not take off or land. Most of the ten "operational opportunities" to deter the attacks involved the failure to share information. And after 9/11, first responders complained that the censorship of online maps and diagrams (for example, of Air Force One) blocked effective emergency response. The FBI complained that the haystack approach of vacuuming up phone calls actually generated hundreds of thousands of unproductive leads, overwhelming the ability of agents to focus on real threats.[40]

By 2005, an emerging consensus began to include overclassification as among the "emerging threats" to U.S. security. A congressional hearing in March 2005 heard estimates of the problem from a number of experts, including the Deputy Undersecretary of Defense for Counterintelligence and Security who answered "50–50" when asked how much overclassification there was. Quoted in the hearing record was 9/11 Commission cochair Tom Kean (former Republican governor of New Jersey). After he finished going through the most recent Osama bin Laden intelligence, he remarked that "[t]hree-quarters of what I read that was classified shouldn't have been." Also quoted was President Reagan's former National Security Council Executive Secretary Rodney McDaniel, who told the Moynihan Commission in 1997 that only 10 percent of classification was for "legitimate protection of secrets."[41] Perhaps it is no coincidence that 2005 also brought the first public notice to the NSA's programs of warrantless wiretapping.

The secrecy hid all the key policy turning points for surveillance after 9/11. The record post-Snowden shows that the NSA received three new authorizations to go beyond its statutory limits on October 4, 2001, based just on presidential commander-in-chief authority. Another policy turning point secretly occurred in March 2004, with the now-famous hospital room confrontation between the White House and the attorney general (backed up by his deputy and the FBI Director) over the e-mail metadata intercept program that was collecting way too much American citizen information. All in secret, that confrontation shook President Bush to the point that he overruled his own staff and scaled back the program, which ultimately (secretly) ended in 2011 on inefficiency grounds. Just as the secrecy debate was erupting in Washington in 2005, the NSA secretly passed a milestone by collecting all the e-mail and phone calls produced in Iraq that year. The newly proven capacity to vacuum up everything became the template for collections not only abroad but at home, supervised by the aggressive new NSA Director, General Keith Alexander. First Iraq, then the world.[42]

The hyperactive growth of the intelligence establishment did not go unnoticed. Perhaps the most innovative attempt to grasp the full dimensions of the U.S. government's spy agencies came with the 2010 *Washington Post* series and subsequent book by Dana Priest and William Arkin, *Top Secret America*. Here, counterterrorism is the driver of extraordinary growth especially among government contractors, with the greed motivation front and center. In effect, Priest and Arkin argue, national security secrecy served mainly to protect contractors' profit margins. The core tools of the ambitious Priest/Arkin mapping process came from contractor job announcements and job descriptions, often containing descriptions of intelligence programs and even code words. Clinching their case was the revolving door created by the first Director of National Intelligence, a centralizing reform of the community pushed by the 9/11 Commission. But former NSA Director Admiral Mike McConnell did not last long in the job, and left the government to take his 1,000 percent raise, as a $2 million a year executive at an intelligence community contractor.[43]

In all this reporting, there were more than hints of what the NSA was up to. In 2005, the National Security Archive obtained through FOIA the NSA's transition briefing prepared for the incoming Bush administration in 2000. That briefing straightforwardly announced that the reality of global networks requires that "senior leadership understand that today's and tomorrow's mission will demand a powerful, permanent presence on a global telecommunications network that will host the 'protected' communications of Americans as well as targeted communications of adversaries."[44] In December 2005, *The New York Times* broke the warrantless wiretapping story, and in May 2006, *USA Today* broke the telephone metadata mass collection story—but with much less impact than the *Times*'s account, at least in part because of the lack of primary source documentation. Edward Snowden would take care of that problem.

THE SNOWDEN TSUNAMI

Out of the "tens of thousands of documents" (Glenn Greenwald's phrase) handed over by former NSA contractor Edward Snowden in May and June 2013 to *The Guardian* columnist Greenwald, the filmmaker Laura Poitras, and *The Washington Post* reporter Barton Gellman, a handful stand out for their shock value. The very first Snowden stories focused on an April 2013 order from the secret wiretap court, the FISA court, mandating that Verizon turn over to the government "all call detail records" not only for calls between the United States and abroad but also "wholly within the United States, including local telephone calls." The order cited Section 215 of the Patriot Act as the authority for this mass collection—news to that Act's authors, who never envisioned such a vacuum cleaner approach. Not only did the document show the government contravening Congress's intent, but the text showed that the Director of National Intelligence (DNI), James Clapper, had lied to Congress only a month earlier, in March 2013, when he answered a direct question about whether the NSA collected information on millions of Americans by saying, "No. Not wittingly." After the Snowden revelations, Clapper told NBC News reporter Andrea Mitchell that he had been trying to provide the "least untruthful" answer—an immortal phrase that will be summoned by teenagers facing irate parents for generations to come.[45]

The Verizon metadata order set the stage for a cascade of contradictions, as the documents and more reporting repeatedly undercut the U.S. government's claims about its surveillance programs. First up was President Obama himself, on the PBS *Charlie Rose* show (June 16, 2013), telling a couple of whoppers, that the wiretap court process was "transparent" (until the Snowden leak, not a single wiretap court order had ever seen the light of day), and that "if you are a U.S. person, the NSA cannot listen to your telephone calls and the NSA cannot target your e-mails." To the contrary, the PRISM documents leaked by Snowden showed the NSA could keep and search for five years any U.S. person's e-mails and calls "swept up as part of the agency's court-approved monitoring of a target overseas." The PRISM documents also showed direct access by the government to the servers of tech companies ranging from Google to Facebook, a revelation that damaged the companies' credibility and their business model for overseas growth. Subsequently, Google, Yahoo, and Microsoft, among others, announced that they would encrypt their data lines between servers to prevent such direct surveillance.

NSA took another credibility hit with the Snowden leak of the BOUNDLESS INFORMANT slides describing the agency's capacity to count precisely how many billions of records were being intercepted. Previously, NSA Director General Keith Alexander and DNI Clapper had claimed to Congress that they could not produce any precise numbers on targets or intercepts or messages analyzed. Subsequently, the NSA removed a series of inaccurate "fact sheets" on its surveillance programs from its official Web site.[46]

The entire administration suffered a hypocrisy hit when the journalists reporting on Snowden's documents published the classified Presidential Directive signed in November 2012 authorizing offensive cyber operations overseas. During this same period, the U.S. government had repeatedly attempted to focus media attention on hacking activity by the Chinese military and security services. Now, the White House press spokesman had to address the U.S. government's own behavior and the complicated policy issues that arise from deliberate state-sponsored attacks on computer networks abroad.

Other embarrassing Snowden documents that kept the White House press briefings lively showed the U.S. government surveilling the telephones of allies (like German Chancellor Angela Merkel, who demanded a public cease-and-desist order from President Obama) and friendlies (like Brazilian President Dilma Rousseff, who canceled her planned summit meeting in Washington). The documents detailed the XKEYSCORE program's capacity from 2007 to today as the "widest-reaching" of NSA's tools, able to capture "nearly everything a typical user does on the internet," including the text of e-mails and all searches, even in real time. In April 2013, according to the documents, XKEYSCORE gave the White House the UN Secretary General's confidential talking points before his meeting with Obama.

The fallout from the Snowden leaks revealed that top officials had lied not only to Congress but also to the wiretap court, to the Supreme Court, and to each other. For example, one wiretap court opinion held that NSA Director Alexander "strains credulity" with his 2009 classified declaration that repeated NSA violations of the court's limits on searches of stored intercepts arose simply from differences over "terminology." The lead author of the Patriot Act, Republican Congressman James Sensenbrenner of Wisconsin, contrasted what he learned from the Snowden leaks with the misrepresentations he said government officials had repeatedly made to him about the way they were using his own statute. The solicitor general of the United States, Donald Verrilli Jr., discovered that his own Justice Department lawyers had misled him prior to a Supreme Court argument. Arguing for the Court to throw out a challenge by Amnesty International and the ACLU (among others) to a 2008 wiretap law, Verrilli assured the Justices that defendants would be notified if warrantless wiretap information was used against them, and therefore could in the future challenge the constitutionality of those searches. Only after Snowden did Verrilli find out that prosecutors did not so notify defendants, and that the Supreme Court had dismissed the prior case on false grounds.[47]

Perhaps most egregiously, NSA Director Alexander's claims—repeated by many other officials and by members of Congress—that mass collection of call data had prevented fifty-four terrorist plots, soon evaporated under close inspection. Subsequent official investigations found that only thirteen of the fifty-four cases were even connected to the United States, that the bulk telephone metadata program had actually broken no such plots, and only identified a single terrorism supporter, whom the FBI was already tracking. The PRISM targeted collection deserved credit for contributing information to those fifty-four terrorism investigations, but the bulk collection program turned out to be little more than what the retiring deputy director of the NSA called an insurance policy.[48]

To President Obama's credit, perhaps realizing that his top intelligence officials were suffering a credibility gap, he ordered his own blue-ribbon review group to look at the surveillance programs, and also encouraged the existing Privacy and Civil Liberties Oversight Board (PCLOB) to investigate. Among other extraordinary findings (such as that the Section 215 metadata vacuum cleaner was illegal, ineffective, and unconstitutional), the PCLOB eviscerated the government's claims over a decade that congressional action—in the Patriot Act, in the FISA Amendments of 2008, and in the repeated renewals of surveillance authorities—meant that Congress had embraced the executive's interpretations. Rather, secrecy had completely undermined the constitutional checks and balances:

> [W]hen the only means through which legislators can try to understand a prior interpretation of the law is to read a short description of an operational program, prepared by executive branch officials, made available only at certain times and locations, which cannot be discussed with others except in classified briefings conducted by those same executive branch officials, legislators are denied a meaningful opportunity to gauge the legitimacy and implications of the legal interpretation in question. Under such circumstances, it is not a legitimate method of statutory construction to presume that these legislators, when reenacting the statute, intended to adopt a prior interpretation that they had no fair means of evaluating.[49]

According to the Oversight Board, George Orwell would find familiar the government's abuse of language and vocabulary:

> [S]anctioning the NSA's [bulk telephony metadata] program under Section 215 requires an impermissible transformation of the statute: Where its text fails to authorize a feature of the program (such as the daily production of new telephone records), such authority must be inferred from silence. Where its text uses limiting words (such as "relevant"), those words must be redefined beyond their traditional meaning. And where its text simply cannot be reconciled with the program (such as its direction that the FBI, not the NSA, receive any items produced), those words must be ignored.

Attorneys for the ACLU took the critique even further, highlighting the fact—revealed by the Snowden leaks—that the NSA was using a completely different dictionary than the rest of us. The words "surveillance," "collect," "targeted," "incidental," "inadvertent," "minimize," and even the word "no" as uttered by James Clapper—all meant something other than the dictionary definition when the NSA employed them.[50] Faced with the cascade of Snowden leaks and credibility contradictions, the Office of the Director of National Intelligence (ODNI) started racing to catch up, declassifying all kinds of documents that the NSA and the intelligence community had fought for years to keep secret. By the time of Obama's speech in January 2014, the President could actually brag that the government had declassified more than forty opinions and orders of the FISA court, as against three that Snowden leaked. James Clapper told reporters that he considered the documents still properly classified but that the damage to national security was outweighed by the public interest, so he was declassifying thousands of pages and putting them all online.[51] To David Ignatius of *The Washington Post*, Clapper argued that the real cost of the leaks was that he had to "throttle back" on collection in order to restore relationships with foreign intelligence partners and corporate partners. However, new documents about Yahoo's resistance to the government's orders suggest many of those "partners" no longer see themselves in cahoots.[52]

Unfortunately, Clapper's declassifications, as laudable as they were, often simply dug a bigger hole for the defenders of the surveillance programs. For example, the wiretap court had blasted the government in a secret October 2011 opinion for misleading the court. Senator Ron Wyden had hinted at the existence of such an opinion in published letters in the summer of 2012 as Congress was looking at reauthorizing the 2008 FISA Amendments (sunset in 2012). So the nongovernmental Electronic Frontier Foundation went to court with an FOIA request based on the Wyden letters, but the government said the whole opinion, eighty-five pages long, was top secret, so not a word could be released. After Snowden, in August 2013, the government released a redacted version of the opinion, and the public could see that one whole section—previously top secret—consisted of the actual text of the Fourth Amendment!

The right of the people to be secure in their persons, houses, papers, and effects, against unreasonable searches and seizures, shall not be violated, and no Warrants shall issue, but upon probable cause, supported by Oath or affirmation, and particularly describing the place to be searched, and the persons or things to be seized.

The other result from the ODNI declassifications, especially of the wiretap court submissions and opinions, was the exposure to public view of the government's almost complete reliance for its legal theory of surveillance and privacy on an obsolete and arguably inapplicable Supreme Court precedent from 1979, before cell phones were even invented. The recent Supreme Court decision in *Riley v. California* in June 2014 on cell phone privacy suggests the 1979 precedent (*Smith v. Maryland*) is in jeopardy, and that mere third-party possession of a person's call data (by the phone company, for example) may not in fact eliminate privacy rights. Such a new standard, which is strongly supported by the PCLOB, might well change the entire legal landscape for the government's surveillance activities.

THE NEW TRANSPARENCY OF THE INTELLIGENCE COMMUNITY POST-SNOWDEN

The intelligence community in general, and the National Security Agency in particular, remain on the defensive after Snowden, their misrepresentations exposed, their dictionary discredited, and their budgets under pressure. This chastened outlook comes through in the public statements by top officials, now that the Snowden frenzy of summer 2013 has settled down. For example, an interview with the new NSA Director, Admiral Michael Rogers, published in *The New York Times* in June 2014, appeared under the headline "Sky Isn't Falling After Snowden, N.S.A. Chief Says: Data Protection Cited: New Leader Calls Leaks Regrettable but Manageable."[53] If true, then we have either undergone a fundamental change in the definition of a secret, or we are witnessing a pragmatic adjustment to a new transparency forced on the NSA (likely the latter). What a contrast to the hyperventilation of Rogers's predecessor, General Keith Alexander, cited by the *Times* as calling the Snowden leaks "the greatest damage to our combined nations' intelligence systems that we have ever suffered."

No small degree of secrecy remorse is also on view. The ODNI's general counsel, Robert Litt, told a law school audience, "These leaks have forced the Intelligence Community to rethink our approach to transparency and secrecy. . . . One lesson that I have drawn from the recent events . . . is that we would likely have suffered less damage from the leaks had we been more forthcoming about some of our activities, and particularly about the policies and decisions behind those activities." Litt went on to endorse closer scrutiny of "what truly needs to be classified," "a mindset of proactively making available as much information as we can"—all because "Greater disclosure to the public is necessary to restore the American people's trust" that the surveillance was "not only lawful and important" but also "appropriate and proportional in light of the privacy interests at stake."[54]

The skeptic should note that this extraordinary reassessment was not driven by congressional oversight, or by judicial restraints, or by internal reformers or external advocacy, but by the public relations hit to the intelligence community's credibility from Snowden's leaks. Thus, as secrecy watchdog Steven Aftergood has observed, "leaks emerge as a uniquely powerful tool for shaping intelligence classification policy, while conventional checks and balances appear all but irrelevant by comparison."[55] The hazard is simply that the window is open right now, but it could slam shut again, with a single terrorist attack. There are only a handful of permanent reforms in place ensuring any greater transparency (the PCLOB, mainly, plus some internal civil liberties monitors in the intelligence agencies), so this breakthrough may well be temporary, but the changing mind-sets are certainly more than welcome.

One of the most eloquent voices on the new transparency came from National Security Agency retiring Deputy Director John C. "Chris" Inglis in his interview with NPR's *Morning Edition* in January 2014. Asked by host Steve Inskeep whether the NSA should have made the bulk collection program public much earlier, Inglis admitted, "In hindsight yes, in hindsight yes." Inglis went on, "I think going forward, what I would change is that we need to continue to move in the direction of having greater transparency about the nature of NSA, what its authorities are, how those authorities are brought to bear."

Even more telling, in the same NPR interview, after Inglis ominously warned that since the terrorists have been alerted to what we can do, they could now take precautions, Inskeep asked if that would really damage our security. Bin Laden had retreated to a house in Abbottabad. He was completely cut off from phone or Internet contact, only communicating via messengers. In effect, the threat of us listening to Bin Laden's conversations sent him back to the Middle Ages and dramatically reduced his capability. Inglis responded, "Well, at the base of your question I think you're right."[56]

Even President Obama, who criticized Snowden's actions for months, finally endorsed the public debate over surveillance, at long last, in his January 2014 speech on surveillance: "One thing I'm certain of: This debate will make us stronger." However, the

President acknowledged only in passing the credibility gap that Snowden had exposed—by saying "we must maintain the trust of the American people," the President certainly implied such trust was lacking at the moment. Inglis put the issue more colorfully during his NPR interview, trying to defend the metadata collection program. When asked about all the programs such as the Merkel intercepts, Inglis came up with an interesting standard for judging the propriety of intelligence activities: "So with respect to the totality of what NSA does, I think that not all of those have withstood the test of the optics, you know, or perhaps you know, the above the fold right side of the newspaper test."

Another test for the new transparency will be the administration's approach to intelligence budget secrecy. For decades, open government advocates had argued that keeping the U.S. intelligence budget secret amounted to a "fetish" that distorted rational secrecy decisions down the line. In 1997 and 1998, under pressure from a FOIA lawsuit by the Federation of American Scientists, then–CIA Director George Tenet finally agreed, since he found himself unable to sign an affidavit that release of the budget number would damage national security. Yet in 1999, Tenet resumed old habits, refusing to declassify the budget, and after the 9/11 attacks, further lawsuits seemed likely to fail. But the 9/11 Commission agreed with the reformers as part of the Commission's overall critique of excessive secrecy, and recommended not only routine declassification of the overall intelligence budget number but also the number for each of the intelligence agencies, so as to enable public policy debate about those agencies' performances and their claims on taxpayers' resources. Both President Obama and Congress ultimately acted on the former recommendation but not the latter, writing into law the routine declassification of the overall number.[57]

The Snowden leaks produced a potential game changer for the budget secrecy debate. Among the documents given to *The*

Washington Post was the top secret fiscal year 2013 budget justification for the intelligence community given to Congress in February 2012. Now a reader can compare and contrast the individual agencies and how they did budget-wise since 9/11. Incongruously, the agency that failed the most on 9/11, by hiding from the FBI its information on two would-be hijackers living in San Diego, profited the most in resource aggrandizement. The Snowden document showed the CIA's annual budget had soared over the period from 2004 to 2013, from $9 billion to nearly $16 billion. In the same period, the National Security Agency also saw significant increases, from $7 billion to $11 billion. Other data of obvious public policy importance in the budget document included the ominous fact that only about 10 percent of the intelligence community's personnel qualified for foreign language proficiency payments.[58] So far, there's been no hue and cry about national security damage from the budget revelations; so there comes a test for the Obama administration in the next year: Will the new transparency post-Snowden carry over to fulfilling the recommendation of the 9/11 Commission and routinely declassifying the intelligence budget at the agency level?

Finally, several of the recent declassifications provide tangible evidence of the mind-set change. For example, on June 26, 2014, the Director of National Intelligence released an actual "transparency report," giving his annual statistics for calendar year 2013 on numbers of court orders, targets, and National Security Letters. One has to read between the lines to understand the data, since a single "target" (say, the country of Afghanistan) could involve millions of people and all of their phone records and all of their e-mail records. But the top secret document was marked for declassification in the year 2039. Instead, the public received it in June 2014, in time for some policy debates and the legislative discussion in Congress about surveillance authorities. That's the Snowden effect—twenty-five years of secrecy undone.

NOTES

1. The official Director of National Intelligence Web site opened in August 2013 for the purpose of posting the new releases is http://icon therecord.tumblr.com/. The most comprehensive count of the Snowden documents may be found at www.cryptome.org.
2. See *Electronic Frontier Foundation Department of Justice*, C.A. No. 12-cv-1441. The Justice Department declaration was dated April 1, 2013— April Fool's Day.
3. For the text of the COMINT Act and an absolutist view of its meaning, see Gabriel Schoenfeld, *Necessary Secrets* (New York: Norton, 2010), 251–54.
4. This metaphor and the analysis behind it may be found in the author's congressional testimony to the House Judiciary Committee, December 16, 2010, "Hearing on the Espionage Act and the Legal and Constitutional Implications of Wikileaks."
5. See www.whitehouse.gov/the-press-office/2014/01/17/.
6. For an extended discussion of the contrast, see Daniel N. Hoffman, *Governmental Secrecy and the Founding Fathers* (Westport, CT: Greenwood, 1981).
7. For a recent argument for secrecy citing Madison, see Cass Sunstein, "Let Public Officials Work in Private," *Bloomberg View*, July 9, 2014.
8. See the invaluable history in Arvin S. Quist, *Security Classification of Information: Volume 2. Principles for Classification of Information* (Oak Ridge, TN: Oak Ridge National Laboratory, 1993), 187 and throughout.
9. Quotations of the Founders are from Daniel Hoffman, *Governmental Secrey and the Founding Fathers*.
10. Harold Relyea, "National Security and Information," *Government Information Quarterly* 4, no. 1 (1987): 11–19.
11. For an extended discussion of this history and the Weber quotation, see Alasdair Roberts, *Blacked Out: Government Secrecy in the Information Age* (Combridge, UK: Cambridge University Press, 2006), 11.
12. Robert S. Norris, *Racing for the Bomb* (Hanover, NH: Steerforth Press, 2002), 253–54.
13. For the Szilárd quote, see Schoenfeld, *Necessary Secrets*, 145.
14. See David Kahn, *The Codebreakers* (New York: Scribner 1996), especially page 591 on the reasons the Japanese missed the story. See also

the discussion in Schoenfeld, *Necessary Secrets*, 132–40, where he argues in favor of prosecution of newspapers that publish leaks.

15. See Daniel P. Moynihan, *Secrecy* (New Haven, CT: Yale University Press, 1998), which builds on the senator's essay in the 1997 commission report at Appendix A.

16. For the most up-to-date account, see Malcolm Byrne, *Iran-Contra: Reagan's Scandal and the Unchecked Abuse of Presidential Power* (Lawrence, KS: University Press of Kansas 2014).

17. These developments and more persuaded the author to call the 1990s the "decade of openness" in the essay "National Security and Open Government: Beyond the Balancing Test," in Alasdair Roberts, ed., *National Security and Open Government* (Syracuse, NY: Campbell Institute, Maxwell School, Syracuse University, 2003), 31–72.

18. The unclassified summary of the case studies is available on the Web site of the CIA's Center for the Study of Intelligence, authored by James B. Bruce under the title "The Consequences of Permissive Neglect: Laws and Leaks of Classified Intelligence," no date, but retrieved by the author on October 14, 2008. https://www.cia.gov/library/center-for-the-study-of-intelligence/kent-csi/vol47no1/pdf/v47i1a04p.pdf.

19. Mark Feldstein, *Poisoning the Press: Richard Nixon, Jack Anderson, and the Rise of Washington's Scandal Culture* (New York: Farrar, Straus and Giroux, 2010), 200–1.

20. Glenn Kessler, "File the Bin Laden Phone Leak Under 'Urban Myths,'" *Washington Post*, December 22, 2005.

21. See the National Security Archive electronic briefing book on "Declassification in Reverse," posted online February 21, 2006, and the *Washington Post* editorial "Classifying Toothpaste" on February 27, 2006, http://www2.gwu.edu/~nsarchiv/NSAEBB/NSAEBB179/index.htm, which includes *The Washington Post*, editorial as well.

22. See, for example, the book authored by Gabriel Schoenfeld, *Necessary Secrets*, and multiple public utterances cited therein by congressional leaders such as the chair of the House Intelligence Committee, Republican Mike Rogers of Michigan.

23. James Risen and Eric Lichtblau, "Bush Let U.S. Spy on Callers Without Courts," *New York Times*, December 16, 2005. Risen helped force the issue by putting his version of the story into a book, but the newsworthiness of the *Times*'s story came more from Lichtblau's account of the Justice Department's reservations—that we now know

extended to the March 2004 hospital room confrontations between White House Counsel Alberto Gonzales and then–Attorney General John Ashcroft.

24. The full Frankel quote may be found, among other places, in Schoenfeld, *Necessary Secrets,* 23.

25. The quotation originally came from Justice Robert Jackson in a free speech case in 1949, and was repurposed by Justice Arthur Goldberg in subsequent rulings. See Linda Greenhouse, "The Nation; Suicide Pact," *New York Times,* September 22, 2002.

26. Rahul Sagar, *Secrets and Leaks: The Dilemma of State Secrecy* (Princeton, NJ: University Press, 2013).

27. Jack Goldsmith, *The Terror Presidency: Law and Judgment Inside the Bush Administration* (New York: Norton, 2007).

28. Jack Goldsmith, "Critical Comments by Rahul Sagar on My Post on Kinsley," *Lawfare,* posted June 2, 2014, http://www.lawfareblog.com/2014/06/critical-comments-by-rahul-sagar-on-my-post-on-kinsley/.

29. See the authoritative overview of U.S. intelligence functions in Jeffrey T. Richelson, *The U.S. Intelligence Community,* sixth edition (Boulder, CO: Westview Press, 2009), with particular attention to the NSA's early years on pages 30–31.

30. James Bamford, *The Shadow Factory* (New York: Doubleday, 2008), for an updated version of his two previous best sellers on the NSA, *The Puzzle Palace New York* (Penguin, 1982) and *Body of Secrets* (New York: Anchor, 2001).

31. For more details, see Bamford, *The Puzzle Palace,* 459, and *The Shadow Factory,* 272–77.

32. Bamford, *The Puzzle Palace,* 317–24.

33. This oft-repeated quote appears as the epigraph to the book on the Snowden affair by Glenn Greenwald, *No Place to Hide* (New York: Henry Holt, 2014). Knowledgeable reviewers such as David Cole have disagreed with Greenwald that such is the government's motive, arguing instead that counterterrorism continues to be the primary driver of the U.S. government's surveillance programs. See David Cole, "NSA mantra: 'Collect it all . . . know it all,'" *Washington Post,* May 18, 2014.

34. See the National Security Archive electronic briefing book 178, "Wiretap Debate Déjà Vu," posted February 4, 2006, including the declassified recommendations of President Ford's advisers, over the

objections of Secretary of State Henry Kissinger and Defense Secretary Donald Rumsfeld, to set wiretap standards in law, http://www2.gwu.edu/~nsarchiv/NSAEBB/NSAEBB178/index.htm.

35. Vera Ruth Filby, "More Beans," *Cryptolog* (February 1978), a TOP SECRET in-house NSA newsletter quoted by Bamford, *The Puzzle Palace*, 390.

36. *American Cryptology During the Cold War, 1945–1989, Book III: Retrenchment and Reform, 1972–1980* (Fort Meade, MD: National Security Agency, 1998), TOP SECRET, declassified and posted online in National Security Archive electronic briefing books 260 (posted November 14, 2008) and 441 (posted September 25, 2013), http://www2.gwu.edu/~nsarchiv/NSAEBB/NSAEBB441/.

37. For the comparison, see Thomas Blanton, "Umbra Gamma Zarf (Above Top Secret to you, pal.)," *Bulletin of the Atomic Scientists* (January–February 2002): 62–63.

38. For copies of the two charts, see "The National Security Agency Declassified," National Security Archive electronic briefing book 24, updated posting March 11, 2005, http://www2.gwu.edu/~nsarchiv/NSAEBB/NSAEBB24/index.htm.

39. See the National Security Archive electronic briefing book 132, "Tonkin Gulf Intelligence 'Skewed' According to Official History and Intercepts," posted online December 1, 2005, http://www2.gwu.edu/~nsarchiv/NSAEBB/NSAEBB132/press20051201.htm.

40. For a summary account with citations to the original reports, see Alasdair Roberts, *Blacked Out*, 42–44.

41. For the specifics of these estimates, and extensive further data and recommendations for secrecy reform, see Thomas Blanton, "Statement to the U.S. House of Representatives, Committee on Government Reform, Hearing on 'Emerging Threats: Overclassification and Pseudo-Classification,'" March 2, 2005, posted online at http://www2.gwu.edu/~nsarchiv/news/20050302/index.htm.

42. See Bamford, *The Shadow Factory*, 331–33; for documents and more details on "collect it all," see Greenwald, *No Place to Hide*, 95–100.

43. Dana Priest and William M. Arkin, *Top Secret America: The Rise of the New American Security State* (Boston: Little, Brown and Company, 2011).

44. National Security Agency, Transition 2001 (December 2000), TOP SECRET declassified and posted online in National Security Archive electronic briefing book 24 (posted March 11, 2005), http://www2.gwu.edu/~nsarchiv/NSAEBB/NSAEBB24/index.htm.

45. For details on the Clapper quotes and the congressional hearing, see the National Security Archive's "Rosemary Award" online posting March 24, 2014, http://www2.gwu.edu/~nsarchiv/news/20140324/ and the story by Al Kamen, "Spy chief James Clapper wins not-so-coveted Rosemary Award," *Washington Post*, March 24, 2014.

46. For details on these and more examples of U.S. government lies exposed by the Snowden leaks, see Greg Miller, "Misinformation on Classified NSA Programs Includes Statements by Senior U.S. Officials," *Washington Post*, June 30, 2013.

47. See Charlie Savage, "Door May Open for Challenge to Secret Wiretaps," *New York Times*, October 16, 2013.

48. See Lauren Harper, "The 'Top 10' Surveillance Lies Edward Snowden's Leaks Shed 'Heat and Light' Upon," Unredacted (National Security Archive blog), posted January 17, 2014, http://nsar chive.wordpress.com/2014/01/17/the-top-10-surveillance-lies-edward -snowdens-leaks-shed-heat-and-light-on/.

49. Privacy and Civil Liberties Oversight Board, "Report on the Telephone Records Program Conducted under Section 215 of the USA PATRIOT Act and on the Operations of the Foreign Intelligence Surveillance Court," January 23, 2014, 101–2.

50. See Jameel Jaffer and Brett Max Kaufman, "Deciphering what NSA officials say (and what they really mean)," *Slate*, August 1, 2013.

51. ODNI Web site may be found at http://icontherecord.tumblr.com/.

52. See Craig Timberg, "U.S. threat led Yahoo to relent: Facing huge fines, firm released data," *Washington Post*, September 12, 2014.

53. David Sanger, "Sky Isn't Falling After Snowden, N.S.A. Chief Says: Data Protection Cited: New Leader Calls Leaks Regrettable but Manageable," *New York Times*, June 30, 2014.

54. Robert Litt speech to the American University Washington College of Law, Collaboration on Government Secrecy, Freedom of Information Day conference, March 18, 2014.

55. Steven Aftergood, "ODNI Rethinks Secrecy and Openness in Intelligence," Secrecy News, March 20, 2014, http://www.fas.org/blogs /secrecy/2014/03/litt-transparency/.

56. John C. Inglis interview, National Public Radio, *Morning Edition*, January 10, 2014.

57. For some twenty years of coverage of the intelligence budget secrecy issue, see the invaluable Secrecy News blog written by Steven Aftergood of the Federation of American Scientists, http://fas.org/sgp/.

58. Office of the Director of National Intelligence, *FY 2013 Congressional Budget Justification, Volume 1, National Intelligence Program Summary,* February 2012, http://www.washingtonpost.com/world/national -security/black-budget-summary-details-us-spy-networks-successes -failures-and-objectives/2013/08/29/7e57bb7810ab-11e3-8cdd -bcdc09410972_story.html. For the language proficiency data, see page 70. See also Barton Gellman and Greg Miller, "Black budget summary details U.S. spy network's successes, failures and objectives," *Washington Post,* August 29, 2013.

EPILOGUE

Ronald Goldfarb

WHEN I CONCEIVED the idea of a book analyzing the aftermath of the Snowden revelations, I had in mind presenting multiple explorations by various experts of the systemic questions raised by his disclosures. *After Snowden* does that, and offers recommendations for reforms. All of the chapters respect and acknowledge the very important societal need for careful protection of our nation's security in a very dangerous time, while they point out systemic problems and offer sensible reform measures to improve them.

Professor Siegel's chapter urges a fundamental change in the judicial treatment of the state secrets defense. That could be accomplished by the Department of Justice simply changing its position of invariably claiming that national security interests foreclose adjudications in all cases questioning secret government actions. In addition, the courts themselves could reform their current practice of thoughtless deferral to that executive claim, acting within its inherent judicial power to do so in appropriate instances. That is not to say that courts should never affirm the government's claim for secrecy, but that it should independently decide when to uphold the claim on the merits.

Congress could improve its oversight performance by adopting the recommendations of the prestigious bipartisan 9/11 Commission. Experts with unique CIA and Senate experience agree that the present system is inadequate and overly politicized. Recent disclosures raise serious questions about the effectiveness of congressional oversight in national security matters.

The wisdom of Hodding Carter's advocacy of a probing press being mindful of its First Amendment mandate is made clear by the Snowden affair. *The Guardian*'s editor Alan Rusbridger suggests that journalism is a "fire service," an indispensable agency for the public when events call for a watchdog. The Snowden affair is a classic case of the press contributing to public understanding of important issues while responsibly curating and filtering what should and should not be publicized.

The suggestions of journalism dean Wasserman, and that of law professor Yochai Benkler (also noted here), that the public interest defense be used in American courts in unusual cases when appropriate, makes sense and ought to be implemented.[1] Whistleblower laws must be improved to weed out the improper claims but to protect and follow up on correct ones. Specific suggestions are offered by Professors Wasserman and Cole regarding the proper times and situations to use or plug leaks and to encourage or silence the whistles. Examples of recent whistleblowers who were victims not of praise but of scorn, not gratitude but hostility, have been documented in the media, most recently by PBS and by James Risen in his new book *Pay Any Price*.[2] Making whistleblower laws more protective of valid claims is very much in the public's interest, and should be a part of any reform. There is a logical disconnect between punishing news sources for misappropriation of property and rewarding their accomplices in media for their role in making that misappropriation public.

According to a McClatchy Washington Bureau report, at the end of 2014 "whistleblowers . . . have served as America's conscience in the war on terrorism . . . of government waste, misconduct, and overreach. . . . Yet the legal system that was set up to protect those employees has repeatedly failed." Since 9/11, over 8,700 defense and intelligence employees and contractors have filed claims, only to suffer retaliation, the report concluded. Few investigations resulted in reforms.[3]

Republican Senator Charles Grassley stated, "There is an inherent bias against whistleblowers in the inspector general's office," and others in Congress, three Republicans and five Democrats, complained that whistleblower laws were interpreted so narrowly as to potentially preclude meritorious claims of retaliation. The veteran legal director of the Government Accountability Project, Tom Devine, said his group advises whistleblowers "to stay away from established channels to defend against retaliation," because that "predictably ends up with the whistleblower as the target."

The recent McClatchy report undermines President Obama's comment after Snowden's leak that "there were other avenues available for somebody whose conscience was stirred and [who] needed to question government actions."

The reporters' game has changed in major ways. Journalists who historically received leaked information from human sources in private conversations or passed documents can now, through sources like Snowden, have access to vast collections of information. Among other consequences, this means the press's governing principles on cooperation with leakers and whistleblowers require thoughtful reconsideration.

The new pervasive technology has changed law enforcement, too. Faced with the shocking assault on the United States on 9/11, it was natural for law enforcement officials, instructed by the highest authorities in government, to take appropriate steps to prevent something like that from happening again. Investigations aimed at limiting terrorism now can be undertaken using highly intrusive technology to gather mountains of information for sophisticated search engines to winnow out the terrorist wheat from the chaff. At the same time it has empowered technically sophisticated people to gain access to that same information in vast amounts, including purposes serving no public interest or serving the interests of our mortal enemies. The present volume of records the government gathers, much of it questionable, it seems, can overwhelm the purpose of their collection, building haystacks of data that make needles of crucial information harder to locate. That should change with refined laws governing the collection as well as the classification and declassification of government records, requiring investigative agencies to coordinate the information they gather, and circumscribing the process with reasonable constitutional restraints.

As Thomas Blanton states in his chapter, our classification system needs to be revised in major respects, so that it is solicitous of real needs for secrecy but radically limits those instances to timely, appropriate, and necessary matters. Major bipartisan studies have advocated less classification, more declassification, and more effective sunset and FOIA laws for decades.[4] A joint intelligence committee concluded so in 2002.[5] Snowden's disclosures should bring this reform to center stage.

Adapting new and evolving technology to aid the needs of law enforcement while protecting personal privacy requires sophisticated solutions that balance public and private needs. The consideration of how to accomplish both goals is now on the public agenda as a result of Snowden's disclosures.

Professor Mills's chapter suggests how we can protect the Homeland and the haystack without unnecessarily exploiting people's privacy. He recommends ways to establish transparency in domestic surveillance; he calls for effective, independent oversight of surveillance practices and advocates an effective whistleblower system that demonstrates abuses without endangering national security; finally, he proposes protecting citizens with Fourth Amendment procedures that are adapted to the new and more complicated nature of communications in the modern digital world. His admonitions provide a starting point in what surely must be a continuing balancing act as the digital world expands, bringing with it new opportunities and new problems.

All these suggestions balance the nation's needs for perfection of our security system with protection of the public's civil liberties. The analyses and proposals in *After Snowden* are sensitive to the country's needs for responsible national security measures. Some of us served our government in positions of responsibility, proudly. We do not question the loyalty or commitment of the members of the intelligence security establishment, and it should not question the loyalty of its critics. To disagree with specific policies or practices is not to question the country's legitimate security interests; to suggest otherwise is to ignore Americans' constitutional rights.

Former NSA Director General Keith Alexander was correct to call for unity in national security matters between the government, technology, commercial institutions, and the public.[6] So was Alexander's deputy and principal adviser, NSA's Chief Operating Officer Richard Ledgett, when he agreed that the security hierarchy needs to be more transparent, and acknowledged the need to protect the public's privacy. Ledgett also stated that Congress "had the opportunity to make themselves aware" of the programs now being criticized.[7] Interestingly, Ledgett was open-minded about the possibility of a negotiated settlement between the government and Snowden.[8]

Might that be possible? And what should such a settlement include? As a former federal prosecutor, I can imagine a negotiated settlement that would be in the interest of both prosecution and defense. Many critical facts remain to be discovered as this book goes to the printer in early 2015. Yet because of the daily drip of disclosures that continue while Snowden remains a fugitive, a stalemate is in neither side's interest, and a negotiated resolution between the government and Snowden would be wise.

The prosecution and defense might agree to Snowden pleading guilty to misappropriation of government property, and returning voluntarily to face a speedy public trial. The government wants its material returned, and where there is a real national security reason it ought to be. Elusive as that goal may be, it is a proper concern of the national security community. If he hasn't retained the material, as he claims, Snowden should tell the government which records he turned over to his select journalists so it can take steps to protect against improper disclosures, short of criminalizing the press. What might the response of Snowden's press connections be if a settlement between Snowden and the government required the description, if not the return, of the stolen secret files? Barton Gellman has already stated that he would publish no information that jeopardized national security.[9] Presuming the good faith of the journalists who have the records Snowden appropriated, the government ought to be able to reclaim those of them that it could demonstrate to a federal (not FISA) court would endanger national security, if the parties do not agree to return the documents voluntarily.

Snowden has asked for a public trial by jury, and the Constitution guarantees that he is entitled to one.[10] Presumably it would be in Hawaii, where his offense took place. Snowden told *New Yorker* correspondent Jane Mayer in October 2014 that he fears a closed court proceeding, but he would return if assured he'd receive an open trial.[11] There is no good reason that should not be the case.

Hawaii state courts permit televised trials; its federal trial court does not, though the federal appellate court covering Hawaii does, and some other federal trial courts do.[12] If there is a negotiated guilty plea, all that remains to be decided would be the sentencing. That hearing ought to be televised as an important way to educate the public. The government could present its case for sanctions, *in camera* before the judge alone when confidential issues arise. Snowden could make his plea for the justification of his acts. Justice is best served when it is perceived to be done.

Federal judge Jed S. Rakoff recently wrote that constitutionally guaranteed criminal trials are a mirage because in federal courts 97 percent of them are determined by plea bargains. As a rule they are negotiated secretly by prosecutors "with no judicial oversight," and Judge Rakoff concludes that this "invites arbitrary results."[13] A public sentencing under the supervision of the presiding judge, in a case as sensitive and notorious as Snowden's, would add legitimacy to whatever the outcome might be.

Edward Snowden has stated, ". . . the status quo is no longer tenable . . . things must change and the public has to have a say in the way its government operates its surveillance apparatus and where the lines are drawn on the boundaries of our rights."[14] While opinion polls oscillate, there is growing public agreement with Snowden's remark.

The New York Times editorialized on January 1, 2014, that Snowden "has done his country a great service," and deserves "some form of clemency."[15] His ultimate sentence, after the government presents its case, and Snowden his mitigations, finally would put into a correct context the demonstrated public costs and the verified values of Snowden's actions. When those facts are finally on the public record, a proper verdict and proportionate sentence could be reached. The salutary reforms of our country's policies, bound to be generated *After Snowden*, will place his daring acts in a full context, whatever the public may think about his methods. Snowden has said he is prepared to face fairly adjudged sanctions.[16] His sentence could include ways for him to contribute to his country's interests as part of that adjudication. Conviction alone would reconfirm the vital precedent against theft. A wise and balanced sentence would demonstrate the value of reconciliation as a central element of justice.

For any court to calculate the excruciating balance between appropriate and competing interests in national security and personal privacy is as difficult as it is important. The choice is *not* either/or. The best national policy requires protection of both important interests. The wisest balance includes the endorsement of the public (through its public and private institutions) to a maximum degree feasible. One hopes that the lessons learned in the aftermath of the Snowden phenomenon will lead this country to a better place, safer and at the same time more attentive to constitutional protections. That was the intent of Snowden's actions, and it ought to be the result.

NOTES

1. Yochai Benkler, "A Public Accountability Defense for National Security Leakers and Whistleblowers," *Harvard Law and Policy* 8, no. 2 (July 2014).
2. James Risen, *Pay Any Price: Greed, Power, and Endless War* (Boston: Houghton/Houghton Mifflin Harcourt, 2014).
3. Marisa Taylor, "Intelligence, defense whistleblowers remain mired in broken system," December 30, 2014. http://www.mcclatchydc.com/static/features/Whistleblowers/ Whistleblowers-remain-mired-in-broken-system.html?brand=mcd.
4. Ronald L. Goldfarb, *In Confidence: When to Protect Secrecy and When to Require Disclosure* (New Haven, CT: Yale University Press, 2009).
5. Joint Inquiry Into Intelligence Community Activities Before and After The Terrorist Attacks of September 11, 2001. *Report of the U.S. Senate Select Committee on Intelligence and U.S. House Permanent Select committee on Intelligence.* December 2002. http://www.gpo.gov/fdsys/pkg/CRPT-107srpt351/pdf/CRPT-107srpt351-ERRATA.pdf.

6. "The NSA responds to Edward Snowden's interview at TED," *TED Blog*, http://blog.ted.com/2014/03/20/the-nsa-responds-to-edward-snowdens-interview-at-ted/.

7. Ibid.

8. Charlotte Alter, "NSA Official Floats Amnesty For Snowden: If the leaker could show the data he took is contained," *Time*, December 16, 2013, http://nation.time.com/2013/12/16/nsa-official-floats-amnesty-for-snowden/.

9. Live chat, "NSA Surveillance: Q&A with reporter Barton Gellman," *Washington Post*, July 14, 2014, http://live.washingtonpost.com/nsa-surveillance-bart-gellman.html.

10. Jane Mayer, "Video: Snowden Would 'Love' an Open Trial," *New Yorker*, October 20, 2014, http://www.newyorker.com/news/news-desk/video-snowden-love-stand-trial.

11. Ibid.

12. Derrick Hinds, Radio Television Digital News Association, November 18, 2014, http://www.rtdna.org/content/cameras_al_id#.VIocwnv9ZVc.

13. Jed S. Rakoff, "Why Innocent People Plead Guilty," *New York Review of Books*, November 20, 2014, http://www.nybooks.com/articles/archives/2014/nov/20/why-innocent-people-plead-guilty/.

14. Alan Rusbridger and Ewen MacAskill, "Edward Snowden interview—the edited transcript," *Guardian*, July 18, 2014, http://www.theguardian.com/world/2014/jul/18/-sp-edward-snowden-nsa-whistleblower-interview-transcript.

15. Editorial Board, "Edward Snowden, Whistleblower," *New York Times*, January 1, 2014, http://www.nytimes.com/2014/01/02/opinion/edward-snowden-whistle-blower.html?_r=0.

16. Mayer, "Video: Snowden Would 'Love' an Open Trial."

ACKNOWLEDGMENTS

Thanks to our editor, Thomas Dunne, for seeing the importance of this book, and bringing it to public life, and to Will Anderson for all his advice and assistance.

And to Gerrie Sturman for her always helpful and professional assistance here and in all I do.